In the Small Places

Stories of Teacher Changemakers and the Power of Human Agency

In the Small Places

Stories of Teacher Changemakers and the Power of Human Agency

Fred Mednick

CHANGEMAKERS
BOOKS

Winchester, UK
Washington, D.C., USA

JOHN HUNT PUBLISHING

First published by Changemakers Books, 2024
Changemakers Books is an imprint of John Hunt Publishing Ltd., No. 3 East Street,
Alresford, Hampshire SO24 9EE, UK
office@jhpbooks.com
www.johnhuntpublishing.com
www.changemakers-books.com

For distributor details and how to order please visit the 'Ordering' section on our website.

ISBN: 978 1 80341 482 9
978 1 80341 483 6 (ebook)
Library of Congress Control Number: 2022952135

A CIP catalogue record for this book is available from the British Library.

Design: Lapiz Digital Services

UK: Printed and bound by CPI Group (UK) Ltd, Croydon, CR0 4YY
Printed in North America by CPI GPS partners

We operate a distinctive and ethical publishing philosophy in
all areas of our business, from our global network of authors to
production and worldwide distribution.

Contents

For my parents, both teachers
For Rosalie, Alanna and Lora
For Dr. Sunita Gandhi, my mentor
For Dr. Jane Goodall, my friend and hero

All author proceeds will be donated to Roots & Shoots
(the youth action program of the Jane Goodall Institute)
and to global literacy programs

Paul Robeson stood
on the northern border of the USA
and sang into Canada
where a vast audience
sat on folding chairs
waiting to hear him.

He sang into Canada.
His voice left the USA
when his body was
not allowed to cross
that line.

Remind us again,
brave friend.
What countries may we
sing into?

What lines should we all
be crossing?
What songs travel toward us
from far away
to deepen our days?

—Naomi Shihab Nye, "Cross that Line," *You and Yours*

Preface

Heads of nongovernmental organizations (NGOs) and college professors have difficulty passing up podiums and microphones. We want to tell everyone what's on our minds. We *lecture*. Lectures are not *inherently* bad. They are, after all, a time-honored and efficient message-delivery system. It's just that they're not always *effective*. The droning and sanctimony (mine included) can be downright taxing. When I feel a lecture coming on, I remind myself of a quip loosely attributed to Lyndon Johnson. It goes something like this (and I paraphrase here): a speech is a lot like peeing down your leg; it may feel hot to you at first, but it gets cold (and old) quickly.

There are better ways to make a point: tell stories. They may not be that efficient, but they can be profoundly effective. Some can get out of hand (mine tend to meander before finding their way home), but a personal, authentic story taps into our *collective* story. Think about stories of dreamers wrestling cynics. David versus Goliath stories. Stories about learning and earning.

A lecture is a roadmap to a destination. A story is a compass, leaving it up to you to navigate uncertain territory. A lecture may make a compelling case for a momentous social change. A story is a book of matches.

True, stories rely upon the unreliable narrator of memory. We often hear, "If memory serves me..." But memory also *fails* us. The sequence of events may not add up. It may *not* have

1

been raining that day. That head of state may *not* have said the words I thought I heard. If memories haven't slipped one's mind entirely, they can still be slippery. Just when you think you've got them firmly in hand, they tumble and bounce out of reach like marbles down a long flight of stairs. You try to gather them up, but several have a mind of their own, rolling away to join all their distant cousins: loose change, puzzle pieces, Bic pens and baby pacifiers at some strange *réunion d'objets* to which you were invited but have, alas, lost the directions.

The teachers I describe in this book have helped fill in my mental lacunae. They tell me that my recollections are "pretty accurate." Not exactly a ringing endorsement, but, then again, Toni Morrison once described the act of remembering as "a form of willed creation."

Sometimes, though, every detail comes rushing back. Racing through pools of rain on a pitted, unlit road in Nigeria from Port Harcourt to Calabar before the bandits take control. The arm of a mannequin propelled through a department store window during the Wenchuan earthquake. A colleague's stoicism after having come upon the aftermath of ethnic cleansing. Those intimidating guards in President Pervez Musharraf's office watching my every move during a series of conversations about Islam and development. That gleefully mischievous Afghan girl peeking through the iron bars at the White House fence, then turning to us to ask if she could meet the king of America.

Acknowledgments

My wife and two daughters are champions of love, connection, and service. Thank you for keeping the faith.

Teachers' natural sense of reciprocity and agency has defined and shaped Teachers Without Borders (TWB) and me. To my colleagues profiled in this book, my boundless gratitude.

Jim Astman, PhD, the groundbreaking and visionary headmaster of the Oakwood School, hired me in 1980, knowing that I would be a project. He has instilled in generations the abiding faith that, given the chance to learn, human beings will make moral choices.

Sunita Gandhi, PhD, introduced me to a network of teachers and has remained my mentor ever since. Without her, I wouldn't have summoned the nerve to fire myself from a respectable job and start this escapade. Her newest initiative is designed to accelerate functional literacy and numeracy for poor communities by leveraging local talent. We work closely together today.

Fernando Reimers, PhD, Ford Foundation of International Education at Harvard University and Director of Harvard's Global Education Innovation Initiative, has been a pioneer in viewing teachers as catalysts for change. He is an inspiration.

John J.Z. Gardiner, PhD, my dissertation chair, warned me that this path would be thorny, but worth the trek. Don Jacobs, PhD, pushed me to remove barriers to connect teachers. Daniel

3

Will Harris, W. Joseph King, PhD, Joel Thierstein, PhD, Laurie Racine, Haviva Kohl, Hilve Firek, PhD, and Lois Fein helped clear away the brush.

The Cisco Foundation's Peter Tavernise, Michael Yutzrenka, Alex Belous and Sima Yazdani took a risk on the idea and promise of Teachers Without Borders. The William and Flora Hewlett Foundation's Kathy Nicholson and Cathy Casserly soon followed and funded our passion to develop free and open educational content and tools. Lynn Nixon and Karen Lewis of the Agilent Foundation provided funding, translators and support to regroup after the Wenchuan earthquake and assist teachers in our efforts to connect science with safety.

Were it not for Konrad Glogowski, PhD, TWB's Chair of our Advisory Board, Teachers Without Borders might have faded away long ago. He has kept his eye on what matters most: measurable change, stakeholder-based professional development, and teacher communities of practice. His intellectual honesty, fealty to research-driven practice, and goodwill have made it possible for so many others to show up.

Colleagues at the World Bank, the Peace Corps, the US State Department, Johns Hopkins University, the University of Washington and especially Vrije Universiteit Brussel (Free University of Brussels) provided invaluable support. I hold special affection for Koen Lombaerts, PhD, Head of the Department of Education Sciences at Vrije Universiteit Brussel (VUB), who has enabled me to work with brilliant and dedicated international students earning their master's degrees and PhDs.

Marta Orellana, a Teachers Without Borders volunteer and editor, provided invaluable editing support. Two students in particular, Valentina Dragičević and Nisa Fatima, provided important feedback and reminders to make friends with the reader.

Dr. Jane Goodall, the preeminent primatologist, environmentalist, United Nations Messenger of Peace and friend, considers me one of her little brothers and reminds me that global service is mystifying, emotionally taxing and never as romantic as it sounds. Indefatigable in her late eighties, Jane recognizes that the human family is at its greatest when we act as stewards of each other, animals and the environment. How can anyone slow down with such a role model? And one more question. When will she receive the Nobel Prize for Peace? I know of no one more deserving.

Thank you, teachers. Please accept this book with my deepest gratitude.

Introduction

The world can feel like a cesspool, but it's filled with generous people. Some of the most generous of all, the ones who carry the world on their shoulders, teach. On a global scale, they are nothing short of a development army. They have always been there. We just might not have been paying attention.

When I ask teacher changemakers what drives them to serve their communities so profoundly, some look at me as if I were an airport security agent noticing their mismatched socks. Most appreciate the gesture but say they have not done *enough* to make a difference.

Before I get ahead of myself, allow me to start with the basics. I once asked a bigwig at the United Nations to define the word "teacher." Without skipping a beat, he responded, "A teacher is anyone with valuable information to share." The simplicity of this statement belies its underlying elegance and depth. *Anyone* also includes those without formal training, but who nonetheless teach what they know. Coaches, parents, preachers and village elders come immediately to mind. There are so many more. *Valuable* is less a commodity, precious and high-priced, than a service, beneficial and productive. The two words, *valuable information*, are dance partners. In a world of fake news, information is not valuable until it's verifiable. *Sharing* demands a conversation and reciprocity, not a broadcast. *Sharing valuable information* is the soul of teaching.

I often ask my graduate students to describe teachers from their formative years. We make a list: charismatic, hippie, fresh-faced, cool, creepy, apathetic, boring, subversive teachers. A student practicing his English blurted out, "Preternatural paragons of patience!" Reluctant authoritarians. Risk-takers. Magicians. Stand-and-deliver and follow-your-dreams teachers.

We knead in the movie versions and the messages these films communicate: a wide range from incompetent to inspirational. Still, it doesn't move the needle toward anything we can use.

Someone invariably raises the question about whether teachers are born or made. I ask them to take sides and argue it out. It usually ends in a draw, like an unanswerable Zen koan. I, for one, shudder at the prospect of an education school admissions test that distinguishes a *born* prospect from a "project." I've tried inviting Alexa and Siri to class and asking them to shed light on this born/made conundrum. Both digital assistants spit back anemic answers.

Why not dispense with the variability and fallibility of the human factor and ask a different question, like can we *manufacture* teachers? Think Chat GPT-embedded iPads attached to Roombas roaming around the classroom sponging up data and offering help, drones measuring facial expressions, or the deluxe version of an all-in-one, teacher-tutor-grader app. DNA test-kit companies like 23andMe can "decipher the human genome" to reveal monumental health indicators such as Type 2 diabetes and skin cancer, not to mention asparagus odor detection, back hair, glossophobia (fear of public speaking, though I would hazard a guess that few teachers carry this) and misophonia (hatred of the sound of chewing, probably running through a majority of the teaching corps). Might these companies produce a breakthrough *in utero* service that identifies an "urge-to-teach" trait? Time will tell.

I have devoted the past 23 years of my 44-year career to a different inquiry: the sweet spot when a community's urgency meets teachers' agency. I'm interested in living, breathing teachers who *show up*.

This book is about teachers who show up at the right time, often at the wrong place, with valuable information to share. They show up for 60 children crowded into Quonset huts without desks, books or water. They show up in odd places to collect discarded bicycle parts, toys and plastic bottles to demonstrate a concept. Teachers without classrooms or even a school, who show up to gather students under a tree or in a cave to scratch out addition and subtraction exercises in the dirt.

I want to introduce you to teachers who prepare and plan for disasters and who, in a crisis, establish child-friendly spaces that foster a sense of normalcy amid all that chaos and horror, and reunite families when an earthquake decimates their schools or a once-in-a-century flood ravages their crops and washes their homes away. Teachers who show up to educate children about how to minimize the likelihood of catching a deadly virus even when conspiracy theorists scream that it's all a hoax. Who bolster civility in an era when our social contract is under siege. Who explore challenging subjects despite book bans and prohibited topics. Who shelter children from school shooters or ideological mercenaries bent on ransacking classrooms and trafficking children. Teachers who show up even when the very act of teaching is against the law.

Teachers are changemakers in our backyards. They don't need Hallmark cards, a PR firm or more bake sales, though funding for education on a global scale is paltry at best. They can do without the corporate-sponsored awards ceremony or, God forbid, teacher talent shows. Teachers deserve that their voices be heard at Davos, at the G8 summit and in the General Assembly of the United Nations.

When that day comes, we will have shown up for them.

Chapter 1

Addled Child

I became a teacher the hard way, by first suffering as a student.

The word "addled" never appeared on our fourth-grade vocabulary list, but its meaning was unmistakable. "Mr. Mednick! You are an addled child!" To this day, I remain mystified by the logic of using the formal salutation of one's last name to humiliate a child. It shattered me. Incidents like these leave fragments. I am still fishing them out.

I should have known better than to cross her invisible chalk line. Likely, she had exhausted all the discipline strategies in her spiral-bound Tips for Classroom Management binder: (#1) "Review behavioral expectations"; (#2) "Offer help strategies"; (#3) "Make eye contact"; (#4) "Speak after class"; (#5) "Rearrange seating"; (#6) "Redirect attention." Just before she unleashed her word-javelin, she had been applying (#7): "Extinguish negative behavior by not reinforcing it," a dubious and passive-aggressive tactic, I might add, that can escalate into a crisis. Here's my Eduspeak-English translation for #7: *she was ignoring me*.

Too busy practicing my Buddy Rich pencil paradiddles against the side of my chair, I was not reading the cues. Too distracted to notice the Hawaiian Punch-colored blotch spreading across her neck. Too insistent on getting her attention. Too busy *being busy* to spot her eyes narrowing like Clint Eastwood's in *A Fistful of Dollars*.

I should have known her nerves were fried. The past few days, she had chastised me several times for following instructions she had never given or answering questions she had never asked. I must have driven right through the universal sign for stop— arm straight, palm at a 90-degree angle like our crossing guard or that trapped pantomimist on the *Ed Sullivan Show*. Tonight, it would be tip #8: "Inform (and enlist) the parents."

My teacher had been asking for a show of hands to see who understood the steps for solving an arithmetic problem on the board. Even then, I thought this teaching technique was suspect. Public voting may work at a local town-hall meeting to approve extra funding for Shakespeare in the Park. But for 9-year-old kids learning arithmetic? The stakes are too high. If most of us raised our hands, why would one or two honest ones expose their weakness and risk their peers' ridicule? If a *dozen* raised their hands, but *two dozen* remained silent, might she feel compelled to teach the lesson differently, or was a 33% get-it-right rate good enough for her? What if she asked us to work in small groups so that peers could help peers? Or asked students to *teach* the lesson, rather than compete for the recognition of having already known the answer?

Worse, I *knew* the answer and I wanted her to know. Dismayed by the red scrawl on my recent homework, I was bound to turn the unfamiliar into the familiar, decipher the logic of fractions and do something right. I was certain my time had come to prove myself worthy and win her over. A nod or even a genuine smile in my general direction would have sufficed. I waved my arms as if trying to flag down a distant cousin at a crowded train station. The more she ignored me (as she had done with stinging regularity), the more I tried to get her attention. *Pick me! I have the right answer!* Wrapped in my chair desk, half-standing, I must have looked as if I were trying to wriggle out of a Halloween costume forced upon me by bullies.

During prior calls home, my parents usually blamed eczema for transforming a cheerful kid into the rash-consumed, squirming menace my teachers saw. My body felt like sandpaper. I sawed, chafed and churned my limbs against the iron legs of my school desk and filed my knuckles and my elbows on the indentation for pencils. If I noticed blood on my shirt, I would sit as still as I could, resisting the impulse to scratch through the pain and make it worse. This time I had painted my own red target.

First came the snarl and the next thing I knew, "addled child!" was hurtling my way. Her venom startled my classmates. I dropped back in my seat. E. Annie Proulx best describes the feeling: "a heaving sludge of ice under fog where air blurred into water." My classmates may have been snickering, but I could not hear them. If they were staring or pointing at me, I did not notice them. If the second hand on the clock was still ticking inexorably forward, time nevertheless stood still. To this day, whenever I hear the word "addled," I feel my heartbeat in my ears. "Addled" is a trigger.

She did not invoke rule #4 ("Speak after class"). By 3:05 I had already reached the alley behind the school, and ran. I stripped off my schoolbag, reached under the doormat for the key and stepped into the cool sanctuary of home. The screen door wheezed shut behind me.

My schoolbag was open. Pencils and erasers must have spilled out somewhere en route, all of them replaceable. I plunged my hand into the bag to fish around for something far more valuable, a talisman as consoling and palliative as any child's stuffed animal: a ruler made of ash, stenciled in red with "Rulers of Baseball" at the top in that distinctive cursive sports script, followed by a list of the greats: Connie Mack of the Philadelphia Athletics, Cy Young of the Boston Pilgrims, Willie Mays of the San Francisco Giants, Hammerin' Hank Aaron of the

Atlanta Braves, and my hero, Sandy Koufax of the Los Angeles Dodgers. On the flip side, the usual picket fence of inch-lengths. The ruler was gone. I couldn't bring myself to retrace my steps.

Outside, I could hear the neighborhood kids on their Schwinns, baseball cards sputtering in their spokes. Today I would not be joining them. I climbed onto the armrest of a couch to pull down the Webster's and search for "addled." Crawling my fingers up the spine, I slipped on the plastic slipcover. The tome fell from my hands, bounced on the cushions and crashed onto a glass coffee table. Miraculously, the glass did not shatter, but the book freed itself from its mesh binding. I accordioned the sides back together, found the divot for the letter "A," and drew my finger down the page. I stopped at "adder" and read the definition. Did my teacher say I was an adder: (n.) a poisonous snake? Insulting, but a snake child made little sense. I didn't slither or bite. I continued down the column until I reached "addled." Addled, from the Old English *adela*, to make or become confused, fuzzy, disoriented. Used as an adjective, addled meant *rotten*. Bingo. I was an addled child. Confused and rotten.

My mother returned home after work and found me slumped on the couch. She noticed the slipcover on the floor, the coffee table slightly skewed, and the dictionary not flush with the growing number of *World Book* encyclopedias, even though I had been careful to use both hands to push it back in slowly, like a surgeon in the game *Operation*. She felt my forehead. I remained silent and sullen.

Calls home usually came when we were doing the dishes. This evening would be no exception. Standing atop the Yellow Pages next to my mother, ready to dry the plates, I wiped my hands on my pants. I knew what was to come. She sighed through the second ring and shooed me away. I backed off to the far end of the kitchen, toeing the curl where the linoleum meets the wall. She snatched the receiver from its cradle.

Imagine, dear reader, a teacher–parent game show featuring a split screen of dueling kitchens wallpapered with sunflowers or a faded farm scene, a Formica table and matching Naugahyde chairs, and a turquoise or black Bakelite rotary phone attached to the wall. Seated at their respective kitchen tables, each contestant has stretched the phone's curly cord to its limit. Who budges first? Who will go too far? Who will win?

In kitchen number 1, the teacher shuffling through index cards of infractions. In kitchen number 2, my mother (also a teacher) straightening her shoulders and reaching for the back of an electric bill and a ballpoint pen.

My teacher offered her saccharin greeting and transitioned quickly to a recital of my misdemeanors, delivered breathlessly and with enough forensic detail to render useless any defense. My mother nodded. She crossed and uncrossed her legs. She opened her mouth and closed it again.

The monologue ended with the usual hackneyed, sitcom suggestions: Fred (strangely, no longer Mr. Mednick) should apply himself more, check his homework before turning it in and restrain from obstreperous behavior. Her closing statement: a bewildering pseudo-psychological insight about being my own worst enemy.

Did my mother think that this presupposition about her son not applying himself or reviewing his homework was a thinly coded way of saying that he was lazy and dull? Should she say she had seen me check and recheck my homework? Would she also add that my impulsive behavior was not aggression but simply a desperate plea for a chance to show what I knew and be acknowledged accordingly? Might she ask, "How do you know about my son's potential if you shut down his motivation to learn?" As for the worst-enemy trope, would my mother ask how one negotiates a peace treaty with oneself? Or will this be a surrender? Why should learning be compared to war, anyway? From the sidelines, I seethed. *My teacher* was my own worst enemy.

Urie Bronfenbrenner, a psychologist and co-founder of Head Start, once wrote: "Every child needs at least one adult who is irrationally crazy about him or her." I wasn't looking for, or trying to be worthy of, unconditional love. I just wanted to be seen. Surely my mother would recognize this and *say* something.

I expected consequences. The signs were easy to read. If my mother bobbed her head like a dashboard hula girl, there would be no transistor radio for a month, which meant no Dodger games. If she rolled her eyes, a lighter sentence was possible: Dodger games only with proof of homework completed *and* checked *and* chores done. If my mother cocked her head, puzzled at what she was hearing or simply not convinced, I might get a lecture. If she felt impugned as a parent, she would straighten up and purse her lips. In that case, the same lecture, albeit abbreviated and halfhearted. The punishment would fit my crimes, never anger or a belt to the backside. Whatever the outcome, eczema would roar back, my body's somatic response for a modicum of pity or clemency.

Just writing this, I get nervous. I was jumping ahead. Let's return to the split screen. The score was Teacher: 1. Mother-Teacher: 0. Child: minus 1. Did my mother think my teacher was tedious and spiteful? Would she agree and assure my teacher this would be handled best at home? I looked for a miracle comeback, like the Dodgers' walk-off win in the second game of the 1962 playoffs against the Giants.

Did she roll her eyes just now? Cock her head? At last, my mother spoke: "May I ask what the class was working on that caused my son to behave the way you describe?" By dissecting the content of the lesson and its pedagogy, was she exposing flaws? Was this a teacher-to-teacher, insider-to-insider tactic? She would never go so far as to shift responsibility from me to the teacher, but she did not seem to be giving the teacher a free pass. By introducing a larger context—how an imperious and unforgiving classroom climate stifles learning—or that adults must act with equanimity and balance toward *all* children, *even* the squirrely ones—was she implying that my teacher harbored a predilection toward character assassination? "He's a good boy," she said. "He reads all the time. He's very curious, sometimes *too* curious. It's just that he doesn't do well when he feels intimidated." Yes! Atticus Finch in mom form!

Who could argue with the notion that frightened kids feel scrambled and then act out? Understated, yet so elegantly irrefutable! "When he feels intimidated" was not so much a counterattack as a reminder that teaching requires compassion. There is no question about it: I was a twitchy, grating, unnerving pain in the ass, but I was trying. Making progress, too.

Allow me to replay the scene, this time with thought bubbles for each side:

Teacher: "I have concerns," followed by offenses 1–3, then unhelpful advice: "apply himself...check homework...his own worst enemy..." Thought bubble: *Kids like yours make me consider early retirement.*
Mother: "Which assignment? What, specifically, was going on?" Thought bubble: *You should have retired last year.*
Teacher: "Disrupted the class...in the middle of my lesson..." Thought bubble: *Your kid has shit for brains and can't control himself.*
Mother: (nodding, readying her comeback) "...when he feels intimidated." Thought bubble: *You should cut my kid some slack, asshole.*

I don't remember who hung up first. The text was cordial, the subtext more combative. It may have been a draw. My mother motioned me over and pressed me against her pleated skirt. I smelled dishwater soap, rubber gloves, chicken and broccoli.

She seemed taller, looking down at her son doing his best to keep himself from crying and scratching the crook of his arm, his lower lip and his knees.

I knew what was coming. No Dodger games, more chores, and homework completed before going anywhere. I was too exhausted to negotiate the start date for my sentence, even though Koufax was pitching that night.

In truth, I *was* a walking, talking, itchy, niacin rush with a built-in on-off switch. I had no dimmer. My mother knew it and did her best. My teacher didn't care. It is challenging to teach kids with attention-deficit hyperactivity disorder. But it is far more challenging to *be* that kid. There was no neurodivergent sensibility back then, no personalization of instruction. Just winners and losers and stigma.

The next day, I also knew the answer to the problem on the board, but I had turned my switch "off." I wanted to be invisible, even though I had been desperate to be known, not simply tagged as a concern. Most children are willing to go to extraordinary lengths, for better or worse, to be seen before they can see, to be understood before they can understand, and to feel free from fear before being free to learn. I made my decision: I was a flawed, feckless fuckup.

The word-spears stopped, though the slow burn of neglect did not. Expectations were low and I sank to meet them. Over time, school felt unjust, unkind, embarrassing and even conspiratorial. I could not help myself from staring outside my classroom window, gripped by an irresistible desire to be elsewhere.

I continued to struggle. I turned every question at the back of a chapter into a knot of impossible complexity. Mathematics was a foreign code without a legend for reference. Suffering in silence, I squeaked by. By junior high, the eczema was gone. I even managed to get serviceable grades. I simply had lost interest.

In high school, our 2-inch American history textbooks favored bite-sized memorizables and minutiae I could easily look up in the encyclopedia or glean from the television quiz show *College Bowl*. It was all a top-down view of the "what," leaving no room for the "why" or "how," or the discovery of patterns or tensions. If I were the teacher, I would find textbooks with opposing positions and ask the students to find the truth and discuss how they got there. I would not separate civics from history. I would start with that day's newspaper and work backward, challenging students to trace contemporary problems to their roots. Anything but this soporific march through time.

I had questions and wanted answers. Why did it take so long to vote the Civil Rights Act into law? Why was there so much discrimination in housing and why so much in the northern states of the US, when I had read that all the problems were in the south? Why did Sirhan Sirhan shoot Bobby Kennedy in my own city of LA? How did war go from being hot-to-cold-to-hot again? Why were 14 Black athletes kicked off the University of Wyoming football team just for wearing black armbands, or members of the Black Panthers shot in their beds by Chicago policemen? Was the "arc of the moral universe" truly bending "toward justice" or veering off to parts unknown?

I was wise enough not to offer teaching suggestions. That would seal my fate. Caught between monotony and curiosity, I propped my textbook on my desk to hide my secret stash: Bernard Malamud's *The Natural*, Vladimir Nabokov's *Lolita* and Karl Marx's *The Communist Manifesto*. Baseball was familiar and comforting; sex was confusing, yet tingly; and revolutionary ideology was a perfect intellectual outlet for adolescent rage. I was convinced school was the enemy. My school did not hand out stars to autodidacts. Naturally, my grades continued to slip. I didn't care.

If my fate would be manual labor, there was no time like the present. I found work at a bagel factory: an abbreviated swing shift on weekdays and graveyard shift on weekends. Training took half an hour. Someone mixes the dough, a machine shapes the bagels, and a worker spaces them out on a floured, rotating plate. My job was to ring one bagel in each finger and gently glide them into a vat of steaming, bubbling water, stir them for five minutes with a baseball bat, use a butterfly net to sift them out, and splay them onto another floured tray.

Standing over a swirl of moist, hot steam from the cauldron and a wall of stifling air from 450-degree ovens, prickly bumps appeared on my arms and spread to my chest and shoulders like a Moscato wine spill. I thought I had long outgrown eczema, but I was back to chafing and churning. The foreman commanded me to step away from my double toil and trouble and strip off my shirt. Rather than toss me a damp towel, he thumbed open an orange box of Arm & Hammer Baking Soda and shook it above my head, like fairy dust, to ease the hives. My sweat turned to white paste. Men running the dough-stirring machine began to chuckle. I rushed to the bathroom, tore away my apron, filled Dixie cups with cool water and doused the back of my neck. I glanced at the ghost in the mirror. I speed-cranked the window for fresh air. Unable to live in my skin, incompetent at school and even worse at work, I hung up my apron and walked out. Once home, I showered off the gunk and broke the good news to my parents. I wanted to go to college. I barely got in.

It only took one teacher to open my world. A Literature and Politics course was an intellectual powder keg and my professor held the match. Depending upon her mood, she wore iridescent, flowered moo-moos or dressed all in black. She paced and smoked Chesterfields through a black plastic cigarette holder. She described every inch of Picasso's *Guernica*, asked questions that spawned more questions, and told stories. "Stories allow us to be known," she said. "They make visible the invisibility of politics. They reveal who we are and what motivates us. Without stories, life is a gritty, incomprehensible mess."

We were a diverse group of students. Autoworkers commuting from a General Motors car plant two hours away, retired folks auditing the course, and kids like me, trying to build back a sense of worth. Most of us felt as if we stood at the periphery of learning, nibbling at the edges. But in that class, once a week, we *felt* intelligent and competent. She might stop in the middle of a passage she was reading aloud, words wafting above us like her smoke halos heading for the ceiling lights. In that intoxicating silence, we constructed meaning. We read more than she assigned. We met in groups more than she expected. We arranged potlucks every two weeks before class. A single course transcended the mechanics of information transmission and assimilation. It became a conversation. We had become a community of learners free to think out loud.

In the last half-hour of the final class session, my mind was *not* elsewhere. I was *not* squirming or chafing or drumming with pencils. I was listening intently. She stopped abruptly again. This time I heard my name. I flushed. She announced that my paper was insightful and alive, and read a few paragraphs aloud. She said she found it honest and *clear*. Let me say it again: *clear*. Clear is the *opposite* of addled.

Public acknowledgment is a thrill for anyone, but for me in that instant, it was epiphanic. My paper, the basis of her last session? Who, me, with something to *share*? In that minute, I had vanquished my own worst enemies. I forgave my elementary school teacher. I even forgave myself. One moment of affirmation is hardly an antidote for the serrated knife of public humiliation, but it was a salve for my thin, pocked skin.

I wanted to be *that* kind of teacher. I wanted everyone to have teachers like that.

Chapter 2

What Do You See Outside Your Window?

Most high-school principals spend their days navigating a blur of real crises or tempests in teapots. They show up early and leave late. Their evenings are not their own. Word of advice to new principals: forget buying alcohol in the same town you teach. People will talk.

As principals go, I was in an enviable position. I ran an excellent independent school secure in its reputation and nestled on a hill in an expensive, leafy neighborhood just around the corner from Kurt Cobain's former residence in Seattle, Washington. Parents did *not* treat me like a piñata. The faculty members were kind, passionate about their subjects and compassionate with their students. Outside my window, a cluster of purple and red rhododendrons would pick up the late afternoon light like a seventeenth-century French garden. It was a dream job.

Still, I was bored. The approaching millennium was upon us, along with the World Wide Web and the promise of a level playing field: universal freedom, ubiquitous opportunity and new connections at our fingertips. Strangers could ask questions of strangers. Websites scrolled down at a painfully slow pace like a wall map pulled down by some sadistic teacher, but for those with access, it was worth the wait. It did not take long to recognize, however, that a digital divide exposed and compounded stark inequalities and privilege. I saw an education divide. A hope divide, too.

The world outside my window was precious, bucolic and removed. Twenty-five years had passed since I'd felt that shared intellectual exuberance in that literature class, and a dozen more since my wife and I had spent a year teaching English in China. I longed to be in and of the world, rather than a mere bystander watching it unfold from afar.

Caught between the exhilarating weightlessness of exploring unknown stars *and* the gravitational pull of professional safety, I scolded myself for my whining and claustrophobia.

I wanted to be a learner again. The faculty understood and took on more responsibility so that I could pursue my doctorate.

Late one afternoon, I turned on National Public Radio (NPR), as I always did at the end of the day, stuffing papers into my briefcase for more work at home. A reporter described how an extremist militia group known as the Taliban had taken control of Afghanistan's capital, Kabul. How could extremism flourish in a world of information? How could Afghan children get an education in a war zone? How do we prepare teens for an irrational world? How might teachers help transform education to meet the needs of a *connected* world? A thesis topic began to percolate.

I pulled out a business card of an education specialist at the World Bank I had met at a conference. I asked her to enlist her network to disseminate a survey about teachers and their visions of the future for my doctoral thesis.

By the time I met with the chair of my doctoral committee, I had launched this question into the internet ether: "What do you see outside your window?" I told my chair about the responses I had received from around the world: windows looking onto tenement buildings. Smashed windows. No windows at all.

He pretended to listen but was visibly worried. As I waxed on about meeting new people, he came out with it: I seemed more enamored with the internet than the topic. My approach was unfocused, improvisational and impulsive. (Did I sense a veiled "addled" reference?) A doctoral survey is not some chatty icebreaker, but a planned, systematic round of inquiry grounded in a theoretical framework. How could I expect teachers to take this seriously?

Had my curiosity screwed me once again? By building a relationship with respondents, was I contaminating the results? I needed *usable* data. Teachers are busy. Stop the ingratiating, folksy banter and get to the targeted questions. While I have always held reservations about quasi-scientific objectivity in survey design, I kept them to myself. I needed the three letters after my name.

Over the next several weeks, more responses arrived. One teacher described someone outside her window who shook a carpet each day at exactly 11:00 am. Another teacher wrote about a colleague consoling a student on a bench and those little arms reaching for warmth. A janitor leaning on a broom, talking with teenagers ejected from class. Windows protected by iron bars, dicing the view into geometric patterns. Windows decorated with paper cutouts to obscure a view of sewage. Windows pasted with pictures of animals bearing each child's name.

Non-teachers responded. A prisoner described what he saw outside his spittle-smeared jail-cell window: the silhouette of a burly guard fingering his keys. A farmer's view of hay bales and tilting barns outside a combine window. A semitruck driver in Texas wrote this haiku:

In front and behind
White lines perforate my state
Are we all alone?

I thanked each respondent and received reply emails thanking *me* for thanking *them*.

I honed the survey to my chair's satisfaction. I asked various rounds of questions and anonymized answers to approach a consensus.

From your viewpoint, what five abilities or characteristics are necessary for youth to take part productively in the early twenty-first century? Please rank them in importance. What challenges and opportunities do you face in preparing students?

More questions followed. I predicted a huge drop-off in subsequent iterations, but somehow, they stuck with it. Several wrote about what they saw coming: a reduction in time for play given the pressure of high-stakes testing. Some identified immediate challenges: violence, public-health emergencies and widening socioeconomic disparities. Some saw more opportunities to bring the outside world into their classrooms. Others wanted to reinforce the sanctuary of the classroom and keep the world out.

In early November 1999, within hours of each other, a teacher from Norway and another from Nicaragua described what they saw outside their windows. Trapped by a tunnel of dark days and an impending storm, the Norwegian pined for a beach in the tropics. Drained by the crucible of hairdryer heat bouncing off corrugated roofs and baking her classroom for several weeks, the Nicaraguan longed to touch snow for the first time and make a snow angel. I connected them. Their interactions were filled with humility, hospitality and invitations to visit. Relationships foster reciprocity.

On 30 November 1999, the World Trade Organization (WTO) meeting at the Washington State Convention and Trade Center in Seattle (my home city) faced 40,000 protestors opposed to anti-labor policies, human rights abuses, environmental destruction, and the hypocrisy of "free" trade declarations that would put developing countries at a distinct disadvantage. Delegates encountered a human chain blocking the entrance to the Convention and Trade Center, surrounding hotels and even on-ramps to the Interstate highway. Opening ceremonies were delayed. President Clinton threatened to cancel the WTO meeting entirely unless something was done. Seattle's mayor declared a State of Emergency. The National Guard and Washington State Patrol were called in. Out came the batons. Fluorescent-orange-taped shotguns fired rubber bullets. Mounted police pushed back the protestors and sealed the surrounding 25 blocks. The "Battle in Seattle" was a turning point. Global issues were household concerns.

On 10 December, Médecins Sans Frontières (MSF) was formally awarded the Nobel Peace Prize. In the Nobel Lecture, James Orbinski spoke of his profound discomfort at an assault on the excluded, about how refugees have been expelled from their countries and denied political status, how inequality is a public-health nightmare. How humanitarianism was far more than generosity and charity; it was a citizen response to political failure and paralysis. And yet, humanitarians alone cannot make peace. Humanitarian action and political will must *converge*.

I don't believe in a higher order or the idea that everything happens for a reason. At the same time, serendipity can teach a great deal. I recalled Flannery O'Connor's short story, "Everything That Rises Must Converge," in which a college-educated son confronts his elderly mother. He tells her, "What all this means is that the old world is gone. The old manners are obsolete and your graciousness is not worth a damn." He continues, "From now on you've got to live in a new world and face a few realities for a change."[1]

Things were, indeed, converging. For three years, I had been listening to teachers uniquely placed to hear their communities' pulse. Teachers are the largest professionally prepared group in the world. They know who is sick or missing, orphaned by disease and at risk for abduction by human traffickers. If the world were a body, teachers would be its acupuncture points. It was abundantly clear: brains are distributed evenly around the world, but education is not.

That night, I thought about the power of the internet, the Nicaraguan and Norwegian teachers, the "Battle in Seattle," and MSF's admonition against complacency.

I made up my mind. I wrote a note to everyone who responded to my surveys, giving them a description of what *I* saw and smelled outside *my* window: a city on edge, the odor of pepper spray just a few miles away, the power of human agency, MSF. Having finished my doctorate that summer, I looked at convergence squarely in the eye and resigned my comfortable job as a principal at the last faculty meeting of the year. In early 2000, I founded Teachers Without Borders (TWB). I reached out to MSF and received approval to use the "without borders" name.

Someday, I hope to meet the two Nicaraguan and Norwegian teachers. I am confident they have no idea how much they have changed my life. They, like thousands of other Teachers Without Borders members, have embraced a vision of courage and dignity and given substance to hope, even during the COVID-19 pandemic, when their classroom windows were replaced by 1-inch Zoom squares.

Chapter 3

Meeting Jane

Three months after I founded Teachers Without Borders in 2000, I cobbled together enough money to attend the State of the World Forum in New York during United Nations Week, the annual opening of the General Assembly. The Forum was billed as a "global town meeting" to encourage dialogue between civil society stakeholders and a who's who of former and active heads of state, Nobel Prize winners, technology wunderkinds, NGO directors, scientists, literary giants and C-suite notables.

The big cigars shuttled back and forth between the Forum, other high-level clusters of cognoscenti, and consultative meetings at the United Nations Millennium Summit to finalize and launch the Millennium Development Goals, a global agreement designed to address the world's most pressing challenges for the next 15 years.

A *New York Times* piece focused on the impact of globalism and the need for collaboration "at a time when national boundaries have become nearly as irrelevant to economic and political tides as they are to infectious diseases or popular music."[2] I liked the sound of "irrelevant boundaries."

I fiddled with my nametag. I am *here*. I leafed through the program's dizzying expanse of topics: disarmament, human rights, child labor and child marriage, refugees, women's rights, environmental hazards, globalism, universal access to the internet, global governance, small arms and drug trafficking, religious and spiritual leadership for the twenty-first century, Indigenous medicine, water wars, media literacy, the ethical consequences of genetic innovation, and satellite radio education for the developing world.

Attendees were urged to complete a short contact-information form for the sake of building a network of "all critical stakeholders." Teachers Without Borders was a stakeholder, damn straight. Muhammad Yunus, the Founder and Managing Director of Grameen Bank, discussed microcredit in Bangladesh, a concept by which small loans made to women could free them from the vicious cycle of having to borrow bamboo from traders but not sell their products on the open market. Yunus tested the idea with $27. All loans were repaid. Six years later, the Nobel Committee awarded Muhammad Yunus the Nobel Peace Prize for his pioneering work in demonstrating the connection between poverty, self-reliance and peace. I had the good fortune of attending his Nobel Prize ceremony. The upper balcony was filled with Bangladeshi women shouting their approval. I wept.

President Mikhail Gorbachev spoke about *glasnost*, the consultative and more transparent measures taken in the post-Soviet era to embrace openness. At the same time, he warned of the consequences of globalism unchecked. Pauline Tangiora, a Maori Tribal Elder, rubbed shoulders with Ted Turner, Desmond Tutu, Colin Powell and the Clintons. I took furious notes. As each heavy hitter stepped up to the dais, my conference program turned into an indecipherable scribble of marginalia.

And then it was Jane Goodall's turn. She leaned into the microphone and let out a guttural pant-hoot, her neck extending upwards, lips pursed, the sound soft, then increasing in volume and intensity until a howl became a scream. She ended with a smile. The chimpanzee's pant-hoot call communicates emotion, presence, identity and excitement. She had both captured our attention and relaxed the room. I stood up to cheer and sat down, embarrassed. All speakers pant-hoot, in some way, to be noticed. Hers was different. It was as if she were saying: "I am here! You are here! We are here! Welcome!"

I remember everything she said. How as a child she took worms to bed with her to observe what they did. How, at four and a half, she hid in a henhouse to see "where on a hen was a hole big enough for the egg to come out." The relief on her mother's face when Jane was discovered, rushing from the barn, exhilarated, covered in straw. How her mother did not punish her but answered her question about how a hen lays eggs, thrilled to save up for books to fuel Jane's curiosity, like the tales of the wonderful Dr. Doolittle, able to talk to the animals. Jane was convinced she could be a better Jane than *Tarzan*'s Jane.

She spoke of saving wages and tips from a waitress job to find her way to Africa and study under Louis Leakey. The Serengeti Plains. Gombe National Park. Lake Tanganyika. The chimpanzees she named: Flo and Fifi, Mike, Goliath, and David Graybeard. The time she discovered that chimpanzees make tools and practice social norms, vacillating from kissing and embracing to patting each other on the back. She described how they emerge from the tree canopy, their relative degrees of swagger, how they protect their young, and the fear in their eyes when trapped in medical research labs or wearing electric collars for the circus: the same look in refugee children separated from their families. Animals have much to teach, she said. She told us how the earth is failing to compensate for industry's wanton disregard for the environment. She spoke of the cavalier destruction of animals and the desecration of Indigenous ideas held in sacred and reverent trust. Progress was winning the battle over sustainability.

She talked about the resistance she faced from those accusing her of blasphemy for having claimed that humankind was not the only toolmaker and for having blurred the line between science and religion, animals and humans. How the scientific community accused her of faulty research for having named the chimpanzees as subjects rather than as objects for study. And yet she was able to laugh about a popular Gary Larson's "Far Side" cartoon in which two chimpanzees are sitting on a branch. Picking through the male's hair, the female holds something suspicious between her opposable thumb and first finger and declares: "Well, well—another blond hair...Conducting a little more 'research' with that Jane Goodall tramp?"

Jane described her passion for Roots & Shoots, an organization she founded in Tanzania to pass the mantle of service and leadership to young people worldwide. "Roots creep under the ground to make a firm foundation. Shoots seem very weak, but to reach the light, they can break open brick walls."[3] Youth of all ages work with teachers, community members and graduates to observe their surroundings and take action. Roots & Shoots provides actionable toolkits for equality and inclusion, the protection of animals, the rights of refugees and displaced people, migratory species, biodiversity loss, responsible consumption and production, and climate change.

Roots & Shoots is a summer camp for changemakers. Its programs have reached community organizations, corporations, families, faith-based movements, foundations, nonprofits, home schools, prisons, senior centers, zoos, aquariums and museums. The program resonates with the deepest of human needs: to be loved, to connect and to serve.

I had to meet Jane and describe my vision for Teachers Without Borders. I had already been inching my way closer to the front, then took my place in a line of networkers. I dried my hands, ready to shake hers. I checked my badge. I fingered my business card.

When my turn came, at last, I shook her hand and forgot to speak. I dropped my card, which fluttered between the legs of an older woman in pearls. I dropped to my knees and patted around her Ferragamos until I found it. I looked up. Jane waited patiently. I thrust my card into her hand and, instead of introducing myself formally, simply said, "I'm Fred." Why hadn't I said my *last* name? My organization?

"I'm Jane," she replied, my hand in hers, and she wouldn't let go. She didn't *look at* me so much as *see* me.

I blurted out: "My friends call me Freddy."

She released me, stared at my card and peered at me one more time. "Thank you, Freddy. Here's mine."

Freddy? Really? Was this some cheap attempt at informality? I returned to my seat, horrified at my lack of professionalism. I could not remember the rest of the speeches that afternoon. At the end of the day, the crowd filed out. I stayed behind, taking notes. Gathering my things, I missed the exit sign and opened a door into a pitch-black closet. Spotting a sharp line of daylight at the bottom of a door, I found my way out to an alley where a group of caterers, dishwashers and maintenance workers on a smoke break pointed to the street. I strode past them as casually as I could.

My embarrassment dissipated quickly. I walked the 37 blocks back to my friend's place in a surreal, late afternoon light. I didn't see Jane Goodall again at the conference, but I practiced shaking with my right hand and handing the card to the big shot with the left, certain to say something complimentary and succinct about the presentation. None of it mattered. I had met Jane Goodall! *Hoo hoo!*

Four months later, a postcard arrived. "It was great to meet you," she wrote, "and I believe wholeheartedly in what you are doing. Just know that it's going to be hard. Don't give up."

I couldn't think of any way to respond other than by handwritten letter, something I hadn't done since sending aerograms in China decades before. Words racing ahead of thought, I tore up version after version. Tell her about the organization. (Too stilted.) Thank her for her contributions to science and humanity. (Too obsequious.) Describe what she means to you. (Too shallow.) What did she see when she looked at me that way? Make it short, punchy and focused.

I described my speech at my socialist-themed Bar Mitzvah held in my backyard rather than in a temple. My father had secretly recorded it. When I told him I was starting an organization called Teachers Without Borders, he transferred it to cassette and dropped it in the mail. My voice cracking and squeaking, I spoke about the need to "help teachers all around the world" and that teachers were the key to peace.

I told Jane about how I wanted to connect teachers, enhance the dignity of the profession, and help to mend and repair a broken world. I confessed I had half-baked answers for the insuperable problems ahead. I promised her that I didn't know the rules, but that I would try to stay the course, just as she had asked me to do.

I practiced my handwriting and revised obsessively. What the hell, I concluded. I am who I am. Seal it. Send it. Don't expect anything. Write from the stomach, not the head.

Her postcards continued, followed up by handwritten letters, random phone calls, and visits. Here is my favorite: as Jane approached the fiftieth anniversary of her groundbreaking work in Gombe, she composed this by a Gombe waterfall:

Dear Brother Fred,

Am sitting, late afternoon by the waterfall, this most spiritual place in Gombe. So much ancient life force. This is where the medicine men used to practice their secret rituals twice a year. How can half a century have passed since then and I first landed here? It does not seem possible. Yet, it is our 50th anniversary on the 16th, tomorrow.

The bombs in Kampala seem so far away, unreal, as I sit here. Another world altogether. A grim world in so many respects, but a wonderful world too.

[She expressed her desire to meet soon and, running out of space, added (as she always does):]

Lots of love,
Jane

A grim and wonderful world. Though Jane Goodall is on the move 300 days a year (except for a break during COVID), we have found the time to travel together, serve on panels and meet an occasional head of state. She is as joyful, warm and sincere in private as she is on stage. Once, near the end of a lavish dinner, Jane excused herself. After a while, a colleague and I noticed that she had not returned. We asked someone at the table to volunteer to check the women's restroom. No Jane. We looked outside to see if she was mingling with autograph seekers. Still no Jane.

Just as we returned to the table, she emerged from the swinging double doors leading to the kitchen. She wanted to thank the chefs and dishwashers and waiters directly for their hard work.

When we get together over Chinese food and a spot of whiskey, I feel loved. We laugh. She tells stories of children and their parents, world leaders, prisoners, machinists, dishwashers and farmers who have held Mr. H., her stuffed monkey. We hug. We take pictures. We promise to stay in touch.

I have seized every opportunity I could to see her again. I am a lucky man.

Chapter 4

My Brother, Jihad

Teachers Without Borders began as a concept looking for a project. Soon enough, that project found TWB. The first partner would be a man named Jihad. It was May 2001.

Pilot projects to bring computers to the people, or bring people to computers, were gaining traction. The prevailing wisdom was, "If you build it, they will come." The idea was to fill the gap between digital haves and have-nots. Machines would help them participate in an increasingly interdependent world. It felt sincere and I wanted in.

"Computers for the World" (C4W) was an after-school service-learning club for computer students who refurbish PCs for use in developing countries, set them up on-site and teach basic IT skills. Students held fundraisers for their travel and shipping so that people and machines would arrive at the same time.

I wrangled an invitation from Rotary International to attend a C4W meeting. When I arrived, students were clearing two tables littered with computer chassis, motherboards, monitors, keyboards, cords and tools. After brief introductions, the computer teacher offered an update on ongoing and emerging projects in Russia, Mexico, the Philippines and Mozambique. Two Rotarians in attendance pledged support.

It was time to choose the next project. Kay Bullitt, born in 1925, a Radcliffe grad, mother of six, and a tireless advocate for human rights and school desegregation, offered a laundry list of compelling reasons to support a new opportunity in Laqiya, a village populated by a Bedouin community on the northern edge of the Negev Desert, close to the bustling, modern Israeli city of Beer Sheva, once the source of Jacob's stairway to heaven and later conquered by King David.

Laqiya had consistent electricity, Kay explained. There were good roads. The community was committed to providing educational opportunities for students to engage in constructive activities after school. Contrary to widely held belief, the community is *not* isolated, nomadic or threatening, but accessible, anchored and friendly. The local leader was trustworthy and motivated. She paused until all eyes were on her. "I have met Jihad El-Sana. He and Laqiya are *not* a threat."

Jihad is a Bedouin professor of computer science and mathematics at Ben Gurion University and a Fulbright Scholar with a PhD in Computer Science from the State University of New York at Stony Brook. Highly respected in his field of 3D graphics, mathematical modeling and augmented reality, Jihad is often cited in his field's most influential academic journals.

He is also one of nine siblings. Throughout his childhood, his mother was illiterate. His father, a truck driver without a formal education, longed for his children to finish school but did not live long enough to see it happen. Jihad had vowed to keep his father's dream alive. He wanted his mother to learn how to read.

Jihad had met with Kay to discuss the idea of a community computer center in Laqiya. His village association agreed to provide the space. Jihad's graduate students would support the upkeep of the computers and teach youth in after-school programs to communicate with their counterparts in the US. Jihad would take care of all arrangements at his end. He simply needed computers.

Kay's idea was rejected. Someone offered: "How about Ecuador?" The mood seemed to change. I slipped Kay a note to reassure her that I was in. She dashed off her response: "Wonderful!"

As people were packing up to go, I announced: "I'll do it!" I had no idea how to start. I had neither a track record nor a plan. "I don't have the details or money for my own travel yet, but I'll do it. The kids won't have to go. We can make the connections virtually."

Kay pressed a note with Jihad's email and her phone number into my hand. We took it from there.

After several conversations with Jihad, I told my wife, "I want to go to the Negev Desert to start my first project with a guy named Jihad. I met him on the internet. Seems like a great guy." I could understand her concern. Fire yourself from your job and then make friends with Jihad? How about *easing into* projects?

This might be a career choice as flimsy as a paper towel. Once it absorbed reality, it would lose its purpose. Could I not find a starter project less fraught with challenges? Did I have to learn everything the hard way? She also sensed my determination. She pulled herself together and said, "Freddy, be careful, but I can't stop you. I won't. Just do the right thing. It may work or it may not." She smiled uncomfortably. "Even if this TWB thing is one gigantic extended manic episode."

For weeks, Jihad and I exchanged ideas and settled on a Community Teaching and Learning Center concept. There would be two rooms: one with computers, the other with bookshelves and pillows. I read everything I could about Bedouin communities.

Suppose all goes well and the computers arrive on time. What about those dust storms that roar in from the Sinai and destroy the machines? What if I get taken hostage? Or eaten by an angry camel, or picked at by a vulture like Warren Beatty in *Ishtar*?

I asked two local universities for computers that could handle 220 volts, monitors and surge protectors. Each opened a storage closet. Microsoft obliged with several computers they used to test versions of Microsoft Office. Others' e-waste became my entry into the world of international development shipping and handling. I cozied up to office managers and assured them they would receive public plaudits for their gesture. It worked every time. A maintenance man led me to a dumpster in a parking garage. There, I retrieved four more used computers. An executive from DHL offered to ship them for free. Kay gave me a pep talk on how to ask donors for flight money.

I landed in Tel Aviv and reached in my pocket for Jihad's directions to take a bus to Laqiya. I handed the driver a slip of paper Jihad had sent over, ingratiating myself to him by asking in broken Hebrew and with my best pitiful face to watch out for my stop. A petite Israeli woman in her late teens took the aisle seat next to me and rested her Uzi across my lap, checking her light-pink fingernails and adjusting her ponytail through her scrunchie.

Close to two hours later, the bus lurched to a stop. There was nothing much around, though I thought I had seen a McDonald's a few kilometers back. *An optical illusion*, I told myself. *This is the desert, though not the cartoon version.* As we approached the next stop, passengers began to clutch their enormous blue tarpaulin bags and suitcases. I loitered near the driver, showing him the note. He held out his hand. "Next one," he said, in English, then told me to sit down.

The bus came to a stop. I stepped off and it sped away. I stood with a suitcase in each hand, blinking from the exhaust, rounds of sweat under my arms and an impressive heart-shaped perspiration blot on my shirt. I looked for Jihad to materialize from behind the dust and bus exhaust. Nothing but a mirage of water as the road curved ahead. I turned to see a modern building. In the corner of the empty parking lot, a camel foraged through a dumpster. Funny, I thought, I had been doing that very thing not so long ago. The camel returned my gaze, then spat. I was impressed by the arc of spittle but pretended not to notice. "Fuck you, too, ship of the desert," I mouthed out of earshot, moving my jaw in a circle in my best camel imitation.

I pushed my suitcases together, sat on them, and contemplated my next move and fate.

I collected my bags and walked to the building ahead. I tried the door. No luck. I peered inside. A building supervisor looked up and opened the door. I offered my well-practiced "*As-salaam alaikum*" (peace be upon you), to which he answered with the customary "*Wa-alaikum salaam*" (and upon you, peace). The supervisor spoke patiently in Arabic. Noting my bewilderment, he switched to Hebrew. Charades would be our lingua franca. I fingered my shirt pocket for Jihad's soggy note, relieved that the words scrawled in pen had not bled into illegibility.

I looked outside. No bus, no cars, no Jihad. I gestured a kind of *mahalo* request to use a phone. He motioned down the hall.

I started to dial, forgetting to drop the country code. I tried again, interrupted by the operator before I had a chance to complete the sequence. I slowed down, mumbling the numbers aloud as I punched them in. *I am genuinely addled*, I thought. I tried again and got his answering machine. I left a message with the number on the phone booth and told him I was inside the building. Hanging up, I smiled pitifully and indicated I would like to sit down. The supervisor nodded his approval. I stared at the pay phone, willing it to ring.

I considered asking him: "Do you know Jihad?" In that setting, the question would have been a reasonable one, but I wasn't entirely sure. If I asked the same question in the United

States, I might get cuffed. Somehow, asking someone if they know Jesus would be entirely acceptable. Jihad? No.

I decided to go with: "I am looking for Doctor Jihad El-Sana, professor," pointing to words for *professor* in Hebrew and Arabic, "at Ben Gurion University." No response. I sat down. The building was a newly built teaching center, museum, lecture hall and library. Propitious, indeed. It was only natural that Jihad would frequent such a place. I picked up a brochure in Arabic looking for pictures of board members, expecting to see his face. I waited. Still no Jihad.

Someone new approached and asked in Arabic and Hebrew who I was. I pointed to the slip of paper drying out on the ledge of the pay phone. He placed his hand on his heart to signify, I interpreted, that he was friendly. In perfect English he said, "You're looking for Jihad? May I help?" He called the number, looking back at me with a disarming smile. No answer. He left no message. Catching a glimpse of my crestfallen face, he tried again, leaving a message in Arabic.

In what seemed like an hour (more likely 20 minutes), Jihad appeared, breathless and apologetic, took my bags and ushered me into his car. His family was waiting for us at home, he said. He apologized for being late. He should have left a message with the teaching center.

It mattered little to me. We had connected and I immediately felt safe. We stopped at a Bedouin market to pick up two freshly killed, unplucked chickens.

At his home, we removed our shoes. He placed the chickens in the sink, washed his hands in a bowl and kissed his mother. She smiled. I knew enough not to attempt to shake her hand. In a room furnished with pillows and a flowered, plastic tablecloth spread over rugs woven by local women, we ate sumptuously. His mother smiled often. Jihad often brought home guests.

The following morning, he showed me the site of the Laqiya Community Teaching and Learning Center. The computers would show up soon, he reported. I deluged him with questions about surge protectors, maintenance, dust, security, program, paint, carpet and supervision. It's covered, he explained.

"Don't be concerned about the Center," he said. "If we need paint or carpet, we'll ask. If we need supervision, we'll talk with the teachers. The program will follow."

Groups of villagers visited Jihad over the next few days. They had secured the building, finalized arrangements for carpet and paint, and created a class schedule once the computers arrived and were installed. Two of Jihad's graduate students appeared in response to a posted flyer on campus. I was surprised at the ease of it all. Jihad looked puzzled. "Isn't this what communities do?"

Jihad wanted to address two pressing issues. The first had to do with increasing youth restiveness following a recent incident in which a group of teens had provoked Israeli police after a controversial film made the rounds. Shot from inside a tent, it showed Israeli soldiers bulldozing an unrecognized village. The police claimed that waste and garbage were fouling the ecosystem of the fields. The community asserted that this was a clear violation of a lease and an audacious excuse for a land grab. Jihad pointed out that youth are easily sucked into a vortex of resentment, setting off a vicious cycle of anger, reaction, incarceration and anger. The Community Teaching and Learning Center needed to be an alluring distraction and a teaching opportunity.

His second concern had to do with a vanishing awareness of identity and history in the Bedouin community. Increasing access to media seemed to underscore a stark contrast between their lives and those of their peers in other countries. They wanted to afford those Big Macs (it had not been an illusion).

The adults considered fast food expensive and tasteless and the chain an insult. He wanted more critical thinking. The digital divide was an education divide. At stake: his culture.

I recalled a conversation a colleague told me about what we mean by culture in the age of globalism. As both an anthropological and biological metaphor, culture can be viewed as "a way of life" (who we are, what we do, how we have learned to act) and "a medium for growing things" (a petri dish, a fertile environment).

We discussed what this might mean for our project. Given that culture is viewed only as "a way of life," how might communities cope with modernity? Languages and customs are rendered extinct every year. At the same time, cultural preservationists may unintentionally marginalize the very people they want to protect by making them appear exotic and helpless.

Jihad explained that globalization is a given and should be embraced, but it can leave whole communities behind, run roughshod over cultural traditions and look distinctly American. Anti-globalization groups claiming to speak for the underserved have told him that poor communities do not need computers but basics. He rolled his eyes. "Tell that to someone looking for where to get the best price for seeds, or how to get a license to start a business, or what they can do to stop their child's diarrhea." I thought of the WTO protestors.

Jihad remained in the village, he said, instead of moving to Beer Sheva or Tel Aviv, precisely because communities bring about sustainable change by marshaling *local* intelligence. That's how paint and carpet can appear overnight. He would keep his promise to his father to become educated and to educate others in return.

He invited me to the wedding of a relative in a tent. We agreed to split the cost of a sheep as an appropriate gift. We sat on ornately woven rugs and pillows, rose for family members, and expressed our appreciation for the meal and our joy at the family's pride.

Our conversation continued. "A way of life and a medium for growing things," he said aloud. "I got it. We'll teach them how to conduct interviews, tape oral histories and photograph portraits to capture the stories of their elders and record our traditions. Then they'll come back to the Community Teaching and Learning Center. We'll put it all together and make CDs. This way we'll record our culture using skills they'll need for the future. The Community Teaching and Learning Center will be the bridge between 'a way of life' and 'a medium for growing things.'"

The Laqiya Community Teaching and Learning Center was born. Later that night, I listened to the percussive sounds of guns fired skyward to celebrate the wedding, like holiday fireworks at a public park.

The computers arrived intact a week after I had returned home. Jihad's graduate students fulfilled their commitment to set them up and served as teachers and camp counselors after school. Over the years, Jihad continued to operate the Community Teaching and Learning Center to connect technology, education and community development. He received his tenure at Ben Gurion University and, to this day, leads efforts to ensure that the citizens of Laqiya are learning not only about who they are but also about who and what they can be. It takes that kind of leader to raise a village.

Four months later, on 12 September 2001, I called Jihad. His voice had none of its former confidence. "We are devastated," he mumbled. "I also want to tell you this, Fred. At dark times like this, we must light a candle."

That night, I lit a Yahrzeit candle, a Jewish ritual for remembering the dead.

A few years later, Jihad and I met in New York. He had been working on an early version of virtual reality programs that included an interactive dimension for patients at children's hospitals to determine whether gaming could help with pain alleviation. I was in Manhattan at an education conference.

He told me that a women's weaving group had moved into the offline room and were selling their wares. "Do you remember my mother?" he asked. "She decided she wanted to learn how to read. With the other women in the weaving group, they found an instructor. Get this, Fred. She's in third grade!"

Jihad and I see each other far too rarely, but it never matters. I love my brother, Jihad.

Chapter 5

Shall We Stay the Same?

I could see Teachers Without Borders because I believed it. I knew that most people would believe it only once they had seen it.

A small pilot in a Bedouin village does not prove organizational viability. The world owes us nothing. I don't believe in karma, a higher being or cosmic synchronicity. There is some credence to the saying that luck favors the prepared mind, but beginner's luck doesn't count. I had fired myself from an excellent job to step out into the unknown. I should expect slammed doors, rejection and failure.

For many, development depends upon replicating and scaling projects. I wanted to take another approach — to replicate Jihad's: talented, good-hearted, unflappable people who think more about removing obstacles than building empires. People with street cred, yet equally comfortable around the powerful. People who can challenge the status quo yet remain humble and question their assumptions. People with valuable information to share.

It also seemed natural that the organization should act like the best of classrooms. If children learn best when they can help shape their learning, then our programs must be led and governed by the talent that created them. If learning is most effective when flexible and personalized, then the same should be true of teacher professional development. If the best classrooms are a buzz of small groups tinkering and thinking together, then a global community of teachers should rely on each other to test innovative ideas. If safe, healthy classrooms function best when they cultivate and foster a moral social contract, so too should we attract those who could help others on a global scale.

That was the pitch. I made my case to anyone who would listen.

I received responses like this: "Well, would you look at the time!" Some feigned interest, but their eyes told me their thoughts were elsewhere. Some were blunt: "Fred, teachers are the busiest people on earth. They have enough on their plates already. Now you're going to dump society's problems on them?" In an exceptionally rugged intimation that I harbored megalomaniacal intentions of being the world's principal, someone said, "Do you *really* think you can expect people to depend upon you to orchestrate global change from a laptop in Seattle?" I said, "No, but..."

Teachers, however, understood and contacted their colleagues. Teachers who had responded to my doctoral survey got on board. I received postcards and handwritten letters about *changing* what was outside their windows.

I searched for one letter to which I had not yet responded: an invitation to visit Ahmedabad, formerly the capital of the Indian state of Gujarat. I dug it out and reread it. Deepmala Khera wanted to summon teachers to introduce the concept of Teachers Without Borders, then turn them loose. She described her sadness at seeing whole segments of school-aged children ignored and underserved. She had long recognized the futility of waiting for authorities to create, nurture and enforce education-friendly policies. She was not asking for money, favors or answers, simply my commitment to help her spark a conversation among teachers. Ahmedabad would be the perfect setting for convening teachers to discuss educational issues that matter to them. She didn't explain why.

Deepmala showed up for those teachers. I had to show up for her.

The Ahmedabad I saw was a *Koyaanisqatsi* blur of honking buses, cars, Tata trucks without side-view mirrors, farm animals, yellow and green tuk-tuks, whole families on motorcycles, bicycles trilling bells, and two-wheeled carts groaning under the weight of rebar, bamboo, blankets, wood, animal cages and folding chairs. The moment a traffic light changed or a police officer decided to give the "go" signal, swarms at cross streets pinballed ahead. This city was a game of Tetris, ping-pong and shuffleboard all in one. My driver's training instructor's mantra came to mind: "Drive defensively, get the big picture and leave yourself an out."

The air was thick with smog, soot, samosas, brackish water, Durian fruit, urine, diesel exhaust, incense and calls to prayer. Steam billowed from grills under blue tarps. Women in navy blue, peach and magenta saris chatted and held bowls of everything above their heads with one hand and children with the other. Couples fanned themselves with newspapers.

I was a stranger in a strange land yet again, dropped off a dozen time-zones away and left holding my bags. I took a cab to Deepmala's neighborhood, but construction barriers and a collision prevented me from reaching her home. I switched to method-acting mode again: the helpless, middle-aged, lost foreigner hoping to find a sympathetic companion to escort me to Deepmala. I pulled out yet another wadded-up address, this one written in Gujarati and English. I drew a small crowd, all convinced they knew the way, some pointing in opposite directions. If you want to be truly multicultural and work effectively in the global arena, learn several languages.

Someone swiped the piece of paper from me and shouted the address to an apartment building. A woman leaned out and, in turn, yelled to someone else across a ganglion of power cables, clotheslines of children's shirts hanging upside down, arms fluttering in the breeze like inflatable air dancers, bras, saris and sari pants, sheets, and sturdier lines holding blankets.

Suddenly, I heard my name: "Dr. Fred! You made it!"

Deepmala was returning from her teaching job, panting, waving. "Dr. Fred! Mr. Fred! Fred Mednick!" A dozen children lagged behind her, some in school uniforms, others in donated American soccer T-shirts and worn rubber chappals. She picked up the pace, pulled by a determined-looking girl wearing a Disney backpack, braids bouncing and swaying, holding Deepmala's key.

Once inside, I saw an open room. In one corner, a stack of folding chairs. In another corner, a single table with baskets of colored pencils and pastels, bottled water and snacks. Early that morning, Deepmala had taped poster paper to her walls from the floor to the height of an 8-year-old on tiptoes.

The children knew what to do when they entered the room. Two boys, Shaival and Dilip, distributed the colored pencils and pastels. Others paired up to work on their shared paper real estate, careful not to trespass on each other's drawings.

"Who wants to draw a bowl of fruit?" "Who wants to draw an elephant?" "Who wants to draw from your imagination?" "Show me!"

As the artists labored, Deepmala circulated among them, cooing as if she had just stumbled upon a breathtaking work of fine art. Should they tussle over colors or compete for her attention, she would refrain from intervening. Instead, she asked questions. "How can you both solve this problem?" "What happens inside when one of you wins and the other loses?" She never raised her voice. Manju, a little girl holding her hand, never left Deepmala's side. When she saw most of the children busying themselves with their masterpieces, Deepmala would hoist Manju on her lap, stroke her hair and read to her softly.

Deepmala kept track of them and knew instinctively what each child needed.

The children came back day after day after day for drawings, games, reading, praise, bottled water and snacks. All children were welcome, whether they attended school wearing crisp uniforms or spent much of their day picking through rags and trash. She had sheltered a few, she whispered, at risk from traffickers. "You cannot protect children without educating them," she said. "And you can't educate children without protecting them."

One evening, before we turned her temporary school back into her living space, she pulled out a roll of pictures and smoothed them on the floor. "I kept these for you. They drew the World Trade Center," she said, "from what they heard on the radio." The buildings had faces. Bodies falling from windows were tears. "It was their choice. I couldn't get myself to ask questions about it."

It was the first day of Diwali, a "festival of lights" in which candles and clay lamps lit with oil brighten homes, places of worship and streets. Lakes sparkle with floating lanterns. Observers clean their homes and create designs in sand, colored rice or flowers, and greet visitors. Deepmala informed me that the fifth day of Diwali, Yama Dwitiya, involves sisters inviting brothers to their homes. All were welcome here, year-round. I was her brother, she said.

* * *

Ahmedabad is the site of Mahatma Gandhi's Sabarmati Ashram, a center of his nonviolent movement for India's independence and his 24-day, 240-mile act of civil disobedience: the Salt Satyagraha, a truth-telling march and global awareness campaign focusing on the single issue of making salt without having to pay exorbitant British Raj salt taxes. Salt became the symbol of the people's sweat and the product of their labor.

The march captured their imagination and catalyzed the transformation from colonialization to liberation.

Inspired by Mahatma Gandhi's leadership of a textile worker strike, the Textile Labour Association (TLA) began in Ahmedabad in 1920. Cart pullers living in the streets and working for Ahmedabad's cloth market sought TLA's help to fight for fair housing and equal rights. In 1954, the women's wing focused on protecting women from exploitation and morphed into the Self-Employed Women's Association (SEWA), a women's trade union founded to defend the rights of exploited and disenfranchised women through a system of cooperatives and networks. It was not easy. Ela Bhatt, a young lawyer, was rebuffed when she and hundreds of garment workers tried to register the organization with the Labor Commissioner of Gujarat. They were told they could not qualify because they were not a formal entity. By stitching garments at home, women were invisible economic contributors and excluded from the census.

With no government structures in place to provide job opportunities, job security or protections, SEWA would organize the unorganized, two-thirds of whom came from rural communities: vendors and hawkers, yarn spinners, dung collectors, rag pickers and midwives, many harassed and attacked as they searched for work. Almost 90% worked in agriculture. Early on, they recognized that empowerment and self-reliance would only be possible through an informal system of sustainable wraparound services on their terms. SEWA campaigns arise wherever women are in need: legal aid, savings and credit, healthcare, childcare, housing, education, capacity building. The *International Journal of Politics, Culture and Society* illustrates SEWA's demand-driven approach:

A good example is the story of Kunvarba, who grows roses for a living with the help of her family members. She picks roses at night for delivery the next morning. Without SEWA, she would hold a lantern in one hand and pick flowers with the other. At SEWA's instigation, engineers designed a headlamp much like a miner's lamp that runs on a solar-powered battery. Kunvarba can pick many more roses and, as she excitedly reports, her income "has gone up faster too."[4]

This was bottom-up democracy in its truest form, where women were heard and in charge: locally *and* nationally. SEWA's model has always fostered interpersonal relationships, recognition for the marginalized, homegrown leadership and the collective wisdom residing in its network. I have always believed that global philanthropy focuses on deficits rather than on home-grown assets. A deficit mentality incubates dependency. An asset mentality emphasizes self-reliance and local solutions. SEWA walked this talk.

Deepmala introduced me to Dhara and Ami, two cheery SEWA workers who joined us for a seven-hour car trip to a northwest region of Kutch, a region caked, dusty, and devastated by an earthquake in the city of Bhuj just eight months earlier. Dhara and Ami passed around triangular cheesy ghughra sandwiches of fresh coriander, onion, and chaat masala. They shared stories of women cast aside by caste, mistreated and abused, along with stories of self-reliance and hope. Two hours in, Dhara handed me a SEWA poster with these words painted on a picket sign:

Our bodies are our wealth
Our houses are our workplace
Our children are our future
Our lives are full of crises

After the government launched a program to reduce the number of diesel buses, SEWA partnered with NGOs and civil society organizations to turn diesel buses into mobile libraries, even entire schools, rather than clog up landfills.

In Bhuj, we walked on streets where multistoried buildings had dissolved in an earthquake that killed over 18,000 people, injuring over 165,000, and destroying or damaging close to a million apartments, many constructed on the cheap by substituting illegal amounts of compacted sand in place of concrete and without sufficient reinforcement or anchors. Out of 1359 schools, 992 were destroyed.[5] SEWA had already distributed learning kits/toys to support the 500 families in the salt fields. They worked with partners to build traditional circular, domed Kutch homes made from local bamboo and wood, and thatched and plastered with mud and dung. The cylindrical shape does not resist wind and is less likely to become unstable from lateral forces. The mud against curved walls helps with cooling, and the dung serves as insulation against frigid winters.

Earthquakes decimate the poorest and most densely populated communities living in unreinforced buildings erected atop known and often shallow fault lines. All of it was preventable. Educational fault lines are systemic structural hazards because illiteracy and the absence of awareness about basic safety measures undermine the foundations that hold society together. The temblors of corruption and neglect put lives at risk. Unsafe buildings, like an inadequately constructed education system, may withstand a shock here and there but are compromised to the point of collapse at the next earthquake or aftershock. Five years after the devastation in Bhuj, Teachers Without Borders launched its earthquake science and safety program. I consider it to be our finest achievement.

The following day, we traveled to a SEWA-run program focused on teaching women to read. Many had never seen their names in print. Dhara and Ami spent several minutes walking about the village, chatting with the women in ways that felt like a visit with old friends, then shooed us into an abandoned stable-turned-classroom. Soon, a group of women assembled.

Dhara and Ami distributed slates (yes, real slates), chalk and small damp towels, then Dhara told the assembled group, "This could be our lucky day." The women looked at each other, not sure they had heard correctly. She continued, "Because today, everybody can feel the joy of achievement." Dhara and Ami both went on to explain that success would be possible only when everyone received a score of 20 out of 20 on the upcoming activity. They were to mark their slates (no iPads here) and help each other during the practice session. The incentive was clear. If we help each other, we all win. This was cooperative learning at its core. Any observer from the West would be awestruck at its elegance: curriculum seamlessly integrated into assessment, an inviting climate for learning, pedagogy that met the moment, peer support and measurable outcomes, all without the latest gadgets or electricity. The absence of Eduspeak was refreshing.

Dhara and Ami were helping women construct and design a resilient foundation for a future grounded in literacy. Should we wish to consider society as we would a building, then literacy is education's rebar.

And yet, SEWA projects were hardly the only examples of educational ingenuity I saw. Back in Ahmedabad, Deepmala introduced me to Dr. B. R. Sitaram, the Director of the Vikram A. Sarabhai Community Science Centre. Sitaram was eager to show how essential science concepts could be accessible using local materials. He taught children principles of motion and the function of a stroboscope by instructing them to glue bhindis onto bicycle wheels. He showed how a pinhole camera worked, and helped children construct their own with cardboard paper rolls and found objects. I watched children hard at work designing a wave machine out of straws, discarded plastic and gummy-bear-like candy.

"Come outside with me," he said. "I want to show you an example of playground science at work." We strode up to a merry-go-round. Dr. Sitaram asked, "What is centrifugal force?" Children grabbed a bar, ran two revolutions and jumped on, leaning against the curved bars. When they came to a stop, a girl peered up at him and described the concept. We walked over to a swing set. Children took turns pushing each other in higher and higher arcs, pumping their legs and increasing their speed. Sitaram asked, "How does that work?" One child responded on behalf of his peers, "We're conserving energy by storing it up!"

Dr. Sitaram said to us quietly, "Well, sort of...but we just started," and explained his lesson on principles of potential and kinetic energy. He had retrofitted the swing set with an extra bar to show the transfer of energy from one swing that has come to a halt and generate enough to propel an empty swing forward.

He explained that a lack of resources is an opportunity to be creative. Using props available, Dr. Sitaram engaged hearts, minds and imaginations. He argued that, while municipalities should not stoop so low as to use this creative problem-solving as an excuse to abdicate their responsibility for funding schools, the lack of funds for science kits or other manipulatives should not stand in one's way. "Besides," he said, "textbook or swing set? You choose." No wonder Deepmala chose him to keynote a conference she had been organizing on behalf of Teachers Without Borders from all sectors of Gujarati society: Hindu and Muslim teachers, government and private school teachers, and teachers from different castes. She had also put the children to work, assembling packets of donated materials she, too, had collected.

Deepmala titled the conference: "Shall We Stay the Same?" True, it was a rhetorical question, but it led naturally to a teacher-led discussion about the status quo and its consequences. Staying still and waiting for help from the government would put education that much further behind. She found formal teacher preparation programs inconsequential and irrelevant. Learning from peers would be the only suitable form of professional development, an opportunity to stretch, interact with colleagues and take risks.

Teachers did precisely that. They aired grievances and sought help from each other. "My students are falling behind in reading. Can anyone help?" "My school director doesn't want anything to change. I feel trapped." "I've tried everything to get children re-enrolled after they drop out, but it feels impossible. What can I do?"

Teachers divided into groups, then generated and prioritized audacious ideas without fear of censure, refined solutions, drew prototypes and discussed the implications of implementation against the realities of intransigent policies and resistance. They spread large sheets of paper on the floor (Deepmala must have had an endless supply) to sketch out presentations and to list questions for further discussion. Completed sessions were pasted on the walls.

She had orchestrated everything. At a break, high-school students performed an original play about feeling empty in classrooms that did not celebrate learning. Clearly, Deepmala wanted this conference to end with an answer to her question. No, things should not stay the same.

By the end of the second day, teachers committed to creating a global, modular, culturally sensitive teacher professional development program available online and offline. They would build teacher communities to supplement traditional teacher education; influence policy; and create materials for teachers free from restrictive copyright restrictions in a form that they could update, translate, adapt and remix to meet local contexts, current needs and cultural orientations.

For a few hours near the end of the third and final day, Deepmala was conspicuously absent, yet the conference no longer depended upon her. However, a robust discussion about building a campaign against corporal punishment in schools was getting louder. The room felt tense. I did not know what to do should this escalate into a shouting match. Rain began to lash against the tin roof and sluice across the windows. I spied her outside under an awning, shielded from the rain. She had arrived with her after-school group of students and street children. Her fellow apartment dwellers had helped her bathe them and hem and patch the finest clothes they could collect or salvage. Boys wore a *sherwani* (a long, silky jacket embroidered with ornate stitchery) and gold pants. Girls wore a *lehenga* (a long skirt) in royal blue, magenta or bright orange.

Deepmala led them into the room, single file. They split into two groups standing on each side of her. She asked for the teachers' attention. On cue, the oldest child lit a candle. From behind their backs, each child brought forth candles wedged into the slot of compact discs they had decorated with flowers, patterns and the words: "Spread the Light." The rain beat harder, but no one seemed to notice. A child walked down the line, lighting each candle.

Deepmala clapped her hands. The children began a song they had rehearsed: "Don't Let the Light Go Out." It was fitting that children would answer Deepmala's question, "Shall We Stay the Same?" Please don't stay in darkness. A minute into their song, the lights flickered and failed. At first, the children looked to Deepmala for direction. She turned to the children and then to those assembled and asked, "How can we ensure that the light does not go out?" Reassured, the children continued to sing and present their CD candles, their faces suffused with a warm glow. The teachers joined in, many in tears.

That was enough for the teachers to agree they shall not strike children and shall campaign to end corporal punishment in their schools. "The right of the child to protection from corporal punishment and other cruel or degrading forms of punishment" was not introduced by the United Nations until 2006.[6] In India, progress was excruciatingly slow. Officials were paying attention, but despite Indian law and signed agreements, violence against children persisted in homes and schools, justified as a socialization process: punishment for being absent, for being ill, for working, for not doing homework, for not paying fees, for not wearing a uniform, for being a girl. A 2015 article in *The Guardian* quoted a 10-year-old girl:

> If we don't study, they beat us. If we ask other children for help, they beat [us]. I went to drink water without asking sir, so he beat me that time. They said all children should come back to class by the time they count to 10 after the interval. But I went home [to use the toilet]. After coming back to school, he beat me.[7]

Unlike many conferences, this one did not evaporate. Teachers saw themselves as multipliers and accelerators of change. Following the conference, educators from 23 countries collaborated with them to develop curricula for another commitment: to create a five-course, free Certificate of Teaching Mastery (CTM) program for educating peers about twenty-first-century teaching, assessment, classroom management, multiculturalism and community development. The CTM has been adapted to meet local contexts, translated into multiple languages, and adopted by unions as an offering on a par with far more expensive and less flexible offerings. Rice University's Connexions and Cisco System's platforms for course delivery expanded its reach. United Nations Volunteers adapted the

CTM for development workshops. The World Bank included a version of the CTM on 30,000 PCs recycled and shipped to country offices.

* * *

I hadn't known much about Ahmedabad before this trip. Deepmala did not spend time filling me in on the city's complicated history. Beneath its surface of mercantilism, culture and development, Ahmedabad has experienced multiple cycles of communal violence.

Hindus have claimed that Ayodhya (a city 860 miles to the northeast of Ahmedabad) was the birthplace of Ram, a significant deity and seventh incarnation of Vishnu. Bābur, a Mughal emperor in the late sixteenth century, replaced a Hindu temple on the site with the Babri Masjid mosque ("Mosque of Bābur"). In 1992, Hindu nationalists rampaged and destroyed the Babri Masjid mosque with sledgehammers, ransacked and demolished hundreds of homes, businesses and places of worship, raped Muslim women, looted shops and killed close to 1000 people. According to a report in *The New York Times*, a former Muslim member of the Indian National Congress party was "hacked to pieces and burned."[8] I was unaware that Ahmedabad had been brewing again. Now I understood Deepmala's impatience.

Three months after the conference, a tinderbox of conflict set Ahmedabad ablaze again. A Sabarmati Express train carrying dozens of Hindu pilgrims returning from a religious ceremony in the northern city of Ayodhya stopped in a town with a high percentage of Muslims. After shouting and provocation, a fire roared through one of the coaches, killing 59: 9 men, 25 women and 25 children. Widespread reports attributed the train inferno to a planned attack by Muslim terrorists. The Gujarati press ran articles with inflammatory, unfounded claims against Muslims, setting off a brutal campaign of politically driven violence: children massacred, women gang-raped, and businesses and homes burned.

A University of Delhi report implicates the ruling party:

> The carefully executed and precisely designed pogrom was meticulously planned and orchestrated...The selective targeting of Muslims, the arson, the rapes and murders were carried out with the kind of exactitude that presumes foreknowledge and advance planning.[9]

The Bharatiya Janata Party (BJP), led by the Chief Minister of Gujarat, Narendra Modi (now India's prime minister), not only refused to confront mobs attacking Muslims but also provided no protection for Parliament members, and waited 36 hours, well into the massacre, before asking the police to step in. Months later, Modi spoke in a district where Muslims were torched in their homes, fueling his version of Hindutva, a Hindu ethnonationalist and Islamophobic movement from the 1920s: "What should we do? Run relief camps for them? Do we want to open baby-producing centers? We must teach a lesson to those who are increasing population at an alarming rate."[10]

Deepmala had convened a conference that represented a diverse cross-section of teachers from a city on edge. Its success was a testament to possibility and hope. Within a week of the conflict, Deepmala received a five-word note from an attendee: "Teachers don't kill each other." They had made a commitment to condemn corporal punishment and to learn from each other. How might we teach peace in a city on edge? A world on edge?

Deepmala reported that Shaival and Dilip, two of the artists, had opened a tea shop and were doing well. Manju, the shy, clingy girl, had stood up and opposed her parents as they tried to force her into marriage at 16. Deepmala confessed, "I feel guilty sometimes that I did not follow through and hold all their hands for just a bit longer."

In 2020, while Modi was hosting Donald Trump in Ahmedabad, nationalists whipped up industrial-strength hate speech, chanted anti-Muslim slurs, vandalized property and once again set fire to mosques. I can picture Deepmala shaking her head, wishing she could do more.

A Teachers Without Borders peace education program would materialize and take hold several years later.

Chapter 6

In the Small Places

In 1948, just three years after the establishment of the United Nations, the United Nations General Assembly adopted the Universal Declaration of Human Rights (UDHR). Translated into over 500 languages, UDHR's 30 Articles have inspired 70 additional human rights declarations, most notably the United Nations Convention on the Rights of the Child in 1989. My graduate students often ask, "What took them so long?" Good question.

Eleanor Roosevelt, the chair of the UDHR drafting committee, wrote:

Where, after all, do universal human rights begin? In small places, close to home — so close and so small that they cannot be seen on any maps of the world. Unless these rights have meaning there, they have little meaning anywhere. Without concerted citizen action to uphold them close to home, we shall look in vain for progress in the larger world.[11]

When I was about 10, I first learned about the Universal Declaration of Human Rights while leafing through Edward Steichen's curated book of photographs of *The Family of Man* exhibition at the Museum of Modern Art in New York.[12] From 2 million submissions, Steichen's team selected 503 photographs to depict the magnificence and tragedy of life in those small places. When the exhibition opened, lines stretched around the block. Museumgoers saw a different world outside their windows. Borders seemed to evaporate.

Painter Ben Shahn, a contributor to the exhibit, mused:

The public is impatient for some exercise of its faculties; is hungry for thinking, for feeling, for real experience; it is eager for some new philosophical outlook, for new kinds of truth; it wants contact with live minds; it wants to feel compassion; it wants to grow emotionally and intellectually; it wants to live.[13]

In the Prologue to the book, Carl Sandburg (Steichen's brother-in-law) wrote:

People! Flung wide and far, born into toil, struggle, blood and dreams, among lovers, eaters, drinkers, workers, loafers, fighters, players, gamblers...

Child faces of blossom smiles or mouths of hunger...Faces in crowds, laughing and windblown leaf faces, profiles in an instant of agony, mouths in a dumbshow mockery lacking speech, faces of music in gay song or a twist of pain, a hate ready to kill, or calm and ready-for-death faces.[14]

I wanted to know more. My parents told me that I would point to images and ask impossible questions. "That man in a tie salting an egg, what is he thinking about?" "Those women at a hamburger counter facing the street, what's making them laugh?" "Why is that woman praying?" "Why is that group so worried?" "Why are they dancing in a circle?" "What kind of sound comes out of that strange instrument?"

A section titled "Learning" included a photograph of a storyteller surrounded by enraptured listeners in the Bechuanaland

Protectorate (now the Republic of Botswana); a tiered lecture hall of students taking notes, an intimate seminar at Berkeley, an old woman practicing her letters, children reading out loud, a monk lost in thought, someone in a hazmat suit holding a lab rat, Einstein at Princeton looking for a calculation under a pile of papers or the key to his bicycle lock. What were they learning? Why doesn't that old woman know how to read?

Childhood looked playful and uninhibited. Kids dressing up in their parents' clothes, playing checkers with a corpulent old man on a park bench, carrying each other on their backs, catching soap bubbles or rain in their open mouths, digging holes at the beach and stretching their arms to make long shadows in the late afternoon sun. I did those things, too.

But childhood also looked painful, poor, angry, afraid, and disconsolate. Children trapped behind barbed wire, hungry, and staggering under an impossible load of bricks. Faces blackened by soot from the mines. Alone in a graveyard. Children without childhoods. This wasn't fair. "Why do some people have to live so horribly and others get to live in fancy houses and eat what they want?" My parents used big words I didn't understand. They said one thing, but their faces told another story. They stole glances at each other. Often, they changed the subject.

Carl Sandburg writes: "I'm not a stranger here." I liked the idea of not being a stranger anywhere. In a two-page spread of seven couples, each caption is the same: "*We two form a multitude.*" The next two-page spread is a wide-angle image of the UN General Assembly and the Preamble to the Charter of the United Nations. I keep the book close by and remind myself, "We *too* form a multitude." I often wonder if any nation or family of nations could function like a functional family writ large.

Despite its popularity, *The Family of Man* did not open to universal critical acclaim. It was panned as Western-centric, vulgar, prurient, sensationalist and sentimentalized.

Nevertheless, the iconic photographer Walker Evans dismissed the exhibit as "bogus heartfeeling." Others scoffed at its promotional claim: "the greatest photographic exhibition of all time." Steichen came under fire for reckless cultural appropriation. Critics sniped: no single art exhibit can categorically and simplistically sum up the human condition. Worse, by portraying East Indians as surreal, emaciated and illiterate, and Africans as primitive, destitute and naked, the exhibit was culturally obtuse and reductionist.

To this day, *The Family of Man* continues to elicit scorn. In a churlish, if not equally racist observation, one critic writes: "*The Family of Man* is not art at all, but a social and anthropological document and ought to be moved from its present location to the Museum of Natural History."[15] Art and photography historian Alise Tīfentāle writes:

> *The Family of Man*...was never an avant-garde or even particularly innovative exhibition. Its general message, that all people are similar in their joys, pain and work, was not especially thought-provoking, unexpected or radical. Its design was attractive, but by no means ground-breaking.[16]

Tīfentāle's "meh" review about its curatorial choices and lopsided representation may have merit, but it leaves me cold. These photographs *invite* wonder. I don't view *The Family of Man* as tragedy porn, an act of Western hegemony, or a callous disregard of the photograph as an art form. Nor do I agree that the exhibition associated pain and poverty with the developing world alone. In Ben Shahn's "Resettlement Administration Client Family, Boone County, Arkansas, 1935," an emaciated woman stands in front of a weather-beaten shack, arms crossed, her face sunken and lined with worry about how to feed her children. Beneath the image, a line from Virgil reads: "What region of the earth is not full of our calamities?" The operative word here was "our." *Our* calamities. *Our* multitude.

The critics make strong points. Nevertheless, I see *The Family of Man* as a unique view outside our collective windows, an invitation to witness humanity working, praying, laughing, giving birth, weeping, killing, falling in love, losing loved ones and tilling the soil. These images, captions, and photographs whisper, "Let these small places enter you." A Sioux proverb alone on a single page has always spoken to me. "With all beings and all things we shall be as relatives." The multitude includes us all.

I am prone to ask the cynic, can you envision the momentousness embedded in these moments? Do you feel afraid when you stare into the eyes of someone whose way of life is fundamentally different from yours? Do you see borders as danger zones or cultural crossings? What is our collective responsibility to the family of women and men and the family of nations? Aren't those small places the heart of the United Nations Declaration of Human Rights?

* * *

Teachers Without Borders was just a few months old when the United Nations formally adopted the Millennium Development Goals (MDGs). All 189 member states and 23 international organizations set out to reach eight broad categories of development within 15 years: (1) eradicate extreme poverty and hunger, (2) achieve universal primary education, (3) promote gender equality and empower women, (4) reduce child mortality, (5) improve maternal health, (6) combat HIV/ AIDS, malaria, and other diseases, (7) ensure environmental sustainability, and (8) build global partnerships for development.

By the close of the MDGs in 2015, aid to support the eight goals had doubled, even tripled. United Nations Secretary-General Ban Ki-moon announced that the number of people living in extreme poverty had been cut in half. Dozens of countries met targets for clean drinking water, stemmed malnutrition, removed barriers to school enrollment, curtailed unsanitary conditions leading to child mortality, and addressed malaria and tuberculosis. Those heralding the success of the MDGs pointed to a dramatic rise in public–private partnerships and government transparency.

By enabling millions to access the internet, we would accelerate the prospect of education for all. The Nike curves illustrating the impact of educating girls and women were incontrovertible. An educated mother could become 50% more likely to immunize her child than a mother without an education. With an added year of school, a girl could earn up to 20% more as an adult and reinvest 90% of her income into her family. Children born to literate mothers were far more likely to survive past the age of 5. Advances in women's education had prevented more than 4 million child deaths.

Enter the critics. The Millennium Development Goals were aspirational, shallow, fragile and hyperbolic, nothing more than a disingenuous global public-relations stunt designed by rich countries and companies to parade their largesse in front of the cameras and, more insidiously, to expand markets and exert political influence. Academics raged about ill-conceived evaluation designs, faulty data-collection techniques, flimsy validity and reliability indices, and spotty monitoring capacity.

Some took direct aim at the MDGs and, by association, the United Nations. That it took more than ten years to recognize the fundamental right to water and sanitation. That halving poverty was hardly an ambitious goal. That in 47 out of Africa's 54 countries, girls had less than a 50% chance of completing primary school. That in the least developed countries, more than a third of young women 15–24 years old remained illiterate. In several countries rated at the bottom of the United Nations

Development Index, the pace of progress toward equity and human rights had not only slowed but regressed.[17]

Some alleged that the MDGs had created a political and financial minefield. Countries with the greatest need were incapable of meeting the fundamentals of human welfare, forced into sucking at the teat of donor countries and global agencies, or teetering on the edge of default attempting to pay exorbitant interest rates imposed by the World Bank or the International Monetary Fund. They were convinced that the MDGs enabled corrupt heads of state to hide behind windy rhetorical allegiances and shameless photo-ops: distributing textbooks in rural communities surrounded by the appreciative poor, or meeting with cheering doctors after the latest announcement about a public-health initiative. Accusations were fierce: "The MDGs have *widened* the chasm between haves and have-nots! You should have known!"

Heady stuff, indeed. But what does it all mean in the small places where it *really* counts?

Led by Raphael Ogar Oko, the members of a Teachers Without Borders group in Nigeria were too impatient to wait for trickle-down development and too suspicious of their country's promises to make good on lofty proclamations crafted in Paris and New York. For Raphael, change must be personal. Global goals would only make sense once they were rooted in the small places, beginning in one's home, at school, and in one's community.

The group organized itself around a set of three inviolable principles. First, individuals and communities must hold themselves and others accountable for their commitments. Second, they were to pool their efforts to model stakeholdership. How might we educate the midwives? Find mentors. Who knows about clean water and can teach about hygiene? Look around, they told themselves, rather than outside, for help.

Third, solutions must be sustainable and homegrown to avoid depending upon handouts, grants, or government subsidies.

Enter the Millennium Development Ambassador (MDA) program, advertised all over the capital city, Abuja. Open to "any individual with the drive and power to effect change," the program was easy to engage with; one need only complete an application and provide a colleague's letter of recommendation. Each prospective Ambassador was issued an identification card. They met for monthly seminars and collaborated on creating practical solutions for reaching MDGs. Raphael challenged them. Are the children in your home/school/community fed and sheltered? Educated? Is your home an example of gender equity and women's empowerment? Will your children be born in hospitals? How will you ensure that mothers get access to quality maternal health? Is your family/school/community educated about HIV/AIDs, malaria and other diseases? What are you doing to ensure environmental stability? MDG 8 is about developing global partnerships. Are you developing *local* partnerships?

He reminded them each month to internalize those three simple rules: accountability, stakeholdership, and consensus.

There were incentives, too. Raphael partnered with the local motor vehicle licensing office. MDA graduates could benefit from a discount on a group life insurance policy and receive an official, personalized MDA license plate. It made complete sense. Throughout Nigeria, safe passage on highways is often interrupted by a maddening number of legal and illegal security "checkpoints." Most drivers expect to press a "toll" or, more accurately, an extortion fee into the guard's hand. MDA graduates replaced cash with their MDA identification cards. Guards would leave the booth and check the license plate against the registry, return to the car, and wave them to go. With a group insurance plan and unencumbered travel, Ambassadors enjoyed a new level of freedom to spread the word about the MDA program itself. A win-win for the small places.

Like most homegrown and home-owned initiatives, it grew. Ambassadors launched microcredit enterprises and small business opportunities for women, supported by community cluster funds designed to lower initial entry costs. Others started village-level hygiene education programs or high school age-level counseling programs on antisocial behavior, violence, and sexual health to encourage more testing for HIV/AIDS. Neighborhoods were cleaner. Local businesses underwrote the Millennium Development Goal Football Cup and Peace Cup.

In partnership with the Ministry of Youth Affairs and the National Youth Commission, a Youth MDA program mobilized universities to connect mandatory voluntary service with specific projects focusing on each of the MDGs. A Youth Summit highlighted the extraordinary contributions of entrepreneurial students. Teachers created a Global Educators for All Initiative and solicited articles from educators in every Nigerian state and in both formal and nonformal settings to examine critical issues facing the implementation of MDGs in their regions. The Teachers Without Borders MDA program expanded to Benin, Ghana, and Sierra Leone, teacher by dedicated teacher, small place by small place.

* * *

In 2015, the MDGs had completed their 15-year trajectory and were replaced by the United Nations Sustainable Development Goals (SDGs). If the MDGs were to halve poverty, the 17 SDGs from 2015 to 2030 would set forth mechanisms by which the world would reach zero poverty, address the critical imperative of reducing economic, social, and gender inequality, build peace, create sustainable livelihoods, and honor the power of an informed citizenry.

While the MDGs focused on quantity—more schools, teachers, textbooks and uniforms—the SDGs focused on *quality*. Without question, the basics remain in desperately short supply. Still, textbooks require quality teaching. Malala Yousafzai, the Pakistani Nobel Peace Prize winner shot by the Taliban for her advocacy of girls' education, does not limit her efforts to getting children into school. Her mission is for *all* children to attend good schools staffed by well-qualified teachers.

The MDGs enabled the building of more schools, accelerated the number of children enrolled in schools, eliminated fees for admission or uniforms, and distributed more teaching materials. The SDGs were to take it to the next level: address the destructive influence of educational inequality and fear on a family's decision-making capacity, support effective and child-focused pedagogy, connect inclusion with equality, and promote lifelong learning.

Enter the critics, once again. The SDGs are non-binding and have no teeth. SDGs add more goals rather than go deep. "Sustainable development" is too abstract a concept to measure. SDG framers should have recognized and addressed the impending collision course between the headlong drive for economic growth and its disastrous environmental consequences that WTO protestors had warned about. The SDGs should have taken into account how easily our agnostic techno-evangelism could dissolve into a playground for state-sponsored propagandists and/or non-state hackers. How quickly freedom could give rise to tyranny, identity theft, fake news, conspiracy theories, human trafficking, weapons proliferation, and the promulgation of far-right extremism and hate.

It's easy to deconstruct systems based upon less-than-ideal results. It's quite another thing to construct something in its place. Flawed or not, the SDGs could benefit enormously by employing the same three simple rules hammered out by a small group of teachers in Nigeria without a project-funded ATM: accountability, stakeholdership, and consensus.

Imagine, too, if teachers were central to the planning. If consulted, a teacher might chime in with a lesson plan. What is our way in, our way through, our way forward? They might conduct a premortem for each of the strategies for implementing the SDGs: imagine ten years from when a grand plan fails. Then work backward from there. Throw in a few what-ifs. Ask people to work in teams to think about the impact of the next global pandemic or devise a plan to procure grain when the supply from *x*-country (substitute Ukraine for now) is cut off from the world because it is under siege. Let them imagine a scenario for addressing depleted or poisoned fish stocks or a yearly flood caused by a change in climate caused by industrial nations. Then ask them to enlist teachers to teach these issues to their students.

This group saw the big picture in their small places because they live the complexity of sustainable development every day. They do not have to look for proof of climate change. Outside their windows, there is too much water, too little water, or water too dirty for drinking and bathing. They know all about access to potable water, sanitation, electricity, and life-saving medicines. Others may articulate the nuances and political machinations of food insecurity. In the small places, they call it hunger and mouths to feed. In those small places, people can take you inside their homes to show you the hole in the roof, the rodents, the mold and the lead. They know the difference between backbreaking work and productive work. They can show you how the ability to sound out words is not enough; they need to learn how to read the fine print *and* author their own stories. They know all too well the gap between surviving and thriving. And they will show you solutions to these challenges, on their terms, in their own homes.

Chapter 7

My "Favorite" Dictator

In September 2006, President Pervez Musharraf of Pakistan made his first of two appearances on Jon Stewart's *The Daily Show*, bouncing out from the wings in a Western suit to cheers and Stewart's upbeat house band. Musharraf saluted the audience and took his seat. Stewart offered Musharraf a Twinkie, made small talk, then leaned forward like a drinking pal sharing a secret and asked nonchalantly if Musharraf could tell him where Osama bin Laden was hiding. The crowd erupted in laughter. Stewart winked. "Just between you and me."

On 2 May 2011, Navy Seals entered Abbottabad and killed Osama bin Laden. In an interview with CNN's Piers Morgan that same month, "former" President Musharraf railed against President Obama for America's arrogant disregard of borders. "Certainly, no country has a right to intrude into any other country," Musharraf told Morgan. "If technically or legally you see it, it's an act of war."[18]

By July, Musharraf was back on *The Daily Show*. Same upbeat entry and cheers. Same Western suit. A more symphonic soundtrack. Same salute.

This time, Stewart offered Musharraf a Gatorade and a Balance Bar, and cut the idle chitchat. "We need each other. Clearly, we need each other in this region...especially because...we have a plan. I really hope that this...obviously, I'm not a general and I'm not involved in high-level intelligence (audience snickers),

71

but we may be leaving Afghanistan (pause) within the next 50 or 60 years (Musharraf and audience laughter) and if that occurs (more laughter), what is Pakistan's interest in the Taliban, you know, what is the situation that, as you see it, with our pulling back a little bit?" Musharraf offered an articulate answer about the artificiality of timelines (especially the implication that the US would withdraw in 2014) that enabled the Taliban to lie low, wait for the Americans to go, and rise again.

Musharraf asked Stewart to visualize an unstable Afghanistan. Stewart nodded, taking it all in: "Well, the problem is…the difficulty for Americans is that Afghanistan hasn't been stable since, I guess, Hannibal" (uproarious laughter). "They don't appear to want to be stabilized." Musharraf reflected briefly, but pushed back by claiming that Afghanistan had been stable until the king was deposed in 1979.

Stewart returned to the subject of Osama bin Laden and asked why no one had wanted to know more about the strange house in Abbottabad that burned its own trash (chuckles from the crowd). Historians and pundits are inconclusive about Musharraf's possible connection to Osama bin Laden. How could it be that bin Laden escaped notice? What did Musharraf know and when did he know it? A weird and unsettling show, especially for late-night television: affable repartee between a bright comedian and an astute military general, head of state, and former boss of Inter-Services Intelligence (ISI), Pakistan's CIA. Weirder still, the circumstances that led to my conversations with President Musharraf about Islam and development.

* * *

It all started at a meeting Jane Goodall had asked me to attend in New York. In her role as a United Nations Messenger of Peace, she decided to convene an array of diverse practitioners for a freewheeling conversation about globalism, climate change, inequality, education and extremism. Dr. Riffat Hassan, a professor of Religious Studies at the University of Louisville, had just received a US State Department grant to gather South Asian Muslim religious scholars, clergy, community activists and their American counterparts at a compound in Islamabad. During a break, she asked me to consider speaking at the University of Louisville and the possibility of joining the initiative, involving several trips to Pakistan.

One would think that reason would prevail over curiosity, but in my case, that is never a safe bet. Curiosity wins every time. Why pick a secular Jew from the San Fernando Valley in Los Angeles, whose only God is Dodger legend Sandy Koufax? My family did not belong to a synagogue. There were legions of people with infinitely more knowledge about the Qur'an. I took it all into careful consideration, then jumped at the chance.

Within weeks after the Louisville talk, I landed in Islamabad for discussions about the establishment of the Iqbal Institute for Research, Education and Dialogue (IRED) — inspired by Allama Iqbal, the poet-philosopher, social activist and "spiritual father of Pakistan."

My name was stenciled on the door. I could stay as long as I liked. Discussions went on for hours, interrupted only by meals and prayers. I offered little to no contributions of my own. I *had* none. Unless escorted by guards Riffat personally knew and approved, we were not allowed to leave the compound.

If I had questions, she assured me, I could ask Dr. Fathi Osman, a preeminent Islamic scholar just a few doors down. I was, however, to prepare my questions carefully. Having earned his law degree from Alexandria University, his master's degree from Cairo University, and his doctorate from Princeton, Dr. Osman served as a faculty member at Al-Azhar University, where he developed a plan to restructure how Islam was presented in higher education.

"Just a minute," Riffat said. She left and returned carrying Dr. Osman's book, *Concepts of the Qur'an: A Topical Reading*, like a Turkey platter at Thanksgiving. I thanked her and staggered back to my room. I had taken one course on comparative religion in college, despite having earned a doctorate from a Jesuit university. Now I needed to ingest a 3-inch thick, 1012-page book. This would be one more act of self-sabotage destined for yet another moment of public reprobation. I could have backed out, but when the going gets tough, the tough get going to the library, going back and forth between the Qur'an, Dr. Osman's *Concepts of the Qur'an*, conversations at meals, books of commentary, and the Hadith—the thousands of notations considered a record of the deeds, actions and references of Prophet Muhammad (Peace Be Upon Him).

It was not difficult to find passages affirming the importance of education as its own reward and as an expression of character: "The angels will lower their wings in their great pleasure with one who seeks knowledge"; "Verily the men of knowledge are the inheritors of the prophets." As for global education: "Seek knowledge even in China." Lifelong education? "Seek knowledge from the cradle to the grave."

But cherry-picking in any endeavor is not scholarship. It's pandering. Even if I managed to cram a modicum of knowledge into my addled brain, it would not amount to thinking.

My true education came from Riffat herself. She asserts that basic rights like freedom of speech, education, faith and choice are fundamental to fulfilling God's mandate. For her, the United Nations' Universal Declaration of Human Rights is one contemporary, secular codification of the Qur'an's higher, more transcendent safeguard of rights over the impermanence of tenuous, negotiated agreements. And yet, she asserts, Islam is associated with terrorism and misogyny. Other monotheistic religions get a free pass for their historical legacy of atrocities. Not Islam.

Riffat insists that feminism is *inherently* Islamic, not an imaginative twist or wordplay. For her, Islam is the path to development for women's internal and external empowerment. She has described the Qur'an as the Magna Carta of Islam for its power to shed light on social justice, human development and universal education, and made it her life's work to take on Islamophobes or those whose misguided views have caused almost irreparable harm to a religion they neither represent nor understand.

We continued to meet and attend conferences back in the United States.

One evening, I was sitting next to her at dinner following a forgettable string of lengthy speeches, when someone brought up a familiar refrain: "Why do the Islamic fundamentalists get all the press?" An innocuous enough question, I thought, even a nice distraction from people's windy justifications for their latest sinecures, so characteristic of gatherings like this.

I expected a few throwaway bromides blaming the media, then a pivot back to the attendees' "my accomplishments" parade. Riffat, however, has never perfected the poker face. She turned to the speaker and spoke bluntly: "I consider *myself* an Islamic fundamentalist," letting the uncomfortable silence sink in, "because the fundamentals of Islam are progressive."

There's a conversation stopper if I ever heard one. *Clever*, I thought, though I wondered how this would land.

Satisfied she had the table's attention, Riffat got straight to her point (I reached for another breadstick): "I align my life with Islamic feminist theology, which is fundamental to Islam."

It is draining to defend one's faith against a steady onslaught of incoming fire from uninformed and gullible outsiders, not to mention aberrant distortions by extremists who, in the words of Karen Armstrong, traffic in the "abuse of a sacred ideal." While right-wing bigots demonize Islam, left-wing sanctimony about secular universality alienates and marginalizes the very communities it purports to defend.

Put yourself in Riffat's shoes day after day and answer a barrage of "But what about...?" questions:

"But what about female genital mutilation?"

Response: No such direct mention in the Qur'an. Male circumcision is required; female circumcision is not sanctioned. The larger point, she emphasizes, is that any interference with Allah's creation (for beauty, to suppress freedom, to punish women for their sexuality) is Satan's work.

"But what about child marriage? Isn't that permitted?"

Response: Not true, she says curtly. Someone might then recall having read that the Prophet (Peace Be Upon Him) married Aisha when she was 9. Riffat would size up the interrogator. If she sensed a sincere and sympathetic inquirer struggling to address questions, Riffat might quote from the Qur'an, followed by ancient symbolic calculations of age and multidenominational numerology and interpretation across several religions. Genesis 5:5 claims that Adam lived to the ripe age of 930. A Hindu example might fit the bill here: "Out of fear of the appearance of the menses, let the father marry his daughter while she still runs about naked. For if she stays in the home after the age of puberty, sin falls on the father" (Vaśiṣṭha 17:70).

"Infanticide?" The Qur'an abolished it.

"Stoning?" Check out your own Deuteronomy 21:18–21.

"Honor killings?"

Riffat has fought against the insanity of leniency for murder in the name of Islam, justified on the flimsy evidence that the act was a reasonable response to a "grave and sudden provocation." She would point out that many of these edicts were derived, often verbatim, from British law. Besides, she made clear that honor killing is by no means limited to the Muslim world. The World Health Organization, NGOs and human rights organizations have documented violence against women *worldwide*: acid attacks, abduction and trafficking, rape, sexual slavery, torture, genital mutilation, forced sterilization, and denial of food.

After all that, she'd make her crucial point: *patriarchal tradition does not define Islam; it defiles it.* The Qur'an asks the faithful why they so blindly continue these abuses, generation after generation, even when one's "fathers did not comprehend anything and they were not properly guided?" (Qur'an 2:170).

The trips continued. On one occasion, I had just set my suitcases down when Riffat gathered us to say: "In two days, President Musharraf will meet with us in his office." Us, I thought, meant the Islamic scholars. I looked forward to a quiet evening. I shot her a look. "All of us," she smiled. Was I now supposed to represent 4000 years of Jewish history, culture and scholarship to a head of state?

Rumors had circulated that terrorists were developing new techniques for targeting official vehicles. Several attempts had been thwarted, but an uptick in violence-tinged chatter on social networks necessitated more layers of protection. After a thorough inspection of our car to detect improvised explosive devices, our Morse code of long and short black vehicles eased out into the street. A kilometer or two on the main highway, we took a detour down a side street lined with barbed wire, and we were ordered out and told to wait. Within seconds, two well-fortified Mercedes pulled up. Each driver was huge. I wondered whether they would have to size us up for Kevlar vests. By far the shortest team member, I figured I would have to strap on a child's size. I straddled a fire extinguisher between two men who could have substituted for defensive linemen on the Seattle Seahawks football team.

We arrived at a circular driveway rimmed by white tents and stopped under a porte-cochère. Giant, fit honor guards with impeccably trimmed mustaches approached and opened all four doors on cue, motioning us to walk between two curtains. I craned my neck to look at them: forest-green berets and khakis, red turtlenecks, red cummerbunds adorned with gold frills and the country seal, white sashes, long white gloves, perfect white spats buckled around their ankles. Others stood shoulder to shoulder, awaiting commands, then marched stiffly toward the next security checkpoint. My seatmates got out, never saying a word.

Up to this point, my nerves had been steady. Once inside, my heart began to race when guards motioned us to take our seats next to individual tea sets made from exquisitely crafted porcelain: teapot, cup, saucer and 2-inch plate resting delicately on an ornately carved table flush with the right armrest. I was told to sit two seats from President Musharraf, who entered the room as guards snapped to attention. Musharraf sat in a throne-like chair set on a 3-inch slab of white marble. I imagined myself making a point and accidentally sweeping the tea set from its delicate perch: plate crashing to the floor, cup hurtling in slow motion toward Musharraf, my face in full Edvard Munch contortion, rifles engaged.

Musharraf was cordial and charming. President Bush called him "my buddy." As I said, he appeared *twice* on *The Daily Show*. I thought, *Dang, whaddya know, a head of state is talking to ME.* During a series of meetings, Musharraf and the scholars discussed the role of ancient faith in a contemporary, politically charged context. I added a few words about supporting teachers with pedagogies to foster critical thinking, collaboration, and service learning. President Musharraf asked the Institute to explore how to popularize "enlightened moderation," his vision of a kinder and gentler Islam, in direct contrast to extremists who had hijacked the language of the Qur'an to justify their repressive agenda.

Dr. Osman was not so easily enamored. He argued that Musharraf's concept of "enlightened moderation" could very well be yet another public-relations stunt to secularize Islam, anoint himself a paragon of goodness and keep America in his back pocket. During animated discussions among the scholars about the strategy or tactics to promote "enlightened moderation," Dr. Osman reminded us that moderation and acceptance are rooted deeply in the Qur'an.

When Riffat returned from a meeting with President Musharraf and asked me to develop an education plan by which teachers can promulgate the idea that progressive, pro-development practices are consistent with Islam, I told Dr. Osman about suspicions communities harbor when they confront international NGOs so bent on showing results that they find faith an impediment. A villager in Pakistan once confided to me, "It's as if they are telling us, if you people would just stop praying so much, you could make something of your lives." Dr. Osman's tireless advocacy for interreligious cooperation arises from a moral conviction grounded in impeccable scholarship of Islam's core tenets. My time with him was precious. True Islam is not the problem, but the solution.

Dr. Fathi Osman passed away on 11 September 2010. The *New York Times* obituary quoted an article he had written on Islam and human rights: "Openness is life, while being closed off and isolated is suicidal."[19]

Soon afterward, the Iqbal Institute for Research, Education and Dialogue eventually folded from criticism, poor management and its association with Musharraf's increasing political troubles. Someone was convinced I was a CIA agent. I never got a chance to see Pervez Musharraf again.

Dr. Riffat Hassan made it possible for me to experience the issues that dominate the world stage by interacting with those in a position to influence large-scale change. These are rare opportunities; in my case, they certainly do not go to the best or the brightest.

As for Musharraf, I'll let history make that call.

Chapter 8

No Fear

Anne Sexton describes the battle between her public and personal personas:

Quite collected at cocktail parties,
meanwhile in my head
I'm undergoing open-heart surgery.[20]

Sameena Nazir, on the other hand, is a different case entirely. Gangs? Political resistance and threats to shut down her work? There may be plenty to fear in her region of Pakistan, but with her it does not seem to register.

Sameena and I had been corresponding for months. She was in Islamabad giving a speech about her organization, The Potohar Organization for Development Advocacy (PODA), a women's rights organization devoted to facilitating the empowerment of people in marginalized, rural communities, especially women. Sameena knew precisely how to frame her work. "PODA's vision is to promote democratic equality based on social justice—a tall order in Pakistan. We focus on economic rights and civil and political liberties. Our role is as a facilitator to empower local communities to articulate their goals and anticipate their needs. Men and women are equal. We work as a bridge between rural communities, stakeholders, resources and linkages." Nevertheless, Sameena faced a volley of tough questions, mostly from men. Her answers were clear, direct, articulate and kind.

I asked her what she thought about the meeting. "That was fun!" she said as if she had just emerged from an inner-tube slide at a water park.

Sameena and I traveled to her village outside the Chakwal District in the Rawalpindi Division, Punjab Province, an hour and a half from Islamabad, to meet her colleagues and see how she connected girls' education, human rights, and livelihoods. Seconds after we climbed into an innocuous-looking car, a pickup truck edged in front of us. Three men wearing "No Fear" T-shirts, each with an automatic weapon slung casually across his chest, took up positions in the truck bed. One guard looked east, the other west, and one kept his gun pointed at the car, all trained to pick off an attacker from either side. What if our driver popped a tire, or something happened that sounded like gunfire? Would they shoot first and ask questions later? From around a corner, a souped-up three-wheeled Bandit S motorcycle brought up the rear. Same "No Fear" T-shirt. Sameena could read my "Yes" fear.

"I'll let you know when it's time to worry," Sameena said, pulling her curls behind her ears. "Where do you think I get these gray hairs from?" She didn't mind that Riffat had ordered this mini militia but found it unnecessary. "Really," she grinned, "there's nothing to worry about. Really, really."

We had time to talk. Rural populations in Pakistan have a literacy rate 30% lower than that of urban populations (44% compared to 72%) and have less access to drinking water and sanitation facilities. While women across Pakistan face gender discrimination and gender-based violence, many Punjabi women face substandard living conditions, elevated levels of malnutrition, and limited employment opportunities. According to Human Rights Watch (HRW), 32% of girls in Pakistan do not attend school, and 87% of those who do attend do not reach ninth grade. An HRW report, "Shall I Feed My Daughter, or Educate Her?", claims: "Twenty-one percent of females marry as children."[21] While Rawalpindi fares much better than other areas of the country, PODA remains a local lifeline. "It's safe here," both girls and women say. "I learn here. I have hope here."

The benefits of supporting education for girls are well known.[22] Educated girls and women tend to be less vulnerable to HIV infection, marry later, raise fewer children and send them to school. In short, more schooling, better health. Better health, more schooling.

At PODA, we watched a group of women wearing smocks inspect clay pots and papier-mâché bowls. On the walls were posters of the UN Declaration of Human Rights and the UN Convention on the Rights of the Child, and pictures of handicrafts for sale. In another room, girls practiced multiplication tables, quizzing each other in impressive English. In the front office, men were doing clerical work, making entries into notebooks, each labeled for its intended use: a meticulous accounting for all the animals, the number of villagers participating in programs, children in school, and vaccinations. In stark contrast to all I had read and heard about Pakistan, here was an ease between men and women, even with women in charge.

PODA was a beehive of studio, school and social movement. Sameena circulated from room to room, seamlessly shifting from offering compliments on the students' art to discussing Article 26 of the Declaration of Human Rights: "Everyone has the right to education."

Another connection made: more rights for education, more education to extend rights. Sameena asked a group of teenagers, "What *is* a right?" They responded by listing words that came to mind: choice, freedom, equality. "Where do rights *come from*?" More responses: they come from me, my village, my government.

A woman broke out in tears. I looked away. Someone held her.

I was ushered outside to meet a group of teachers sitting on rugs under a canvas tarp. A gust of wind swept through, billowing the tarp trampoline-like, up and down, straining its poles and anchors. A man and a woman jumped up to steady a small chalkboard on a flimsy easel. Women covered their eyes and mouths with scarves or the sleeves of their shalwar kameezes. Sameena would join us soon.

I smiled and nodded awkwardly until someone blurted: "How are you, Mr. Fred!" I brightened up and pointed to myself: "I am fine!" a bit too exuberantly, leaving room between each word as if I were teaching English. Someone shouted: "I am fine!" Then another, even louder: "I am fine!!" Still another, straining, the loudest of all: "I am VERY, VERY fine!!!" Sameena appeared with a few staff.

Teachers prepared topics for open discussion. A notetaker summarized each on the chalkboard. Sameena made certain I understood what they were saying.

"If education is the responsibility of the state, why doesn't the government stop extremists from attacking schools?" Someone wrote: *Government responsibility / attacks on schools.*

"Why do Americans condemn madrassas for teaching children to memorize the Qur'an, but then say it is OK to run 'fundamentalist' Christian schools?" I blushed. The blackboard scribe wrote: *American hypocrisy.*

"People say that technology is a low priority for the poor. Why do they think they can make those decisions for us?" *Technology is OUR choice* was added to the list.

"Pakistan's constitution says that all children can go to school, but they don't try to enroll children. Why do they turn a blind eye when children don't attend school?" Another gust fluttered the tarp. Dust swirled. Next line: *Enrollment / government doesn't care.*

No tribal leader was lurking or casting a foreboding shadow. This was a serious, critical discussion among women empowered to assert their ideas and think like development professionals. Male workers leaned on shovels and rakes to listen in. An older woman made certain to make eye contact with me and said, "Men here understand that educating girls is good for the entire family." Sameena added, "Could you give an example?"

The woman continued: "My son told me a story of a man who had saved up to purchase farm equipment. He didn't have the collateral for a bank loan but was convinced by a loan shark that he was getting a good rate. The lender had come to collect the first installment. The farmer did not have as much money as the lender expected to receive, so the farmer called his son over to check the calculations.

"His daughter was nearby, but he was embarrassed and told her to go away and stoke the fire. His son did not know percentages. Overhearing the lender and her father, the girl came back and tried to intervene, having looked over her brother's shoulder for months while he had been doing his homework. She knew the answer but once again was dismissed. The lender insisted on collecting. The daughter persisted, telling her father she could help. At the last minute, her father relented. She solved the problem and saved the family money. The father fished out the correct payment and warned the lender that he would be reported [facing a punishment of up to ten years' imprisonment with a fine of Rs. 500,000] if he tried to scam anyone else. Word like that gets around."

The blackboard notation: *girls + math = money literacy.*

We broke for a meal and prayers, then reconvened. The discussion took up where it left off. They began to explore each of the chalkboard prompts. Sameena added her vision of Pakistan as a society of equals. It would have to start here, in this village.

Somehow, however, they quieted down abruptly. Even the wind had died down. Something must have caused this conversation to deflate so abruptly. Was I the reason? Though the discussion was candid, was I supposed to say something? Sum it up and answer these questions? All too often, I have been put in that position as the expert from the West, duty-bound to "enlighten" the rest. By just being here, listening in, had I crossed yet another invisible line? By not saying anything, did I make them afraid? Had I overstayed my welcome? I tried to pick up social clues.

I noticed that a few women had been looking past me. I twisted around. The four guards who had escorted us to the village had returned. They had parked the truck and the motorcycle at a distance but looked impatient. Sameena leaned in and giggled: "It's the 'no fear' guys." She spoke rapidly to the women, informing them that I needed to return to Islamabad, thanking them for their honest conversation and interesting questions, then something else I could not decipher. They tittered and cackled, some breaking out into a belly laugh. A woman shouted in English, "No Fear!"

Sameena spoke with the guards and returned. We would be leaving in a half-hour, she informed me. She would like me to do one more thing: take a walk with her father. "He's blind. Hold him close, just you and him. He speaks and understands English perfectly."

"He's over there," Sameena said, pointing to a man under a metal awning, sitting in a blue and white webbed aluminum lawn chair, asleep. She walked me over to him and introduced me. He stood up erectly and bent his elbow. I hooked my arm through his and we started our stroll. I didn't know how this would go, but he broke the ice by asking me to circle the village with him and tell him what I saw. Was he testing my observational skills? That feeling passed quickly. He seemed genuinely interested. I described the water buffalo, the color of the fields, birds skittering across a murky pond and veering off, a well that looked unsafe. He asked me about my family. I told him about my mother, born in Vienna: how she spent her afternoons in a candy store her mother owned, how they fled to the United States in 1938 as Hitler was gaining power, and her career as a French teacher. I told him about my father's childhood in Washington Heights, New York, his brief acting career, his war years, meeting my mother, their move to Los Angeles, falling in love with international folk-dancing, and attending college as the oldest student in his class both for his bachelor's and master's degrees.

Sameena's father told me about the village and Sameena's strength. How she could motivate her classmates to do anything. I steered him away from a puddle and a pile of bricks. I wanted to know more, but he asked about my wife. I told him of her work as an art therapist for the elderly, tough kids and sick kids. I turned the conversation back to PODA's work to connect art, human rights, literacy and livelihoods for women, but he interrupted me to ask about my two daughters, their schools and where we live. He squeezed my arm affectionately.

He wanted to do another circle and I was happy to oblige. This time, there were fewer questions. He just wanted to take it all in. I described a bird perched on a water buffalo cooling off in a swamp, chickens gossiping and skirting around corners, light flickering in the trees. I noted menacing clouds on the horizon. "I smell rain," he said.

As we made the final turn toward the cars, he told me about his own childhood, his belief in a pluralistic Pakistan, the tragedy of extremism, and his faith in youth.

I made out Sameena ahead, motioning to us with both hands as if she were guiding a plane to its appointed gate. I leaned in to say that the boss was telling us to pick up the pace. He smiled. "Get used to it," he said. He returned to the topic of Sameena, how she supports the village yet seeks to continue her graduate studies in the United States. "She is my eyes, my heart."

At the office, I settled him into a chair. He patted my arm. "It will rain soon," he said. I told him that, as a dancer, my father could predict rain, too, when his legs ached.

The women from the circle waved and smiled. The motorcyclist started up and revved his engine, belching black smoke. A few more chickens protested loudly at the intrusion. The three No Fears led the way. Sameena waved, holding on to her father's arm.

Not two minutes outside the village, I heard a hard thud, as if a rock had hit the windshield, then what I imagined was an enfilade of bullets pinging across the hood and through the windows. I ducked. No, we were not someone's target practice. This was a summer storm. Five years later, I would know what rain like this would portend for Pakistan: floods that would plunge 40% of the country under water.

That night, I called Sameena to thank her and ask for her candid assessment of the day. She said the encounter with her village was a success. "The teachers told me that, when you met with them, you didn't sit on a chair, though they were sitting on the ground. You sat with them."

"Is that it?"

"That's it. My father likes you and tells me to ask you to come back soon," she said. "But next time, lose the guards."

Chapter 9

Forklift Humanitarian

Well into morning lessons, a 7.6 magnitude earthquake, centered 19 kilometers northeast of Muzaffarabad, the capital of Pakistani-administered Kashmir, struck with enough apocalyptic fury to rattle bones as far away as Kabul and Delhi. Dislodged by aftershocks, boulders tumbled from cliffs and flattened communities below. Muzaffarabad, the largest city of Azad Kashmir and close to the epicenter, was inaccessible, blocked by landslides. School buildings collapsed, burying children.

Eighty-two kilometers away, in Islamabad, internal and helicopter video captured the implosion of the posh Margalla Towers. Only five of its seven floors had permits. Bribes took care of the extra two floors. It took six years to charge the builder of the Margalla Towers with criminal negligence for substandard construction. Apartment owners were eventually compensated, *including* the builder, who also owned four apartments. A 2011 *Express Tribune* article, "Earthquake 2005: Faulty towers — cursed by nature, haunted by apathy,"[23] exposed ongoing corruption and negligence. Twelve years later, survivors were still clamoring for the release of a 1600-page report held from public view. There were too many other tragedies like this one waiting to happen. There was little mention of shoddy school construction.

Underfunded emergency response teams did what they could. Rescue workers airlifted into remote regions were unsure they had landed in the correct place. Armed with picks, shovels and essential debris-moving equipment, they pawed at everything: bricks, beams, glass, shouting updates to each other, aware that they must reach 90% within the first 24 hours.

Radio reports informed villagers that their best hope of survival was to find their way down into the valley to seek shelter, water, food and medical assistance. Communities had long abandoned the belief that authorities would protect them and took matters into their own hands. Sameena called to say that the road from Village Chakwal to Islamabad was jammed with cars, trucks and villagers on foot, not so much from people fleeing the hardest-hit areas but from those traveling *toward* the disaster to deliver supplies to trapped communities.

The snow would be coming soon, she said, after which all would be lost and the area sealed off and entombed. Without winterized tents, blankets, water and food, whole communities would freeze to death. Her voice quivered with exasperation, exhaustion and fear. "We're working day and night to help. We must get them what they need now, then set up child-friendly spaces."

United Nations Secretary-General Kofi Annan made repeated and increasingly agitated appeals for immediate global assistance and international cooperation. The development and global aid community was worried about donor fatigue. An earthquake measuring 8.9 on the Richter scale, located under the sea near Aceh in northern Indonesia, had generated a tsunami caught on hundreds of video cameras. And less than six weeks earlier, Hurricane Katrina smashed into New Orleans's Ninth Ward and St. Bernard's Parish.

Pakistanis would wait for no one. Sameena called again with my marching orders: "I've got a lousy connection here and two minutes before I must share the phone. Please gather tents, clothes, winter clothing and sanitary supplies. Sweet-talk a shipping company to get it to New York. Pakistani Airways will take it from there. Bye."

There is nothing as motivating as a deadline, especially when lives are at stake. I could not fail her, her father, the village, PODA, Pakistan or myself.

The Pakistani community had already mobilized a tent and blanket drive in Seattle. I found several local leaders and invited them to my home. I arm-twisted friends to join them. That night, we coordinated our efforts. We'd call it "Warmth Without Borders."

DHL agreed to waive all costs for shipping up to 18 pallets to New York and transfer them to a Pakistani Airways cargo plane by mid-November. Sameena worked her magic on the Islamabad side, having secured permission to waive customs fees and expedite delivery.

My local post office and the fire station agreed to reserve space for donations. We printed "Warmth Without Borders" flyers with the collection time and place and the urgency of the deadline. Mail carriers slipped them into mailboxes. Volunteers snapped them under windshield wipers. Supermarket managers pinned them on public bulletin boards. A small team cold-called camping stores and showed up at churches, synagogues and mosques.

At a principal's office, I plunked down the front page of *The New York Times* on his desk. "Look at these people. If we don't get the tents and blankets to them, they will die." He scanned the faces of the dusty, the dazed and the bereft. Wait for it, I said to myself. It worked every time.

Every school principal in my community convened parent meetings where I could talk about "Warmth Without Borders" and hand out an updated shopping list. Every school in my community publicized the urgent need to save lives in Pakistan. Rotary International chipped in to solicit supplies. One of the Rotary officials and I found ourselves in the dumpster of a recycling center, looking for boxes and bubble wrap.

This operation was Robin Hood, Karl Marx and the Catholic Church all rolled up into one. The rich could afford it, and it would make them feel good. The poor needed it. I dusted off Saul Alinsky's *Rules for Radicals*: "Pick the target, freeze it, personalize it and polarize it" and always "keep the pressure on."[24] I avoided politics. Pakistan scares people. I implored everyone to respond humanely to this unfathomable catastrophe.

At times, leadership must be visionary: above the fray, transcendent and transformational. At other times, it is all about cracking the whip. In this case, the supply chain. I began to bark orders: "I need you three people to call the camping stores in Seattle. Give them this list of things we need: winterized tents, space or wool blankets, and warm clothes: mostly children's sizes. Show them the tax write-off receipt, appeal to their better selves, get the name and phone number of those who make a commitment, and follow through." I pressed harder. "Two days after you get a 'no,' go back to them and ask again."

I would not be deterred. "Wherever you go, bring a prop: pictures of winterized tents, blankets, shoes, newspaper articles. Allow donors to feel like heroes for pitching in. Thank them profusely and publicly. Leverage the donation of one neighbor to inspire another. The folks down the street just donated *five* blankets! Make sure that everyone knows the deadline for donations, after which the plane will leave and the place will turn into a tomb for the lost and abandoned."

At the post office, a supervisor granted me permission to hang a "Warmth Without Borders" banner across the building and cleared a space outside to drop off unmarked packages. We erected a tarp to protect the boxes from Seattle rain and simulate a temporary shelter. After only a few days, boxes were stacked precariously high. The fire station next door told us that we could not obstruct entry to the post office and then proceeded to free up their own meeting room, now that the voting booths had been cleared away.

The local thrift store combed through its own donations and dropped off winter coats. Middle school students volunteered, giggling when they came across lingerie or high heels. We labeled boxes for sealed bandages, sanitary napkins, toothpaste, toothbrushes and soap. Drivers rolled down windows to hand us checks, $20 bills and pizzas.

On the last Sunday, a succession of 20-foot Ryder trucks arrived right on schedule, some waiting in a line of cars still dropping off supplies. Without any prompting from me, a human chain formed naturally — people lifting boxes from car trunks, sifters separating hygiene items from clothes, packers giving way to sealers and labelers to those arranging boxes in the trucks. Once filled, the trucks took off, each with a volunteer, for a DHL office on the tarmac at SeaTac airport. DHL employees were ready, stacked boxes on pallets, instructed volunteers on how to use the shrink-wrapping machine, and loaded pallets onto a conveyor belt headed straight for the cargo hold of a Boeing 737-300QC by mid-morning the next day. The flight was scheduled for 2:00 pm.

I announced our tally of tents and sleeping bags, coats and medical supplies. I promised to inform everyone when the supplies arrived and were distributed. Cheers and high-fives all around.

Late that afternoon, I eyeballed one more truck's worth of supplies. This might be doable. I promised that both the area outside the post office and the fire station would be spotless. We had never obstructed the free flow of operations, but the warehouse staging area at the fire station was a particular disaster. I pleaded with the dispatcher for one more day. He grudgingly obliged. I would pick up a Ryder or U-Haul, wrangle a volunteer or two to help me pack it up by noon, then head out for the final delivery to DHL. Even then, it would be tight.

No one could make it on Monday. The other collection groups had long since met their deadlines. Truck rental places were closed and most would open too late on Monday. I found a 22-footer from a sketchy company *if* I paid in cash. I did as much loading and prep work possible until I was asked to leave the warehouse. Despite his promises, the owner of the truck said I was too late for one with a lift. That night, I tried, without success, to drum up volunteers. No luck. This would have to be a solo job.

I approached the fire station at sunrise just as fire trucks screamed past me. The red aluminum doors were open, but the station was empty. I stepped inside gingerly, expecting to see a dispatcher. No one was in the office. I spied a dolly and hand truck but was reluctant to use them. Outside, I saw at least ten more boxes beneath the "Warmth Without Borders" banner. Someone must have cleared out a cellar and offloaded their junk. Instead, I saw shoes, children's clothes and store-bought toiletries.

The post office door was open for access to safe-deposit boxes, but the room to the public counter was locked. Around the back, I searched for someone loading those ubiquitous white, boxy Grumman mail trucks. No luck. I straddled two newspaper stands to tear down the sign.

Once the post-office obstacles were removed, my attention turned entirely to the fire station. I began to balance a box on the trailer hitch, then into the truck, climbing into the cabin to arrange them. I assured myself that someone would soon arrive.

Alaska Airlines called to do a phone interview about Teachers Without Borders because I had been chosen as a "giraffe" by "The Giraffe Project," a Pacific Northwest organization devoted to highlighting the work of people "who stick their necks out." My neck was on the line. Trying to catch my breath, I gave the interview, squeezing the phone between my neck and collar as I lifted boxes, disconnecting the phone several times, calling back and apologizing.

By 9:30 am, I had yet to make a dent. The post office was open, but the workers were too busy to help. Yet another moment of panic, embarrassment, self-loathing and "I-am-an-addled-child" syndrome, mixed with the major sin of do-gooders making promises they can't keep. This international shipment required that I be ready at the tarmac by 1:30 pm at the latest to sign the bill of lading and other forms taking personal responsibility for the contents on pallets. A faxed copy, including my signature, would not suffice. My choice was clear. I could take off with the quarter-full truck so that DHL could load the pallets, fly to Kennedy and meet the Pakistani Airways cargo plane; I would ask the Salvation Army to pick up the rest. Or I could fill this truck up, somehow.

I hurried the interview to a close just as a box fell off the truck, bouncing off my shoulder and splaying its contents on the floor. I didn't know what to do. Wiping tears and sweat, fighting off a flash of rage, I decided to quit, apologize to the fire station, expect to pay a fine, and hope that time would assuage my acute sense of guilt for not having clothed more children or helped replenish a rapidly depleting supply of basic hygiene supplies.

The floor was littered with unpacked pup tents, toiletries, markers, half-assembled cardboard boxes, dolls and toys. Someone had been shouting "Hey!" but I was too consumed with self-hate and disappointment to hear him. "Yo, little guy!"

I turned to see someone wearing a headlamp, leaning over the cab of a forklift. Facing the mechanical stegosaurus bearing down on me, I raised both arms, as if I had been caught red-handed in the act of burglarizing the place.

"You're the little guy who made this mess! I heard about you!" I started to stammer my apology, but he wasn't listening. "Look," he said, "I've got shit to do. These guys told me to show up and put the place back together." I started to plead with him that I had to get the truck to the tarmac for a humanitarian effort. I pointed to my watch. I waved the DHL papers. He rose in his seat. "Sit down! Over there!"

I followed his finger to a folding chair in front of open lockers as if remanded to purgatory outside a principal's office. I checked my watch. After about five minutes, I decided I would jump in the truck and make a break for the airport. I imagined a comic version of a slow-speed O.J. Simpson chase. The neurotic carrying camping gear and warm clothes. In hot pursuit, a one-eyed dinosaur calling for backup.

"Lil guy, back up the truck!" He whirled around, pushing boxes toward the center of the warehouse, turning on a dime to push them together from the side.

Within minutes, he had swept up the remaining boxes and began sliding them into the back of the truck, an inch or so from each panel wall and the ceiling, nudging them next to each other. He was a Jenga genius. It took him about 20 minutes. "OK. Truck packed," he mumbled again. "What did you say this was for?"

I told him about the earthquake, the impending snowstorms in Kashmir, PODA, and the deadline for the flight. I pulled the *New York Times* article out of my jacket.

He stepped down from the dinosaur. I hugged him.

"You mean I helped?" he said. I told him he did more than simply help; he was responsible for saving lives. By sharing his skill, he was making a difference.

He smiled. "Not bad. Damn!"

I made it to the tarmac on time. DHL loaded the planes and left on time for New York. Pakistani Airlines picked up the pallets. PODA signed for them in Islamabad and trucked them to camps for distribution to relief agencies and directly to families. Sameena sent images of displaced families in warm coats and sturdy shoes. Blue tarps were stamped with logos for PODA, Teachers Without Borders and local partners.

A week later, the snow began.

Most people think they have nothing to offer. They may work in a cubicle, on a farm or beneath a car. They may have unlimited resources or the keys to unlock storage closets with perfectly usable yet discarded supplies people need. The office worker with a passion for graphics who can design a flyer that captivates attention for a cause. The assembly line worker with a ham-radio hobby capable of doing a voice-over for a podcast. The people who fix things. The artist. The immigrant studying for citizenship with expertise in document translation. The refugee carpenter, once an engineer, who escapes injustice or war for a better life. Forklift drivers. We just must ask them for their help. Most will say yes.

It's all good news, but within a few days, I was discomfited by the nagging feeling that our efforts continued to *follow* a disaster. Teachers Without Borders was not a relief agency. Friends and colleagues presented rational arguments: why deprive people of the exhilaration of service? How could we *not* support a colleague pleading to help people in need? I was not convinced.

I had seen the ruins of buildings made of sand and shoddy cement after the earthquake in India and could only ask questions. For Pakistan, at least we provided some temporary relief. It was necessary, but it was not sufficient.

We had to be proactive and educate communities about earthquakes. Education must save lives before those lives are mercilessly sacrificed. This warning is not new. Around AD 65, Seneca, in his *Naturales Quaestiones*, wrote:

> We have just had news, my esteemed Lucilius, that Pompeii, the celebrated city in Campania, has been overwhelmed in an earthquake...For what can anyone believe quite safe if the world itself is shaken and its most solid parts totter to their fall? Where, indeed, can our fears have limit if the one thing immovably fixed, which upholds all other things in dependence on it, begins to rock and the earth lose its chief characteristic, stability?[25]

What could we do to educate for safety? The answers came soon enough.

Chapter 10

Bulls and Mosquitoes

On 12 May 2008, at 2:28 pm, schoolchildren were about to pack up their satchels when a magnitude 7.9 earthquake struck Sichuan Province in China. Reports from a relatively new microblog site, Twitter, broke the story before any of the news agencies. Once again, children died at their seats.

Those closest to the epicenter heard a thunderclap of subterranean fury. The earth had turned over as if by an enormous, invisible spade. Boulders the size of trucks tumbled onto and engulfed villages below. Rivers dammed by avalanches caused up to 800 "quake lakes."

My local radio jazz station was interrupted by breaking news about an earthquake in China, though little information was yet known. Switching stations, I searched for more. There was a quake in Sichuan, China. More news rolled in. The earthquake was centered near Dujiangyan, an ancient city known for having constructed a unique flood-control project in the third century BC to harness the longest tributary of the Yangtse River and prevent it from rushing down the Min Mountains and flooding the Chengdu Plain. The flow of the river could then be channeled and divided via a levee in the shape of a fish's mouth. Still in use today, this engineering marvel was named a UNESCO World Heritage site in 2000. Some say it is an achievement that rivals, if not surpasses, the Great Wall.

Teachers Without Borders had been collaborating with Chinese science teachers in Dujiangyan on professional development sessions in science-inquiry methods at the middle and high school levels. Just two weeks earlier, we had finished our last session for the year and took group photos. Now, within minutes, whole villages were razed. Twisted roads. Buildings flattened. By the afternoon, tourists on foot and on motorcycles posted the footage: it was unmistakably Dujiangyan.

All that past week, National Public Radio's Melissa Block and Robert Siegel had been recording interviews for a piece called *Chengdu Diary* (Chengdu is an hour and a half away from Dujiangyan). I had been following the story with keen interest. My wife and I lived and taught in China in 1984 and I wanted to hear their take on China's growth, politics, culture and economy. When the earthquake struck, Melissa Block was on air discussing the issue of religion just outside a church. "What's going on?" she asked as the ground rumbled, doing her best to maintain her reportorial equanimity. "The whole building is shaking. The whole building is shaking. My goodness!"

"Oh my goodness, we're in the middle of an earthquake?!" her voice a combination of question and alert. "The whole block is shaking. The...the top of the church is falling down! The ground is shaking and all the people are running out into the street." She continues: "We're standing here. The birds are flying. The ground is undulating under my feet. The cross on top of the church is swaying violently...People are huddled here on the street. The shaking seems to be slowing down. I can still feel vibrations underneath. Everybody has run out in the street. There are crowds gathered. Somebody is naked..."[26]

I raced home in time to hear Alex Chadwick, the NPR reporter in DC, reach Ms. Block and ask: "Where are you now?" Reporting from a car, she responded: "We're trying to get to the city of Dujiangyan. Buildings have crumbled into a heap of white dust and glass." Tofu buildings, as many later described them.

"Screams everywhere. Parents rushing to the schools, wailing." The names of the schools were made public. Xinjian School. Juyuan Middle School. I knew immediately that we had lost children, teachers and schools. I could not sleep or eat. My wife asked me to stop looking at the same videos over and over again. I couldn't tear myself away.

It was impossible to reach my colleagues in Dujiangyan. The only colleague I knew in the US with an insider's view was Yong Zhao, Distinguished Professor at Michigan State University's College of Education and a pioneer in the field of globalization, technology and education reform. We had been in touch only once. I knew he was born in Chengdu, the capital of Sichuan Province. Surely, he could fill me in. I couldn't get through to him either.

I glanced at his speaking schedule. In a bizarre coincidence, I learned that he was in Seattle. I raced over to the lecture just in time to reconnect, hear his speech, and offer to take him back to the airport.

We spent a few moments at a diner, both of us wired and talkative or silent and shell-shocked. I gobbled up my sandwich nervously. He pushed his food around. Yong Zhao had managed to reach his family but could not connect to his friends. We compared notes. We promised to stay in touch.

Hundreds of children were trapped under rubble at the three-story Juyuan Middle School. There were no confirmed reports yet on how many had died. Without an appointment or plan, I drove to the University of Washington and knocked on doors until I found Professor Steve Harrell, an anthropologist, who was holding an open forum in a few days to discuss how his students studying at Sichuan University were responding. They had already formed an impromptu organization, China Earthquake Aid, to assist relief efforts with water, tents and quilts, coordinating their efforts with a stream of military trucks dispatched to the region.

For three days, every hour from 5:00 pm west-coast time to midnight, I called the Director of Education for the region, Zhang Qing, with whom I had built a close relationship. No answer. Finally, a message arrived from his interpreter with these three words: "Can you help?" I wondered how. Relief wouldn't do. Teachers Without Borders had to rely on its central mission to connect and serve teachers. To educate. Still, I had no plan.

I landed in Chengdu two weeks later. Streets were blocked off and some buildings had collapsed. I saw cracks everywhere, but for the few hours there, the city did not look like the war zone I had seen on television. The next day, a colleague and I started for Dujiangyan. The high-tech corridor seemed relatively intact, though there was a clear military presence. The closer we got, the more damage we saw. Billboard advertisements were painted over and replaced by red one-line Chinese phrases encouraging citizens to be strong and work together.

Getting close, traffic began to slow. Up ahead, emergency personnel wearing luminescent orange vests with bands of reflective tape directed traffic to pull over to leave room for caravans of People's Liberation Army trucks to pass or return to base for provisions. Having completed 24-hour shifts, exhausted soldiers leaned against metal railings and smoked, others asleep standing up. Outside my window, a massive assembly of ecru and khaki tents stretched for at least a square mile. After the caravan passed, we inched closer until asked to hug the shoulder again for another caravan.

At our turnoff to Dujiangyan city, we saw the edge of the apocalypse. Crushed apartments teetered above vacant stores, window frames bent and bowed into parentheses. Concrete chunks hung from smashed ribcages of hotels, stores and schools. In the middle of the street in downtown Dujiangyan, I spied a white limb of a mannequin, its hand strangely clenched.

Whole families' possessions made rudely public were plowed to the side of the road like filthy snowbanks after a freak storm.

My throat began to burn. It was hard to breathe. A headache bore down on one side of my head, then the other, like a metronome of mallets. The order of life can't just shift like this. Children are supposed to outlive their parents.

At the site of a school reduced to concrete slabs, scattered bricks, splintered wood and paper, we came across a shrine constructed by grieving parents. Bamboo poles and siding held up a tarp protecting a plywood wall and shelves filled with framed photographs of their children. Above the shrine, a painted bedsheet bore words expressing the community's rage: "Painful Mourning for Underserved Children."

Two tables in front of the shrine held water and flowers for sons and daughters in heaven. On either side, handmade easels supported wreaths. Daypacks were splayed everywhere: pink ones with Disney characters, shredded ones spilling out steno-pads, workbooks, and colored pencils like a riot of pick-up sticks. We watched a young boy twist and wriggle through a temporary chain-link fence and walk tentatively toward the shrine. He stood in front of it, bowed, stood up and bowed again. Catching sight of us, he scampered away. No one spoke. I took deep breaths to ward off my nausea. Here was a school standing tall one day, filled with kids, then crushed like Tinker Toys under a bully's foot the next.

A member of Director Zhang's staff escorted me to an office building he assured me was structurally sound enough to reenter. Once inside, someone offered tea but made no eye contact. Outside, the *wee-ooo, wee-ooo, wee-ooo* of an ambulance raced past. Zhang entered, a changed man: distant, pale, weary, distracted. His family was safe, he said, then looked away. Our meetings customarily lasted at least an hour, followed by a meal and celebratory shots of *baijiu*, a high-octane clear liquor customary for making multiple toasts to friendship and good health.

After a short briefing, he asked that I accompany him to a shelter and temporary school. Zhang took call after call, sometimes lowering his phone to speak to an interpreter. On more than one occasion, the interpreter whispered, "We have found another child." He looked directly at me and said, "Director Zhang said that there is no need to save face. We will show you everything. Please take a moment to go inside yourself to prepare."

At Juyuan Middle School, the grounds were sealed and guarded, though we were allowed to travel along an access road to see up close. Zhang motioned to a guard to open the gate. No closer than 75 meters away, we could see *through* the rooms.

At each school we passed that first day, I saw stairwells without classrooms and classrooms without stairwells, as if separated by an immense, blunt knife: six stories of chalkboards, panda paintings, benches and mangled rebar. This was a war zone.

We arrived at a temporary school in an area bulldozed for tents and 40-foot shipping containers. Students were queuing up for lunch outside a tent, metal tins in hand.

Zhang's team identified a man supervising the lunch line and asked him to tell me his story. The man started slowly, methodically, clinically as if he were under oath: each event of that day stamped, minute by minute. The interpreter relayed every word. At 10:15 am, my class was doing this. At 1:30 pm, my class was doing that.

As he approached the events leading to the earthquake, I expected some level of sadness to take over, but he remained composed. He explained that every other day, he and another colleague switched rooms. His students would go to the language lab outfitted with tape machines, while the other teacher would use his classroom for math lessons. "At 2:20..." He started to wobble. The interpreter caught him and propped him up. He continued. "At 2:20, my daughter was there." He pointed to a concrete platform. A folding chair appeared. Two colleagues held each elbow and guided him to the seat.

"Why couldn't it have been me?" His face lost all color, then reddened again as if he had come down with the flu. He gripped the sides of the chair, his face convulsed in pain. "May the twelfth was a Monday. Why couldn't it have been a Sunday?" Someone brought him water.

Zhang could not meet with me again on that trip, so I relayed a message that I would return soon. A member of his staff replied: "Mr. Zhang says that he appreciates your American saying, 'A friend in need is a friend indeed.' He suggests a change in your program. Could you focus now on earthquake science and safety?" I had no idea where to start, but Teachers Without Borders had to do more than support relief efforts *after* the fact.

Without hesitation, funders for our science and safety program approved the shift in focus. I turned to the Teachers Without Borders network and found Solmaz Mohadjer, a TWB member from our early days. As a graduate student conducting geodesy projects in Pakistan and Tajikistan, she observed that students and teachers knew little about the geology of their terrain, potential building collapse, and damage from moving or falling objects. There were no earthquake drills. Simply put, when the earth shook, one faced one's fate.

She would know. Ninety percent of her native Iran is crisscrossed and surrounded by tectonic activity, more specifically a north–south convergence (collision) between the Arabian and Eurasian plates. P-waves (primary) zip through liquids, solids and gases, causing small jolts and light shakings, followed by brutal, roller-coaster S-waves (secondary) traveling along the surface of the earth, wreaking havoc. With all those folds in layered rocks the seams come undone.

After the devastating Bam earthquake in 2003, government officials considered moving the capital to somewhere other than Tehran. Iran is a seismologist's stochastic nightmare.

Having been jolted awake by mean-spirited quakes far too many times as a child, Solmaz decided she would wear shoes to bed, clearly a geophysicist in the making. For her, preparation and planning can be the difference between life and death.

In a brilliant TED-X talk, "How to Disarm Earthquakes,"[27] Solmaz tells a story about Tilly Smith, a 10-year-old from the UK vacationing with her family during winter holidays in Phuket, Thailand in 2004. Strolling with her parents and her younger sister at Mai Khao beach, she noticed that the tide had receded dramatically. People looked around, amazed. "Tilly saw the water begin to bubble. Staring off to the horizon, she could see boats bouncing like yo-yos. She knew exactly what was happening. She remembered a lesson her geography teacher gave two weeks ago in which she learned about plate motions, earthquakes underwater and tsunamis." Hysterical, Tilly screamed to everyone to evacuate the beach. People heeded her call. Her family made it to the top floor of their hotel, a distance from the beach. According to the California Institute of Technology's Tectonics Observatory, it took 20 minutes for 100-foot tsunami waves to flood and drown Banda Aceh at the speed of a Boeing 737 climbing to cruising altitude.[28] The hotel withstood three large tsunami waves. Tilly's warning saved the lives of at least 100 people.

Solmaz explains: "More than a quarter of a million people lost their lives on this day. Millions were injured and, even more, displaced and became homeless." Even though the UK is not known to be prone to earthquakes and tsunamis, Tilly knew what was going on.

During her fieldwork in Pakistan, Solmaz was told by several people that God chose who lived or died or what gets destroyed, and that "one of the reasons for an earthquake were women, inappropriate behavior and dress." Her lightbulb went off in Tajikistan. When she asked students what causes earthquakes, several told her variations of this theme: earthquakes occur when a bull, down in the earth, bothered by mosquitoes, thrashes about and causes the ground to roil and rumble. They had never given it a second thought. She began to develop a program for earthquake science and safety.

Earthquake origin stories are certainly not limited to Pakistan, Tajikistan or the developing world. The United States Geological Survey (USGS) has been cataloguing "Earthquake Legends" to understand how people around the world perceive natural phenomena. Sins cause earthquakes, the devil causes earthquakes, spirits cause earthquakes.[29]

Solmaz tested her science and safety curriculum with middle school students in Dushanbe, Tajikistan's capital city, where earthquakes and aftershocks were so common that the community no longer noticed them. Young people, however, remained afraid.

She had no intention of taking the bull by its proverbial horns to dispel long-held beliefs, but rather to teach about what happens to the earth itself and let children come to their own conclusions. The challenge was to seize upon their stories as an opportunity for scientific exploration and reflection. Therein lies the magic of her short film, *Between Bulls and Mosquitoes*.

She spoke their language. She knew when and how to introduce and move through topics. She used props to explain what happens in an earthquake. Students loaded sand, soil, gravel and flat rocks on a cookie pan, then rocked it back and forth. They added water to make mud to simulate heavy rain or snow. Hard-boiled eggs illustrated the earth's layers. They demonstrated the general properties of vibrating waves at low and high frequencies by waving spaghetti of assorted sizes with a raisin on top. They manipulated springs and local toys to demonstrate the physics of tension. They combined popsicle sticks, connectors and rubber bands in a competition to build the strongest structure, then shook them until they fell apart.

Her students began to think like scientists. They identified variables that could influence the experimental outcomes. They simulated hazards and mitigation strategies. They made predictions and tested them. They collected, recorded, interpreted and evaluated their results. They worked in small groups to produce questions about their school's structural integrity. She concluded lessons with a book-making project so that students could show others what they had learned. They were becoming earthquake safety advocates.

Post-assessment interviews with students revealed an extraordinary level of retention and commitment to safe schools. Something else was sparked, too: curiosity about science itself. In a video of one of her wrap-up sessions, a student said that now she had learned about earthquakes, she wanted to know about astronomy.

In Tajikistan, students and their parents insisted that community buildings be submitted to vigorous inspection and reinforcement. The students themselves were not only thinking scientifically but also emerging as activists.

Imagine if earthquake science and safety were embedded into the curriculum in schools in seismically vulnerable communities around the world. Imagine if teachers could explain geological factors underlying the earth's movement, the physics and engineering of poorly constructed buildings, and the hazards of objects dislodged and flung about like ping-pong balls in a storm. They would be best positioned to communicate what to do to prepare and plan for disasters. By emphasizing safety, teachers could effectively transmit earthquake preparation and planning to families. Solmaz showed up at the wrong place (an earthquake zone) at the right time.

In one seismically vulnerable and poor community and country after another, Solmaz would conduct pre-assessment interviews with the same appalling and devastating results. In the absence of knowledge about the origin of earthquakes or preparation strategies to mitigate their impact, lives were lost. With science on her side, however, she was on solid ground.

She adapted her curriculum to meet the context and science of each setting. "Not all earthquakes are created equal," she explained. "Earthquakes are complex scientifically and regionally specific. In earthquakes, some buildings sway, others sink." In many cases, an automatic "drop, cover and hold" response alone, without understanding the terrain and the buildings, could result in death. Her message could not be clearer: teachers and students must be empowered to know the fundamentals of geological science in their community, prepare for the eventuality of earthquakes, pass their knowledge along to their families, and, as a community, make noise until voices are heard, changes are made and corrupt builders are held to account.

We returned to China, armed with her Quake Science and Safety Program in Chinese. Li-Hong Xu, an English teacher from Chengdu, mobilized teams of colleagues to learn the trade of earthquake science education. She engaged Chinese seismologists to ensure scientific and cultural accuracy. She connected with our surviving network of science teachers. With the help of Cisco Systems and Agilent Technologies, she coordinated language communities and distribution networks to remove all barriers to accessing the curriculum and appropriate teaching strategies. She found illustrators to incorporate each science lesson into drawings that included familiar Chinese buildings and faces. She negotiated a plan by which new backpacks issued to children included a pocket guide on earthquake science and safety. The William and Flora Hewlett Foundation supported the creation of a course available to the public without cost.

* * *

The 12 January 2010 Haitian earthquake took over 200,000 lives. Around 1.3 million people flooded into hastily constructed camps just weeks before the rainy season. Clean water was almost impossible to find. Cholera took hold. Up to 80% of Haiti's schools collapsed. Haitians describe the quake as if it were a locomotive bearing down or, more onomatopoeically, as "Goudou Goudou," the roar and shake of the earth, followed by the sound of people and animals screaming.

The United States Geological Survey (USGS) and the Earthquake Engineering Research Institute (EERI) have reported that, at the time, "Haiti had no seismograph stations during the main earthquake," a "lack of detailed knowledge of the physical conditions of the soils (for example, lithology, stiffness, density and thickness)," and, you guessed it, "poor construction practices."[30]

In an article for the *Journal of General Internal Medicine*, a doctor spoke his heart:

> After seeing a third child this week die of pneumonia, or dehydration, or cerebral malaria, we clearly understand that this country existed in a state of emergency long before the earthquake: an emergency without enough witnesses. The earthquake has exacerbated an existing bleed. The country is now hemorrhaging.[31]

He continues: "In the midst of the fog of all that is chaotic and difficult, I witness an awe-inspiring collaboration." He asks:

How the hell are the Haitian people so tough? How did they absorb the brutal shaking of the earth into their bones and still endure? The last few days reveal what they have always had to deal with—death from dumb, treatable diseases.

In an earthquake, one would think that the school would be the safest place in one's community. Not so. For years after the Port-au-Prince earthquake, many Haitians were too building-phobic to send their surviving children to school. And yet, our interviews with Haitian teachers who *had* understood the physics of earthquakes showed they had already taken matters into their own hands. An engineering teacher had prepared his students but was traveling during the earthquake. His students followed his instructions. No student of his died that day.

These teachers are an exception to the same tragic story: densely populated communities, unreinforced schools, powerful earthquakes, bureaucratic obstructionists, and little or no earthquake science and safety education. Fifty percent of children who perish in earthquakes die in their schools.

There is plenty of blame to go around, much of which centers on greed, graft, corruption, massive urbanization and poorly built structures. Place a clear map of seismic zones on a table, then lay atop one that shows educational fault lines: neglect, poor literacy rates, a lack of support for teachers; it's an unsettling match of fault lines.

Communities throughout Haiti, Afghanistan, India and Pakistan adopted Solmaz's Earthquake Science and Safety program. Volunteers translated the curriculum into seven languages. Geologists approved the proper use of scientific terms. Solmaz organized professional development workshops and enlisted maintenance workers who became heroes for securing objects that would otherwise dislodge from walls and cause severe injury or death. Parents have held contractors to account for shoddy construction.

We posted all content in the public domain. In Haiti, a poster campaign provided an extra level of community access. *Scholastic Magazine* published "The Haitian Earthquake of 2010" and chose Solmaz as the content consultant.[32] The Interagency Network for Education in Emergencies (INEE) and Prevention Web, two leading organizations in the field of education in emergencies, posted Solmaz's earthquake science and safety content. Scitable, an online collaboration space run by Nature Education, added further credibility by highlighting the science content. The Undersecretary for Education for the Obama administration and the William and Flora Hewlett Foundation acknowledged the Earthquake Science and Safety program for its commitment to open educational resources, public safety, information portability, community outreach and international diplomacy.

Teachers Without Borders would no longer ask helpless questions or send relief packages to earthquake zones after the fact. From that point on, we were out of the shipping and handling business. We were educators, and educators can save lives.

In 2011, Solmaz founded ParsQuake,[33] an organization devoted to "earthquake education in the global Persian community." ParsQuake bridges "the gap between scientists and the public in regions of high geohazards risk exposure." It matters most to Solmaz that communities can protect themselves from catastrophic earthquakes. "We cannot prevent them," she will say, but "we can disarm them," strengthen buildings and know what to do in an earthquake. Today, teachers are training other teachers to use whatever materials are at their disposal to demonstrate the nature of earthquakes. In Afghanistan, students color pieces of cardboard to show layers. In India, teachers easily find scrap material to construct shake tables to show the properties of structural integrity.

The country and context may change, but Solmaz ensures one constant: "to cultivate, support and revive elements of indigenous safety consciousness" through science and safety preparation and planning. In Tajikistan, many may believe a bull, bothered by a mosquito, causes the earth to shake. Today, students now know how to protect themselves in advance and, when an earthquake strikes, what to do next.

That's education from below the ground and up.

Chapter 11

A Country Under Water

Six months after the earthquake in Haiti, July monsoon rains pounded Pakistan with no sign of letting up. In 24 hours, Peshawar recorded 10.8 inches. By August, whole cities were submerged. Comparative satellite images of the Indus River basin did not look the same. In 2009, the basin anatomy looked like a heart and a main artery extending north to south. In 2010, the same region looked like those arteries had been cut, creating blood lakes.

News agencies captured photographs of panicked children and parents marooned with their livestock, looking for higher ground. Their fertile land was washed away, taking with it grain, cotton, rice and sugarcane. I heard an aid worker remark, "Pakistan is living a tragedy in multiples of 2s: 2000 people and 200,000 livestock killed. 2,000,000 bales of cotton made useless. The flood upended the lives of 20 million people. 20% of promised relief funds were made available for a country, 20% of which was under water."

Over 10,000 schools were destroyed. The aid worker continued. "I've never seen anything like it. How do you triage for a country under water? But do you know what? The Pakistanis have regrouped before. They'll do it again." Many weren't so sure. Pakistanis and donor agencies were losing confidence in the government's sluggish response to disasters. They feared that the Taliban would flourish in the breach. Others rejected all help from the West. Donor fatigue was setting in.

Price gouging, crime, and incidents of cholera made normalcy unattainable. Critical infrastructure had collapsed. Relief would not be enough. Education couldn't wait.

The development community had convinced aid agencies that teachers were vital assets in disaster intervention. Relief was no longer limited to food, sanitation, shelter and clothing. Teachers are indispensable members of first-responder teams. They count children, reunite families, establish child-friendly spaces and prevent human trafficking. It has become a part of global policy.

Sameena called me. I called Solmaz. Solmaz called Li-Hong. The three developed a plan to focus on child-friendly spaces so that parents could start the process of reconstructing their lives. For a community in shock, child-friendly spaces are familiar, safe and structured. Children can sing and draw, hear stories, use manipulatives for learning, play with toys, play football and do what children *should* do: play.

Child-friendly spaces depend upon the ability to map local resources and sustain an intervention over an undetermined amount of time in an area often difficult to reach. Families are traumatized and suspicious. Without communication and coordination between government authorities and parents, grandparents, religious leaders, women's groups, NGOs and local authorities, they fail.

Those who create and sustain these spaces navigate between the formal and nonformal education system because the crisis itself upends basic assumptions of what constitutes a school and who can be qualified to teach. They must leverage local expertise in the absence of textbooks, address cultural orientations toward integrating girls and boys, and build a climate that values human rights and gender equity. In an emergency, a child-friendly space must establish norms of inclusion and foster hope amid the chaos.

PODA, Teachers Without Borders, the Pakistan Association for Mental Health and the Roshni Helpline for Children erected a counseling center, child-friendly spaces and a women-friendly space in the Kemari Internally Displaced Persons Camp near Karachi. Sameena, Solmaz and Li-Hong engaged with a wide cross-section of Pakistani stakeholders: workers, nurses, students, psychologists, teachers, journalists, doctors, human rights activists, artisans, lawyers and community development professionals. In short, they reached the people who reach the people.

Aid workers outfitted each child-friendly space with toys, furniture and educational materials, supported by staff trained in children's rights education and basic skills. PODA staffed the counseling center with psychiatrists, psychologists and physicians who supplied outpatient care for panic disorder and depression, treated injuries, scabies and diarrhea, and trained local paraprofessionals.

Our network was now sufficiently strong to enable teachers to find each other, share resources and mobilize quickly. A new form of professional development was emerging: a community of practice seasoned in the real world, facilitated by technology and connected by common objectives. The vicious cycle of earthquakes and floods was met by a self-generating, reciprocal, virtuous cycle: just-in-time support, ad hoc, focused and practical. The teachers shared what they learned.

We cannot prevent or even predict earthquakes or floods with certainty. More, given the preponderance of research on the disproportionately negative effect of climate change on poor populations, disasters are only growing in intensity and deadly force. With preparedness and planning, however, educators can prevent a disaster from turning into a catastrophe. The world would be wise to take heed.

Chapter 12

Time Is Not on Our Side

By the time one particularly Shyamalanesque day had ended, I had gained firsthand knowledge of the ten plagues, in no particular order, as well as insight into my own demons.

Within 15 minutes of our 245-kilometer odyssey from Port Harcourt, Nigeria, to Calabar, the car plunged into a crater-sized pothole filled with brown-gray rain. The driver jumped out, lowered himself knee-deep, lifted the hood, swatted away the steam, fiddled inside and swore. He asked for help to pull the fender away from the driver's side front tire. He called a dispatcher for another car. A small crowd in flip-flops gathered to gawk. Bicyclists, white and blue buses, and cars slalomed around us. He told us to collect our belongings from the trunk in case the carcass sank any lower into the sludge. Someone offered to hose us off. Before we could say no, he had already thumbed the nozzle.

The police arrived and directed traffic around the car. Someone started screaming about corrupt contractors. Another car arrived promptly so that we could continue our journey. We handed the driver our bags and tiptoed through the slosh to climb in. A motorcycle whizzed past, speckling our backs into a Rorschach made of mud. This car had towels and water.

For the first hour, we threaded through a knot of commerce. Trucks faced each other in a standoff, leaving no room to maneuver past abandoned or immobilized hulks straddling the road and a ditch on either side. Here, streets are called "free-for-alls," every object in motion and out for itself. Street children jockeyed for the best place to sell phone chargers. An ambulance driver leaned on his horn and turned on his siren, but could not get through the crush of everything. A paraplegic man propelled himself forward on a child's bed frame outfitted with shopping-cart wheels. The air was thick with a queasy, noisome smell of petrol, urine, garbage and humidity.

I was in Nigeria to meet with a high-school math teacher, Raphael Ogar Oko, who had embraced the Teachers Without Borders vision during its infancy. We often spoke about leadership, UN goals, Nigeria, and teacher networks. For Raphael, dependence upon foreign aid was anathema to development. It had to be homegrown or bust. He was clearly in charge. He was simply looking for a global companion and he would take it from there.

Federal Senator George Thompson Sekibo of Rivers State sat in front. The new vehicle did not have government plates, so no police parted the sea for us. Senator Sekibo was not pleased but had his government card with him. That should do the trick.

With one hand on the horn like everyone else and the other directing traffic and waving away vendors, our driver wriggled through, then thrust us forward like a rocket shedding its boosters. Within minutes, the engine stopped. He started it up again. The road smoothed. We had been traveling for 45 minutes and had covered only 8 kilometers. Straddling the median, a car swerved past us.

The sun was strong, but I could see a distinct bank of dark low clouds and toothpick streaks of rain ahead. Outside my window: swampland, shops, clotheslines, corrugated roofs, billboards, and women balancing washbasins on their heads filled with jugs of cooking oil, sheaves of grain and rags, followed by more farmland, plumes of hay and trash fires.

At each checkpoint, Senator Sekibo flashed his ID. Guards nonetheless poked their heads in to look around before allowing us to continue. He told the driver to "speed up before it got too late."

"Too late for what?" I asked.

Silence. "Darkness," Raphael muttered. Plague. The driver straightened to make eye contact in the rear-view mirror and finished Raphael's sentence. "And bandits."

I changed the subject from the race against impending doom and asked Raphael about our itinerary. "Several stops," he said. "Each one is a project."

Raphael described our ultimate destination, Old Calabar, host of the largest street festival on the African continent, a city known for its public art and a port indispensable to the trade of palm oil and slaves: 25–30% of those sold to the New World during the seventeenth to nineteenth centuries.

From 1967 to 1970, Calabar was known as the Republic of Biafra. Cultural, religious, political, ethnic and economic tensions led southeastern Nigerian provinces to attempt secession, stimulating coups, countercoups, blockades, and the Nigerian Civil War, which left in its wake a trail of death, malnutrition and starvation. Close to 3 million people dead. Media broadcast images of headless bodies abandoned on trains and emaciated children with bloated bellies. Locusts. Blood in the water. Plagues.

Our first stop was a program for pregnant teens, all of whom had made a vow to continue their education. They rose as Senator Sekibo entered the room. Raphael and the lead teacher took the floor and talked about education as the key to women's health. The young women sang a welcome song. The room felt softer, a shared space. Raphael excused himself and headed off with the driver. He would be right back, he said.

Each young woman told us what she wanted to do with her life and what she was learning. They felt seen. They had value. They were not castaways. After sharing sweets, a young woman wearing an "I'm Not a Victim, I'm a Victor (1 Corinthians 15:57)" T-shirt showed me a small stack of books, pointed to one and said, "This is the one I am writing." I didn't have time to ask her what her book was about. Raphael was shooing us back to the car.

The sun gave way to rain. The driver picked up the pace. I pretended to look at the scenery when he switched lanes to pass cars. Raphael handed me a fist-sized meat pie wrapped in wax paper from Mr. Bigg's, a ubiquitous fast-food chain. My first bite spurted meat and sauce onto my shirt. As if on cue, the driver flipped a napkin over his shoulder. Rubbing made it worse.

Patricia Acquah, a fiery graduate student and committed activist for women's and children's rights, squeezed in and joined us for the rest of the journey. "Time is not on our side," Raphael said. On both sides of the road, abandoned tires looked like half-eaten chocolate donuts wading in pools of stale coffee. There were advertisements everywhere: for cellphone and gas companies, Hennessy brandy, legal services: "Just because you did it doesn't mean you're guilty," churches, UNICEF posters about proper hygiene, and a new highway billboard campaign encouraging people to get tested for HIV.

Our next stop, a school, was not accessible by car, so we walked up a hill, following schoolchildren bearing desks on their backs. They would be using their furniture at school *and* at home. Students and teachers were rapt as Patricia explained that teachers are not civil servants but the backbone of society, how teachers worldwide were mobilizing to talk with one another and share ideas, and how there was hope.

Despite a lack of facilities, the school was expanding and literacy rates were improving. The principal met with us in a tidy office and offered her vision of a school centered on how children learn, rather than on what they must memorize. For her, it was the teacher's responsibility to find a way to access the forms and mystery of each child's developing strengths rather than to expose weaknesses. "Schools have learning disabilities, too," she said. Her bookshelves included outdated UNESCO literacy primers and Bibles donated by a drive-by missionary group from the UK. "It doesn't matter *what* they read as much as they *understand* what they are reading. They need to lift words off the page, build phonemic awareness and decode what is in front of them. Reading is about making meaning. It is their ticket to understanding everything else."

We toured classrooms and lingered in a room identified as a science lab: tables and chairs, a few beakers, and a single poster on the wall, "The Story of the Cockroach." I imagined several cockroaches scurrying about, looking for a piece of Mr. Bigg's. Several children were scratching their heads. I suspected lice. Plague.

Raphael told me how we would secure science equipment. He had already started a fundraising campaign. In the following months, he navigated through both legitimate and corrupt customs offices, worked the system and oversaw the details. Jihad's words rang in my head: "The community will take care of it."

On our way again, Senator Sekibo reached for the radio and swooshed through static AM stations until he landed on a news channel. After the sports and weather, a reporter mentioned my name, along with a clip from an interview with Raphael.

Senator Sekibo turned around in his seat and smiled. "Did you hear that?"

Raphael said: "Fred, Teachers Without Borders is on the map!"

I returned a halfhearted smile. He looked puzzled, noting my dour expression. Was I along for the ride to add white legitimacy to these projects? I asked, "How did they know?"

Reading my mind, he answered: "Use it, Fred. The public will forget our names. We're messengers, that's all. But they will remember Teachers Without Borders and they will take to the idea."

Patricia smiled. "To make a difference here," she added, "we need friends like Senator Sekibo...and you. This has never been about the Great White Hope." I looked at her suspiciously. She continued, "It's about being international."

I was not convinced, but had little time to reflect. The sky unleashed drumrolls of rain strafing across the hood, the windshield and the trunk, bouncing around the car and dissolving into caramel puddles. It felt like hail. Plague. Our windshield wipers thwumped and scratched across the windshield in a futile attempt to swat away the onslaught. I heard something bounce against the roof. I kept staring ahead, too petrified to look, fully expecting something like the four-minute frog storm scene from *Magnolia*. Plague.

"Time is not on our side!" Raphael shouted again over the din.

"No fear," I whispered to myself.

We reached a teaching hospital in Abia State to deliver handhelds loaded with ePocrates RX, a freeware app with FAQs about public health and a cross-referencing tool for drug interactions. Raphael was making arrangements for a Community Teaching and Learning Center to serve patients and add a technological component to the medical library.

We entered a gated reception area to wait for a physician to give us a tour. A doctor asked the receptionist if he could see a notebook. He took his time, piquing my curiosity. I stood up to stretch my arms and legs and peeked over his shoulder. Sheets of paper with uneven vertical ruler-drawn lines designated columns for the patient's name, age and HIV/AIDS diagnosis. I stared at the doctor's hand as he flipped through page after page of people in their twenties and thirties, accompanied by the notation, "HIV+." After no more than a minute, he closed the binder slowly and patted its cover as if he were consoling the notebook for having to record the news: a Tibetan Book of Living and Dying, Nigeria version.

Raphael motioned to us to follow a doctor down a hall and into a lab for HIV testing. On a piece of tape across an oblong white-plastic specimen tube, I saw the name "Fred" and a set of numbers written with a magic marker. Plague.

We walked through a corridor lined with beds, all occupied, like planes waiting to take off. We entered the children's wing. A nurse placed a swaddled infant in my arms. At first, the baby seemed to breathe rapidly but then began to seize, shake and cough. Just as quickly, she became limp. I looked up. A doctor motioned to a nurse, who thrust her hands under my own and whisked the baby away, returning later to see us off. She looked drained. Plague.

Raphael explained that negotiations were underway to supply computers for a Community Teaching and Learning Center at the hospital with a particular focus on health information and patient advocacy. We entered a conference room to discuss it further. I don't remember the conversation, except for a nervous teenager who entered with a tray of warm Orange Fanta and paper cups. I could not pay attention.

"We need to get to Calabar before sundown."

"I know," I said curtly. "Bandits."

Raphael replied, "Time is not on our side."

We drove past fields of oil and gas refineries and flare stacks belching yellow, orange and red flames swirling around black smoke like an enormous, out-of-control birthday cake. On each side of the road, more flames rushed furiously from open pipes, as if all this were an attempt to relieve pressure from an active volcano.

We drove on a service road parallel to a tributary of the Niger River. Senator Sekibo talked about environmental degradation, increased toxic-related illnesses and cattle pestilence due to greed. Plague. Catching the afternoon sun, the iridescent sheen on the water looked like food coloring in salad dressing: kaleidoscopic, viscous, bubbling, hypnotizing. "Animals and the people drink, wash and bathe in this."

He waved his hand to draw our attention to the expanse of farmland ahead. "The soil was so rich here. You used to be able to throw a cassava seed in the ground and it would grow. Now, the soil can't produce. No yams, no cassava, no bananas, no work." I smelled a strange mix of sweetness, rotting vegetation, fish, mold and gas.

"Some foreign oil companies know well that they have caused all this, so they give 40 percent back to the country. Some efforts are a sincere attempt to tighten their standards. What do these corrupt leaders do with the money? Turn this revenue into schools and hospitals? Not a chance. This is ecocide. And who suffers the most? The people who work and live here. It's a damn shame."

When we arrived, Senator Sekibo got out, slammed his door and marched toward a group of women, who recognized and greeted him warmly.

Patricia and Raphael chatted with a few villagers. Children in trees waved to us. Senator Sekibo informed us of legislation he was introducing to demand health and education services and stimulate redress against environmental degradation.

Women were taking matters into their own hands, he explained. He wanted to stir the pot.

He turned to look at me. "You saw it. You smelled it. Don't forget it."

On our way back to the main road, Senator Sekibo announced: "Filmmakers are arriving here within a few weeks." Powerful *agitprop* films like *Poison Fire* and *Sweet Crude* would eventually follow, bringing global attention to a growing group of ecofeminists and catalyzing public outrage.

The driver followed signs toward Calabar. Senator Sekibo spent the rest of the time on the phone. We arrived in Old Calabar and dropped off our overnight bags at a roadside motel. The driver looked relieved. No bandit attacks. No cavernous sinkholes. No flat tires. Mere annoyances. Nevertheless, I shook his hand overzealously. A van with two graduate students doing fieldwork and two men in ill-fitting suits and Foster Grants were waiting. I thought of Dan Aykroyd and John Belushi from *The Blues Brothers*. The drivers shook hands. Driver #2 unloaded box after box of Styrofoam takeout dishes and a small folding table. Senator Sekibo was the first passenger to step out of the car, followed by Raphael, Patricia and me. Senator Sekibo could not stay for dinner, he said. He shook hands with us and promised to stay in touch.

"Let's eat," Raphael commanded, "but..."

I interrupted again. "Time is not on our side."

Out came a bucket and towels for washing hands. We gorged on plantains, oversized scoops of jollof rice, chicken and beef skewers, spinach, and *fufu* (made from cassava) for scooping up fish and meat from soups. The Blues Brothers distributed napkins.

At sunset, the buildings, roads and sky were shrouded in a tangerine smoke-smog haze. We packed up quickly, hardly making a dent in our provisions, and drove down leafy streets past a huge concrete sculpture of hands, roundabout statuary and verdant public parks.

We bounced along a dirt road headed toward an abandoned commercial area donated to the Calabar municipality to accommodate a Displaced Persons (DP) camp for 3600 people caught up in ethnic violence. Raphael rattled off a list of challenges: gender-based violence, psychological abuse and distress, fear of retribution, theft, extortion, kidnapping and even mines. Here, too, time was running out. The camp would be dismantled unless plans were in place for a range of social services for 150 families.

Patricia scampered out of the car and met her husband, who had been coordinating relief services on-site. He hugged her and seemed to deliver distressing news. She began to step back. He held her steady. Most of the village was in a woody area at the far end of the complex. She took a breath and told us to wait, then whispered something to Raphael. "They have just buried a child," he said. "They will be here soon."

Two-story, dilapidated buildings lined one side of the road. Their street-facing walls were not yet complete when the construction company abandoned the property. The buildings looked like downtown Dujiangyan after the earthquake.

We could make out silhouettes of about 80 people walking in our direction. Once they had gathered around us, Raphael expressed our condolences and said we were there to support Patricia's husband, a trusted friend. The Blues Brothers took their glasses off and said they were there to inform Senator Sekibo about plans for the future. Patricia held on to her husband's elbow. The grad students and I smiled weakly. Once again, a baby was placed in my arms. I rocked him back and forth, but after taking one look at me, the baby started to scream. Someone came to the rescue. Why do people hand babies to me? Someone shook my hand as if to console *me*. Children peeked out from behind their parents' legs.

The village elder expressed his appreciation. Raphael said he would be mobilizing Nigeria's National Youth Service Corps, comprised of graduates of universities and polytechnics fulfilling their mandatory one-year community service obligations. The Blues Brothers took notes. The students said they were ready to tell their friends.

We said our goodbyes. Patricia stayed back with her husband. Turning from the gravel path to the street, the driver turned on the radio. I asked him brusquely to turn it off. We drove in silence through a tidy neighborhood of upscale homes.

[*Dear reader, it is only right to warn you about the cringeworthy part of this story that follows. I'll explain once you get through it.*]

I blurted: "Stop the car!" The driver looked at Raphael in his rear-view window for instructions. Raphael looked horrified but complied and asked the driver to pull over. The words tumbled out of my mouth: "Give me your money."

"Fred," Raphael protested, having never asked me for a dime. "I don't understand."

"Just turn the van around. We're going back to the DP camp." Looking at everyone directly, I said, emptying my wallet, "Here's my own money. Now I want some of yours. It's not for me, damn it, it's for them."

Intimidated, the graduate students searched for spare naira (Nigerian currency). I took half. The Blues Brothers complied grudgingly. The driver leaned back with his own crumbled bills. I closed his hand around his wad and pushed it back at him. "Not you." I turned to the graduate students and the Blues Brothers. "I will pay you back." Raphael looked dejected and embarrassed.

He began to speak. "Fred..." Raphael had always been in charge, but I interrupted. "Raphael, we are going back, *now*."

Raphael relinquished his naira. I straightened the bills. The driver made a U-turn.

When we arrived, the village elder approached, shielding his eyes from the car's headlamps. Patricia and her husband had left. I reached over the grad students, wrenched open the van door and climbed out. "Here, take it." He was reluctant, looking at Raphael. I pressed it into his hand. Patricia and her husband were approaching. Raphael tried to intervene, though I wondered how he might navigate through my impropriety and abruptness. The village elder headed toward Patricia Acquah's husband with the cash in both hands, as if he were holding an injured bird. Patricia hurried to catch up. Raphael huddled with Patricia, her husband and the village elder. Patricia took the elder aside and spoke to him, walking away from us. A few people inquired about the commotion. The elder waved them away, emptied an envelope into one pocket and placed the money inside. It was settled. We drove away in silence.

All day, I was afraid of bandits. Now I had become one.

I knew well how the international aid world reinforces dependency rather than self-reliance. I had contradicted all my convictions about how effective development must be conceived and led by local brains who can build stakeholder support, develop strategies and partnerships, and produce a plan for sustainability. This was a paltry, patronizing quick fix.

Clichés flooded my mind, each one a stark reminder of the sins I had committed. The sin of the handout rather than the hand up. The sin of giving others a fish instead of teaching them how to fish. The sin of a pound of cure over an ounce of prevention. This was no random act of kindness; it was my superficial and desperate attempt to feel better.

In a 2009 TED Global Talk titled "The Danger of a Single Story," storyteller and novelist Chimamanda Ngozi Adichie defines *nkali*, an Igbo word for power. She explains: "It's a noun that loosely translates to 'to be greater than another'"[34] by telling others' stories and, in so doing, asserting one's authority over them.

Dear reader, this is no unctuous wink to burnish my image as a reflective guy. My impulsivity had occluded my judgment. Everywhere we had gone that day, I had expected the worst and ignored the agency and creativity at the heart of change. I had stolen their story. Even this book of stories can be viewed as *nkali*.

When we arrived at the motel, Raphael handed me a Styrofoam container. He saw I was in no mood to debrief the day.

Back in my room, I flipped the fluorescent lights and ceiling fan switches, then curled up on a thin mattress supported by two-by-fours. The lights flickered on. The fan began to pick up speed but then began a bleating, plaintive sound as if it were straining too hard against its better judgment.

I tried to console myself. I would apologize in the morning, but I knew the damage had been done. I could not dislodge the day's images and tried to distract myself. How many baseball stadiums had I been to? How many animals could I name in alphabetical order? What were the most memorable events in each of the past five years? Baseball didn't matter. I couldn't get past leopard. All the events of the past five years ran into each other. Besides, I only recalled the funerals.

Untethered, unmoored, undone, I felt a full-blown panic attack welling up like those gas flares. I gulped down a bottle of water on the nightstand to calm my nerves. Knowing well that a full-blown panic attack was welling up like one of those gas flares. I walked to the washbasin and kept dousing myself as if to wash away everything I had seen, heard, smelled and felt (those two babies in particular), all compounded by my abject hypocrisy. I remembered the panic I felt in the bagel-factory bathroom. Once again, I was a flawed, feckless fuckup.

The following day, Raphael consciously avoided any mention of what had happened. The Blues Brothers and graduate students had all gone elsewhere, so I had no chance to apologize to them. After an uncomfortable silence, Raphael described what lay ahead — developments he hoped I might see soon. TWB colleagues were training volunteers to manage a rent-to-buy microloan program of foot-powered sewing machines for pregnant teens. He would solicit science equipment for the school and begin negotiations to establish the Community Teaching and Learning Center at the hospital.

In the weeks and months that followed, Senator Sekibo would follow through with his commitments to support public health and education for those impacted by the ecological disaster. The national service corps got to work at the DP camp.

There was much more to come. Raphael articulated a strategy for attracting universities to the Certificate of Teaching Mastery program to secure state endorsements and official accreditation. HIV/AIDS educators fanned out to encourage testing. He raised $7000 to wire funds to me so I could defray costs for a shipping container full of donated computers, science equipment and books for several projects. DHL stepped in again to ship the supplies. He stocked the School of Nursing and Midwifery, Gwagwalada, Abuja, with books, journals, magazines and other educational resources on HIV/AIDS. The Rivers State Library Board added a section on HIV/AIDS. Benue State approved the opening of a Community Teaching and Learning Center. He built a unique educational program to empower the disabled to become skilled, self-reliant and useful to society. He retrofitted a van outfitted with literacy primers, notebooks, writing utensils and a dry-erase board to create "The Wall-less Classroom," a mobile literacy program for cab drivers. In the car-jammed sprawl of Jabi Motor Park in Abuja, Nigeria's capital city, he supervised volunteers to teach reading under a rented canopy.

He launched a *Voice of Teachers* journal and solicited academic submissions on regional educational issues. The Certificate of Teaching Mastery grew and was respected by universities in dozens of Nigerian states. Courses morphed into seminars on HIV/AIDS, problem-solving, community organizing, hygiene, information technology, early childhood development, gender equity, intercultural and intergenerational relations, mental health, mentorship, microfinance, sustainable development, sports, and volunteerism. He conducted "teaching tours" in 12 Nigerian states. Raphael was walking the talk of community stakeholdership I had just undermined.

Beaten by gangs, ostracized, dismissed and harassed, betrayed by those attempting to extract money from TWB members or cast aspersions on his leadership and character to promote themselves, Raphael continues to show up.

Where I saw plagues, Raphael saw possibility. Where I raised the specter of my own *nkali*, he raised the stakes on local change. "Time is not on our side," he continues to say, "but I'll use the time we've got."

In 2010, Ashoka, a global network of changemakers and social entrepreneurs, and the William and Flora Hewlett Foundation initiated an open voting system to acknowledge individuals who have made a tangible difference in Africa. From over 400 submissions from 30 countries, Raphael received first prize, the Champion of African Education award, and $5000. He promptly poured every cent into the *Voice of Teachers* radio show.

Chapter 13

Peace on the Radio

You can teach courses on peace. You can create safe classrooms so that students learn in peace. You can march for peace. But if you want peace to flourish, you must provide a platform to be heard. Raphael considered the radio to be as good a platform as any.

Every Monday for 45 minutes, close to 1.6 million listeners tuned in to his radio show, *The Voice of Teachers*, on Kapital FM 92.9 Abuja. He began with music, followed by education news, community announcements and a showcase of innovations. There was plenty of room for call-ins.

The switchboard lit up each time. If listeners were unable to get through, they sent text messages to a team of volunteers who responded directly or sent them to Raphael to add to the following week's show.

The Teachers Registration Council of Nigeria, a federal government entity responsible for licensing teachers in Nigeria, endorsed the show, enabling him to reach his funding goals for the following season. The Federal Radio Corporation of Nigeria syndicated *The Voice of Teachers* to Niger, Plateau and Kaduna states. Raphael told me you could hear it from tinny speakers on buses during the afternoon commute, from car doors open on both sides so that others could hear, and from transistor radios at the public market.

Raphael has long known about Nigeria's own grotesque horrors, stirred by a barrage of messaging and intimidation. Boko Haram (translated as "Western education is evil") had taken hold in northern Nigeria. The group's logo is comprised of two crossed AK-47 rifles in a V shape. Between them lies an open Qur'an, above which is a flag bearing the *shahada* ("There is no god but God, and Muhammad is the messenger of God"). Their crimes against humanity have not been limited to the kidnapping of hundreds of girls in Chibok. They seek to impose the strictest form of Sharia law against what they see as government corruption. Boko Haram have robbed banks, burned down schools, and conducted execution-style murders of officials, police, Christians and any Muslim who would oppose them.

On an afternoon filled with meetings, followed by an evening event (for which I had turned off my phone), Raphael had left four messages, his latest one time-stamped at 6:00 pm in Seattle, 3:00 am in Abuja. When I finally reached him, it sounded as if he were under water. I couldn't seem to piece together what he was trying to say. The call dropped several times. We persisted.

When the line cleared, he spoke slowly, his tone flat and sepulchral. Silences between sentences lasted so long that I had to ask often if he was still on the line. He recounted how he had traveled to Benue State to visit his mentor, Joseph Hungwa, who had been taken ill. Hungwa's credibility and depth of knowledge had attracted hundreds of teachers to attend Teachers Without Borders seminars about the right to literacy and the ability of any community member, regardless of background or financial capacity, to gain the skills necessary for active participation in civic life. His Community Teaching and Learning Center at Vandeikya in Benue State was a magnet for the curious.

After the visit, Raphael traveled to Jos, a cosmopolitan city located in Nigeria's Plateau State, to observe an emerging Teachers Without Borders program. Plateau State has been portrayed as a center of peace and tourism. However, there were reports of unrest in the area and he wanted to ensure that his colleagues and friends were safe.

He had arrived in time to witness the aftermath of a massacre. Villagers had fled. News reports were graphic: screaming, blood, machetes, a church on fire, stony faces, people wailing, huddled, groups clustering to pray, a community ripped apart. He was unsure whether this was the work of Boko Haram or other groups.

After having hosted months of *Voice of Teachers* broadcasts, Raphael simply wanted to be heard by an audience of one. I remained silent, thunderstruck, mortified. I don't remember if I said anything consoling. When this first conversation ended, I urged him to call every day. Over the next two weeks, I may have uttered 50–100 words.

We studied everything we could about peacemaking through education, success stories about reconciliation, grassroots efforts and top-down strategies. The more we researched, the more we saw layers upon layers of connections between state and non-state actors and violence, religious tensions, deep inequalities and injustice, the weaponization of food, neglect, barriers to access of government services, abuse of girls and women, suppressions of freedom, teachers attacked, and schools closed.

I began to realize that Teachers Without Borders had learned to play it safe. I had been promoting the hardly contestable, sanitized idea of supporting teachers around the world. We had embraced the larger picture of education in emergencies, but I was hesitant about assuming we would be able to make a case for the connection between teachers and building peace. It felt grandiose and self-aggrandizing.

And yet, this entire time and in his own polite way, Raphael had been screaming, "Time is not on our side." I could not betray him. Then again, he certainly did not need my approval. Joseph Hungwa soon succumbed to his illness. "He worked for peace," Raphael wrote. "To honor the idea of his rest in peace, we must become educational ambassadors for peace. It should be our duty, our conscience talking."

Raphael's next *Voice of Teachers* broadcast was devoted exclusively to call-ins and SMS messages. He invited me to listen in. I gathered colleagues to join me. We spent the remainder of the day lost in our thoughts, too numb to speak. It was immediately evident that we did not have to create an all-encompassing peace program. We needed to appeal to the collective wisdom of teachers. They would show up.

After a series of posts on our website about the radio program's focus on the catastrophe in Jos and an appeal for peace education and the view outside teachers' windows, stories started flooding in. Escalating, drug-fueled violence in Mexico, drive-by shootings in the United States, attacks on teachers in several countries, torture of human rights educators in the Congo, Myanmar and the Philippines, and police violence.

We contacted organizations cataloguing attacks on teachers and schools. Konrad Glogowski, TWB's Executive Director, reached out to our network. Stephanie Van Hook, a Peace Corps volunteer in Niger and graduate of the University for Peace, showed up to help Raphael and inquiring teachers develop a curriculum adaptable for communities to use anywhere, on their own terms. Konrad organized TWB members to contribute content. They sent in curricula for all grade levels, opinion pieces, links to research, teacher professional development exercises, and examples of homegrown peace efforts. Within a few months, TWB launched the Joseph Hungwa Memorial Peace Education program.

We reminded ourselves of our value and mission: that brains are evenly distributed, that given the right framework, teachers can find ways to build peace in the small places. We would rely on collective wisdom rather than dispense solutions. The vision of peace was to be firmly in their hands, not ours. Our best contribution would be to convene teachers and then get out of their way.

In South Africa, Nyasha Mutasa completed the Joseph Hungwa Peace Education program and engaged her colleague Patrys Wolmarans, Director of the South Africa National Peace Project, to conduct workshops in primary schools. In Mexico, Deyanira Castilleja adapted the program for teachers living and working in gang-infested communities. In Kenya, Uganda, the Democratic Republic of the Congo, the United States and Canada, in online courses and offline community meetings, on the radio and in podcasts, the Joseph Hungwa Memorial Peace Education program grew because it was a shared enterprise.

Raphael created a football and peace-building program for youth. Peace teams with sponsorships sprouted in schools, churches and senatorial districts. He established a community peace football academy and peace football commissions. Teams adopted "play in peace" policies to build good character in sports (no violence, no arguing with refs) and penalties for racism or demeaning statements. Accompanying campaigns raised awareness about the role of education, sports and peace-building. The "most peaceful player" award would go to the individual who best demonstrated three central qualities: (1) mind/body harmony—character, (2) teamwork—cooperation and citizenship, and (3) non-forceful ball control/possession— creativity. Conversations with teams addressed the winners-versus-losers relationship (peaceful competition), sacrifice for one's team (harmony) and acknowledgment of the opponent ("support your enemy"). All teams were encouraged to serve as

Football Ambassadors for Peace and given a handbook on how to get started.

The radio was a great medium for inspiring peace and yet, 6000 kilometers across the continent, an Islamic military group in Somalia utilized the radio for another purpose. At the time, Al-Shabaab had been running a radio quiz show for 10- to 17-year-olds. *The New York Times* reported that the top two winners received "AK-47s, some money and Islamic books. The third-place winner was given two hand grenades."[35] I pity the children who didn't score well at all.

Al-Shabaab barred aid groups during a famine, and forbade gold teeth, dancing and football, deeming them un-Islamic. A truck bomb detonated at a government building killed students simply awaiting the posting of their exam results.

The article continues: "Sheik Muktar Robow Abu Monsur, who is widely considered a moderate Shabaab leader, proudly said, 'Children should use one hand for education and the other for a gun to defend Islam,' according to Somali accounts of the event." School bells were torn down because they sounded like church bells.

Textbooks included arithmetic exercises that "ask students to calculate the number of explosives a factory can produce...or the number of Shi'ite Muslims or 'unbelievers' that can be killed by a car suicide-bomber," yet had removed the plus sign (+) for its similarity to a Christian cross.

Al-Shabaab waged war on the radio. Raphael sowed seeds of peace on the radio and built a community of teachers whose classrooms reflected the world they would like to see outside their windows. The word *teach* (v.) is derived from the Proto-Germanic word *taikijan*, meaning "to show." I would add this: to teach is *to show up*.

Raphael set the peace football in motion. Teachers from around the world passed it on. In 2018, Teachers Without

Borders was awarded both the Luxembourg Peace Prize and the Ahmadiyya Muslim Prize for the Advancement of Peace. Despite my inquiries, the organizers of these prizes have never revealed how we measured up enough to be so acknowledged. These accolades are due in large part to Raphael.

Chapter 14

Jabriil, Angel of God

The taxi arrived at 3:45 am sharp. While the driver scampered out to collect my roller bag, I noticed that the passenger side was occupied with books bound with a bungee cord. We exchanged pleasantries. I took my backpack off and shoved it into the back seat and climbed in for a long stretch of anonymity and negotiations ahead: three flights, two middle seats, and layovers too long for comfort and too short for sightseeing. Settling in, I unzipped the pockets of my backpack to check for my passport and paperback, untangled and rewound my charging cords, thumbed through my itinerary and glanced back wistfully at my home.

On the freeway, I pulled out the *New York Times* bulging from a side pocket and scanned the headlines. Below the fold, one article caught my attention: a Dick Cheney diatribe impugning the integrity of Senator John Kerry. For reasons I still cannot fathom today, I read it out loud, followed by a disapproving grunt. From that point on to Departures, I found myself outmatched in an intellectual tennis match in which I, the pitiful amateur, lobbed ridiculously easy serves to a Wimbledon opponent.

At this hour, who the hell was I to presume that this guy would concur or feel chatty after God-knows-how-many airport runs and obsequious gestures to anxious riders seeking free therapy? He mumbled something I could not hear. I took it as an affirmation. Betraying my own advice to leave it at that, I prattled on about Cheney's infuriating smirk, his immoral no-bid Halliburton contracts and his all-around smarminess.

I started to apologize, but then he offered the following five unambiguous words: "Cheney is *possessed* by evil." Half a minute passed. He continued with six more: "He has been *overtaken* by evil." I decided that my own silence would send a message that this was just an awkward exchange. I would ride this out. But then I thought, how can Cheney simply be a host for deeper, malevolent, forces? I seethed. Folks like Cheney deserved no pity. His decisions were deliberate and deadly, for which he should be held accountable in a criminal court. Before I had a chance to respond or change the subject, the driver said: "I know what evil looks like. I am from Somalia."

I weighed my options. Option 1: feign sleep. Option 2: serve up something with a little more *oomph*. I didn't have Option 3. Without a reasoned follow-up in place, my impulsivity took over: "Evil? You mean *pure* evil?"

His answer was *yes*. He launched into an exposé about evil as something inexorable and distinct from character, something that transcended choice. His intensity was unsettling. I fiddled with my phone, hoping he'd pick up on my discomfort and leave me alone, but he had returned my serve and was waiting for a volley. He adjusted his mirror to look at me directly.

I returned his gaze, a pulse beginning to intensify behind my right eye. I wanted coffee and one of those oversized, overpriced airport muffins. But Option 2 it was. "Cheney knows exactly what he's doing. He's deliberate and responsible for all the havoc and pain he causes. I can't accept that it's simply out of his hands." Before I could stop myself, I quipped, "The devil made him do it?" I instantly regretted my attempt to channel comedian Flip Wilson's Geraldine Jones character, his stereotype of the sassy Black woman that, years later, made him cringe. I pivoted to "I don't buy it." I warned myself to leave it there but continued anyway. "So, if Cheney lies, he can't stop himself? Cheney is evil *because* he lies, intentionally so. His motives are clear: power and greed." Who the hell did I think I was, lecturing this guy? I should have known better. If this topic came up in a course, I would have asked questions rather than asserted my views.

"No," he said, clearly indicating that it was his turn. "You're wrong. Some people are evil by nature. That's why they rape and kill. Reason has nothing to do with it. The world tries to assign reason to evil, but attempts to do so always come up short. Evil is evil, plain and simple."

"Reason has *everything* to do with it," I snapped, surprising myself with my ferocity toward anyone, no less someone I had just met. "How can someone be born inherently evil? They learn evil. They could have been traumatized as a child. Maybe a brain scan would show pockmarks like the moon instead of what a normal frontal lobe should look like. Or they've been brainwashed or drug addicted." I was evening up the score. I forgot about my coffee and pastry cravings. "There *must* be reasons. I don't believe there is an evil gene or evil for evil's sake. Without addressing the root causes of an evil act, we condone it." I regretted that last line. Too facile, pedantic, unyielding.

He changed lanes abruptly. I was not sure if he had consulted a rear- or side-view mirror to see if a car was too close to the space he had so abruptly chosen to occupy, if this was how he drove, or if he were acting out of anger. I expected someone to flash a middle finger. I knew I had gone out of my own lane, too.

We drove for about 30 seconds in silence. Without boundaries, touchy subjects such as good versus evil or nature versus nurture rarely end well. When, dear reader, was the last time you participated in, or witnessed, a conversation between two opposing positions that resolved itself in an epiphanic moment in which someone says, "You know, you're right. Wow, I see your viewpoint in a whole new light. I'm convinced." Under these circumstances, the very least we can do is exercise a modicum of restraint and civility. This was not going to be one of those times. I was not going to give in. There is nothing like a belief under attack to activate those adrenals.

"I just don't buy it," I protested.

"You don't have to *buy* anything," he quipped. I wondered if this guy thought that Americans frame everything in either commercial or mechanical terms. If we want someone to agree with us, we go for a "buy-in" or a "win-win." Gullible people drink the "Kool-Aid." Something confusing or complicated has "lots of moving parts." If we want more details, we "drill down." If we don't have time or have lost patience, we "don't have the bandwidth." If we want to assert our will, we cut directly to "the bottom line." A worldview driven by money and machines.

I lowered my window an inch both for air and for the white noise of the freeway, but the thrumming sound it caused was not helping the headache. I closed it, trapped.

"There *has* to be a *reason*," I repeated plaintively, "even if we can't find it yet." I had veered way too close to the topic of faith. What audacity and hubris! In tennis: a flagrant, forced error, yet I continued. "Without an understanding of the root causes for human cruelty, we will be unable to address them, and they will fester. Dictators will exploit and strip away our right to choose our own fate. It makes their crimes that much more abhorrent." Gratuitous and affected. A double fault.

We drove on for another 30 seconds of silence. Was he giving me time to realize how ponderous and hackneyed this was? Assign logic to ethnic cleansing, genital mutilation, death camps, people who filet other people, school shooters, the invention of napalm, tiki-torch-wielding Nazis, and any other act of reptilian indifference to human suffering? It felt petulant and obtuse.

I spied a highway sign with an airplane icon up ahead. Had he given up? Had we reached an intellectual détente? He was simply reloading. My hunch was correct; he was going to turn my argument on its head. "Humanity's history of savagery and sadism *defies* rationality. It continues, unabated, despite all our attempts at reason." I felt taxed and queasy. I craved a blueberry-and-cheese Danish with those three perfect swirly treads of icing, the kind you get at 7-Eleven.

To lighten things up, I considered singing a stanza from *West Side Story*'s "Gee, Officer Krupke," about being depraved on account of being deprived, or boring him with a soporific about the marginalization of youth by institutions that do nothing to support their "bringing upke." How might I convince this guy that he has it wrong? Who am I kidding?

A lesson plan came to mind. "OK. Here's a thought experiment I'll try out on my students. I'll ask them this: 'Is Jerry Sandusky, the football coach who abused dozens of kids, sick or evil?' I'll tell them that they can't choose to say he is *both* sick and evil or that one causes the other. It has to be either sick *or* evil. Then they'll have to defend their argument without trying to defeat an opposing opinion. If we ever meet again, I will tell you what the students say." Why did I think this would satisfy him?

"Evil," he said.

This match was heating up. I responded: "We have a vocabulary for sickness, even words for how we try to understand why human beings commit acts of genocide. There is evidence that child soldiers, extremists or cult members can be rehabilitated and deprogrammed. Change *is* possible. But we *don't* have a vocabulary for describing evil. The evil argument shuts down all conversation. It's too pat an answer." What kind of response was this? Who had crowned me line judge? Why presume that those who believe there is pure evil have no solution?

"Sir, some are touched by evil and some are not. Freud wrote that man is a savage beast to whom consideration towards his own kind is something alien. Dostoevsky said we get a demented pleasure from hurting others, and that inside of us all is a hidden demon, full of rage." Glancing at the road and down at his seat to untie the bungee cord, he opened one of his books. "Here it is: the 'lustful heat at the screams of the tortured victim, the demon of lawlessness let off the chain.'" Yikes. Those books in the front seat were not for show.

OK, this guy believes that demons transcend reason. I believe there are reasons that propel our demons. On a normal playing surface, this would look like a fair match, but not on this court. His mastery of Freud and Dostoevsky felt definitive and impenetrable. A clear winner in the scholarship department. A set point. I was getting trounced.

We dipped under the departure sign and slowed as cars converged into a single lane. I tried one more shot at humor. "I think it was Woody Allen who once said, 'If it turns out that there is a God, I don't think that he's evil. But the worst that you can say about him is that, basically, he's an underachiever.'" I thought this would make him smile. I noticed a slight turn of his mouth, but it might have been wishful thinking. He is quoting Dostoevsky and I'm making jokes.

We arrived at the terminal. "I'm United," I smiled. "That's my airline, not an agreement." This elicited a chuckle at last. I was sure of it. But, then again, I have been illiterate at reading social cues since I stepped into this cab. He might not do jokes easily. I could respect that.

He jumped out, popped the trunk and pulled out my suitcase. "United," he said, lips tight, eyes warm. "Funny." I peeked at the meter and dug out my wallet for the fare and tip.

Walking my suitcase to the curb, he said, "I don't want your money."

"What? Why?" I asked. My heart fell. I truly *had* offended him.

He answered, "Because when my friends ask me to take them to the airport, I just take them," he said.

"I don't understand. This is ridiculous," I said. "I can be your friend, but I'm a customer now and you provided me, a perfect stranger, with a service for which I am obligated to pay. It's only fair." He said nothing. I pleaded, "C'mon, man, a fare is fare" (in embarrassing air quotes). "Fair is fair."

He shrugged it off, but a genuine smile formed. "No," he said. "I haven't had a good old-fashioned argument in a long time." He handed me a slip of paper with his phone number. "Next time you need a taxi to the airport, call me. No *extra* charge." He pulled up my roller-bag handle and returned to the driver's side.

I ran after him. "This can't happen. You're very kind. Probably *born* that way." He smiled again. "But this is not right. Here is the fare and tip." He would not move his arms from the door handle to take my money. "I insist," I said. "Why should *you* pay for providing a service to me?" I looked back at my bags on the sidewalk and walked to the driver's side of the car. After a struggle, I pried open his fist. "That would make *me* evil."

He flashed a brilliant smile and took the cash. I added, "And I don't need a receipt."

"Good journey, sir!"

I had won a battle. *This* time, I got the money thing right. I was more than happy to concede the war.

"Sir? One more thing about what you said. You're wrong, terribly naïve and so American. You think everything will work out fine."

I couldn't argue with that. I answered back, "You're probably right." I looked at the slip of paper with his phone number and asked, "Who should I ask for when I call? What's your name?"

"Jabriil," he said. "You can call me Gabriel, the archangel entrusted to deliver revelations on God's behalf. And yours?"

"Frederic," I said. "I think it means 'peaceful ruler.'"

I thanked him again and slipped my backpack over the handle of my roller bag. He leaned his lanky frame over the top of the cab and shouted. "Goodbye, Frederic, king of peace!"

I turned around to see him wave. I waved back. "Bye for now, Jabriil, angel of God!"

Inside, airport security was smooth, even cheery. I found a coffee and pastry kiosk just as a steel gate rolled up. The sugar and caffeine tightened up the screws for my long journey ahead to Burundi, then Rwanda.

I settled into my middle seat, pulled out the article about Cheney and stuffed it into the seat-back mesh pocket. Jabriil had both unnerved and inspired me. His voice was in my head now. He had spoken with conviction, experience and knowledge. There *could be* such a thing as evil in some pure form — ineffable, deep, and independent of reason. I got up to let the passengers on the window and aisle take their seats, buckled up, and scrolled through the movies to find something distracting for Burundi, just ten years removed from its own genocide. I would not be initiating any more conversations today. Relieved they had an entertainment system, I scrolled through the sitcoms. It was all I could handle. It was my lucky day: a season of *The Big Bang Theory* I had not yet seen.

Surely these Cal Tech guys would have all the answers.

Chapter 15

The Time of the Running

Up ahead on a long gravel road leading to our teachers' conference in Bujumbura, Burundi, three organizers and I made out a man wearing a felt hat, white shirt and oversized khaki pants. He looked as if he were stepping out of a William Faulkner novel.

He propelled himself forward by swinging his suitcases as if he had rowed himself here. He had yet to notice us. At one point, he twisted his wrist. One suitcase careened into his leg, but he managed to regain his rhythm and the swinging began again. Fifty yards later, he lowered his bags to the ground, removed his hat with his left hand and, with his right, gave a decisive judo chop in the center to keep the fold intact before balancing it on one of his suitcases. He sat on the other, pulled out a handkerchief from his front jacket pocket and wiped his brow, carefully folding it again into a proper white triangle before returning it to its proper place. He reached in his pants pocket for a cloth to buff his shoes, took off his hat to check the crease, placed it firmly on his head, bent his knees and stood upright, holding his suitcases. Taking a deep breath, he carried on. His elegance and composure were captivating.

We waved to him. Catching our gaze, he quickened his pace. We met him halfway, shook hands and handed him a bottle of water. An organizer pulled out a clipboard and asked for his name in Kirundi, French and English. "I am Saloman, from Rwanda, and I am here for the Great Lakes Teachers' Conference!" He pointed to the registration form. "Here I am! I am Saloman! *Ndiyo! Oui!* Yes!" he beamed.

Someone shouted: "Find Saloman a mattress!" I wondered how long he had been on the road.

A young man hurried ahead to grab his suitcases. But Saloman would not relinquish them easily. The young man understood not to push and motioned him toward lodgings nestled in a low grove of banana trees. Saloman was tall, erect, wiry. Up close, his eyes were red from dust and his brow creased as if he had taken many of these same journeys through all kinds of weather, toting these same heavy suitcases, wearing this same hat. His voice betrayed his weariness, but otherwise one could not detect signs of fatigue or any of the insults and indignities of travel: officials overreaching their authority, missed buses because the fare wasn't exact, blisters, wrong directions. His enthusiasm, all exclamation marks, was infectious.

"We're glad you're here," I announced.

"Thank you!" he responded.

"You're very welcome!"

Teachers arrived all day, some pouring out of cars and vans, others walking in groups. They came from Burundi, Rwanda, the Democratic Republic of Congo, Tanzania and as far as Uganda, similarly exhausted and exhilarated. From a distance, two women looked as if they had just come from church, their hats gold, beaded, extravagant, proud.

That evening, one of the Ugandan delegates sharing a room with Salomon told us that Saloman had been traveling for three days. He was not the only one. The teachers from the Democratic Republic of the Congo had navigated through treacherous territory to reach a dock where they could travel by boat over the tip of Lake Tanganyika, take a bus to the center of Bujumbura and walk the rest of the way.

We expected about 25 teachers in total, but by late afternoon the ranks had swelled to over a hundred. Youth volunteers marshaled more mattresses and bottled water. An organizer on his mobile phone paced and negotiated, doubling up rooms, cajoling cooks to stretch meals, sending teenagers to look for more chairs and additional housing.

Several months earlier, a Burundian teacher had contacted me about convening teachers from the Great Lakes region. The Great Lakes Teachers' Conference would be one of the first of its kind in Burundi. He had already secured a facility without cost. Small grants and a homegrown auction at a neighborhood church were enough to cover basic expenses. Haviva Kohl, TWB's Executive Director, and members of partner organizations in Seattle and Boston supported Burundian teachers with the concept and coordination.

Organizers set some initial ground rules. This would not be a reconciliation or "peace" conference. No "kumbaya" platitudes about getting along, no lectures and no press. Just honest conversations about teaching and learning, and an opportunity to share experiences about how teachers can best serve their communities.

This meant that the conference structure would have to change. We would dispense with pre-set agendas, approved-in-advance research papers, greatest-hits biographies with postage-stamp photographs of keynote speakers, and second-tier plenary sessions. If development flourishes when rooted in local knowledge and driven by stakeholders, so too should form follow function, and function would foster freedom.

At the full session, anyone could introduce an idea but must also take responsibility for convening a group of the willing. The collective would group similar topics under a single heading. Bored? Leave. Is someone dominating the conversation? Leave and cross-pollinate another group.

It would be a risk. Consensus building and community inclusion have been an instinctual staple of community elders for millennia, but have faced withering resistance from those who regard such practices as inattentive to detail and a time-consuming obsession with process over product. Critics claim that alliances and factions undermine progress, enabling shrewd elites and interventionists to manipulate others into embracing their own legitimacy. In short: left-coast, touchy-feely, aphoristic, magical-thinking bullshit.

I raised the issue with the organizers. "Will this feel Western or lazy?"

The response was confident. "Don't let *your* fear cloud *our* judgment. We'll take care of it." Jihad had given me this same lecture. Deepmala had already shown the effectiveness of organic, self-regulating conferences. Why question it again?

Within 15 minutes of the first session, topics flooded in and were grouped by affinity. How to build hands-on learning in a classroom with little space to move around. How to write grant proposals. How to reach children with special needs. How to reach parents who cannot read. How to get things done despite incompetent leadership. How to change policies that undermine the profession. Physical and mental abuse. Indifference. Gatherings like these can easily devolve into a whirlpool of despair, but these teachers had traveled too far to leave it there.

Sessions grew increasingly personal. In a discussion about school feeding programs, a Burundian man broke down and described how he was not certain he could feed his family. The United Nations Development Programme indicators for multidimensional poverty (deprivations across ten indicators aligned with UN Development Goals in three domains: health, education, and standard of living) place Burundi at "185 out of 189 countries and territories."[36] UNICEF reports that "69% of children [in Burundi] live below the income poverty line."[37] Just over 40% of the country's children complete basic education. Around 62% of the population can drink and cook with clean water, and 46% have access to basic sanitation. His issue was real and as valuable as any other.

This man's concerns led to a topic no Western conference organizer would have included in an official program: animal husbandry and teachers' survival. Discussions took off on how to cool chickens by ventilating cages with leaves, how to deal with brooding hens that did not produce eggs, or hens that pulled out their own feathers to keep their eggs warm, constipated hens, hens with mites or lice, aggressive hens...

Another session turned into a training session on using MUAC (mid-upper arm circumference) tape to diagnose malnutrition. Someone said, "If enough teachers measured their students *this* way, as much as they were mandated to measure students by their scores on irrelevant tests, they could advocate for feeding programs and nutritional supplements."

"It's not that our students aren't keeping up or capable of learning," she continued. "They're *too hungry or sick* to learn."

At the first dinner, Burundian and Ghanaian youth volunteers announced that they had discovered a boom box and suggested that groups from each country prepare to demonstrate and teach a dance if they had brought music with them. Their idea met with thunderous approval for the following evening.

The following morning, music poured out of cabins and cars. During breaks, teachers practiced their performances. That evening, after we had cleared dishes and moved tables and benches against the walls, everyone stood in a circle. Youth volunteers opened the large screen doors, as if for royalty. Sister Donata Uwimanimpaye of Muramba, Rwanda, entered with six others from her convent, each wearing their white-and-black habits. Their arms moved like elegant birds. They bent their knees in a rhythm of one large accented step, followed by two rapid short steps, as they snaked their way through the center of the room. If my father (a folk-dance teacher) had been there, he would have leapt out of his chair to join this Rwandan waltz, take a nun's hand and add his own Serbo-Croatian or Greek flair in a wave of joyful syncopation.

Teachers cheered and formed a conga line. Sister Donata was beaming. We all were. Later that evening, I asked her if I might visit her in Rwanda and talk with more teachers. Saloman leaned over to tell me that plans were already in the works. Her dance was followed by others from the Great Lakes region: dances performed at weddings, to celebrate the birth of a child, in gratitude when crops are ready for the harvest, and for fun after a grueling day of work.

The following day, I received word that President Pierre Nkurunziza had requested a meeting. Nkurunziza's mother was a Tutsi Protestant. His father was a Hutu Catholic. A former physical education teacher and football coach, Nkurunziza was teaching at the University of Burundi when Hutu students were attacked and killed. He went into hiding and joined a Hutu military group. He lost all five of his siblings during the Burundian Civil War and became a born-again Protestant, convinced that his rise to power was his destiny.

Nkurunziza's long reign was marked by corruption and the settling of scores. In 2010, his election to a second term by a vast majority was not due to his popularity, but because opposition leaders boycotted the polls.

Nkurunziza banned "outdoor jogging" in 2014 because he believed that illegal demonstrations were organized among the runners, and subsequently sentenced 21 supporters of the opposition movement to life imprisonment for "jogging" their way to violent protests.

According to Reuters' less-than-flattering 2020 obituary for Nkurunziza:

Burundi withdrew from the International Criminal Court in 2017, shut down the United Nations office on human rights last year and expelled the representative of the World Health Organisation last month amid criticism of the government's handling of the coronavirus pandemic.[38]

His wife was admitted to the hospital on 29 May 2020 with COVID symptoms. President Pierre Nkurunziza died 11 days later. The official announcement said it was cardiac arrest.

I had little interest in a sycophantic photo-op, but if I could draw attention to the challenges Burundian teachers raised, it would be worth it.

We entered the reception room of the presidential compound, awakening a guard slouched under a gigantic painting of the president and a tapestry of a caveman wrestling a bear. After the customary frisk and bag search, we took two flights of dark stairs to a landing outside the president's office. A guard circled us, then opened two large doors to a narrow, unadorned office. Nkurunziza entered. We stood. He told us to take our seats. He did not ask for introductions, choosing instead to prattle about Burundi's economic and social progress. He expressed his appreciation for the conference. He neither asked nor solicited questions. There was no Musharraf give-and-take. I separated his mouth from his face, like commercials with talking dogs. He told us to rise and stand in a circle for a silent prayer. I bowed my head and complied, mumbling the words. We stopped for a group photograph under his official portrait. I wanted out of there.

We arrived back at the conference site to learn that a hand grenade thrown from a cattle truck had exploded not more than 80 yards from a group of teachers returning from an afternoon outing. Miraculously, no one was hurt.

That night, the dancing resumed.

On the final morning, teachers filled the room with posters of challenges and recommendations for improvement. Several sheets outlined a grant proposal for conferences in Kenya, the Democratic Republic of Congo, and Uganda. There were no grand pronouncements about reconciliation.

Teachers sang goodbye songs and exchanged contact information. Several attempted the dance of a different country. Some might have arrived alone, by foot, but no one left alone. Twelve women hugged each other before squeezing into two tiny cars. One woman leaned out a window, holding her hat, and shouted: "Can we take Haviva with us?"

I never inquired about the backgrounds of those who attended the conference in Burundi. Were they Hutu or Tutsi? Did they represent government schools or private schools? What mattered was that they were teachers, traveling at their own expense through dangerous checkpoints and over unfamiliar ground, to learn from and with each other. They shall never stay the same.

In Rwanda, Salomon's territory, he took charge. Once we entered Kigali, the capital city, I spotted Toyota and Daihatsu pickup trucks filled with soldiers careening down opposite hills and converging on us. They were brandishing sticks or broom handles or rifles, rising and falling above the cab. I could not tell if this was a military exercise, an emergency, or civil unrest. I imagined "No Fear" T-shirts beneath their uniforms.

I turned to Salomon. "What's going on? What's happening?"

He smiled. "They're planting trees! They're singing!"

The trucks whizzed by, ends of shovels popping up and down, men enjoying the breeze after a grueling day of digging and reforesting. How was it possible, I mused, for human beings to descend into such hell and appear so upbeat a decade later?

A winding road dips into a small valley and rises again to reveal what looks like an upscale home or church in the

Hollywood Hills: palm and banana trees, a small pool oasis, brick driveway, stone patio and white gate. The Kigali Genocide Memory Centre stands at the top of the hill as a beacon of remembrance for up to 250,000 people interred on its grounds.[39]

The Memory Centre consists of three permanent exhibitions. Exhibition 1: "The 1994 Genocide Against the Tutsi" focuses on life before colonization, followed by the massacres, stories of survival, the heroes who intervened, and efforts to ensure justice and reconciliation. Exhibit 2: "Wasted Lives" documents massacres that have not yet been recognized internationally as genocide. Exhibition 3: "The Children's Room." Enough said.

I steeled myself for the irrefutable video footage of carnage to come: the whoosh of a machete swing, ditches littered with hacked parents and children, skulls. Found words, rosaries, mountains of shoes.

It had been only a decade since a plane carrying two heads of state — Rwanda's president, Juvénal Habyarimana, and Burundi's president, Cyprien Ntaryamira — was shot down by rocket fire as it approached the runway in Kigali. Soon afterward, state-sponsored militiamen bludgeoned, dismembered and disemboweled 800,000 people over the course of 100 days and burned their victims' identity cards to eradicate any trace of identity or memory. Throughout the Third Reich, enemies of purity were called *Lebensunwertes Leben* (or "life unworthy of life"). Here, Tutsis were "cockroaches" to be crushed.

Ten years, too, since the Gikondo massacre on one of Rwanda's picturesque hills in a rural, red-brick church where over 500 worshipers were unable to protect their children from a killing frenzy that took place over the course of two days: children ripped from their parents' arms and dragged away shaking and screaming, pulled from beneath pews and decapitated. I imagined Jabriil appearing by my side and asking me if my faith in reason had started to wobble, hearing me stumble to find reasons: generations of colonial rule, aggression, injustice, rage fueled by scarcity, demoralization and retribution.

The following morning, we started our journey to Muramba to reunite with Sister Donata at the College of the Immaculate Conception. The first several kilometers were paved, but for most of the trip we jostled our way on a red dirt road through a quilt of terraced hills planted with banana trees and corn.

Muramba is perched in the fertile Gisenyi Region, close to the Democratic Republic of Congo. During the genocide, Sister Donata's convent was attacked by armed fighters streaming across the border. Schoolgirls were ordered to divide up into ethnic groups, Hutus on one side, Tutsi on the other. They refused. The men ruthlessly opened fire, killing 17 and wounding 14. A Belgian missionary nun, Sister Margarita Bosmans, the director of another school nearby, tried to stop the assassins and was murdered, along with four lay people.

Salomon commented: "Here, we call it 'the time of the running.'" No exclamation mark this time. The people of Muramba, in their search for safety, were caught between the Interhamwe (a Hutu paramilitary gang) and forces of the Rwandan Patriotic Front. I did not ask him for details.

The killing in the area continued well into 1998.

Sister Donata greeted us and conducted a tour of the convent, including the rooms where screams had been heard and bodies found. She explained how Engineers Without Borders (EWB) was planning projects for rainwater catchment and solar panel-powered electricity. Having met with EWB leadership at their base in Colorado, I knew they would follow through.

We met other nuns who spoke about how children conscripted as killers remain lost, traumatized, and too old for their grade in school. How schooling must be redesigned to reconstruct the self and, in so doing, find a sense of common purpose. How a curriculum could be a tool either for deepening old hatreds and blind obedience or for engaging minds in the thrill of ideas. How schools must be learning centers that include public health, parenting and psychological services. How policymakers must be held accountable not only for the basics but also for the quality of support for teachers. How teachers' voices must be heard.

Sister Donata and Father Ubald launched the Association for Christian Peace Values in Education (APAX), a peace project designed "to contribute to the reconstruction of the social links ruined by violence."[40] Devoted to building a sense of wholeness for those who continue to suffer—autistic children hidden by their parents, disabled children bullied and neglected, the bereaved and permanently traumatized, and anyone left behind—Sister Donata blended her graduate work in peace psychology and theology from Fribourg University in Switzerland with a focus on the power of a spirituality of unity, cultural mediation, compassion and "Christian listening."

Sister Donata never speaks in aspirational generalities. APAX has trained a cadre of village peace-workers and opened community centers devoted to vocational skills in handicrafts, agriculture, knitting and sewing.

Most of all, she makes one point explicitly clear. Social fragmentation is a failure of education to teach reading, practical skills, critical thinking, collaboration, self-respect and the cultural values of peace.

The sun was setting. Saloman was ready to go. Haviva had made more friends. Sister Donata insisted that we stay the night in the nuns' dorms. Food came out of nowhere. Soon, a sister issued us each a candle and a plain matchbook. We followed her silently to our tiny, windowless rooms. Once inside, I lit mine, watching shadows play across the walls and smiling at the thought of an atheist Jew feeling at peace in a Rwandan convent.

After meeting several teachers from the conference, I asked to visit the Kigali Genocide Memory Centre again. I wanted to see it anew after having spent time with Sister Donata. I returned to the chronology of horror, but somehow took a wrong turn and stepped into a room I had not seen during the last visit. I expected more exhibits of atrocities, or a brightly lit prep room crowded with graduate students wearing cellulose facemasks and blue gloves, probing skulls or pinching remnants of fabric with tweezers. This room was neither. It was white and empty, smelling of drywall and fresh paint. A guard entered behind me.

Could this be a meditation room for museumgoers to reflect on the grisly artifacts they had just seen? The sentry cleared his throat. *"Vous êtes perdu?"* (Are you lost?) He stared at me and continued, "Do you speak English? Are you looking for something?"

"No. Thank you," I replied and headed for the door through which I had come. But I had to ask: "What is this room for?"

No answer.

"What, sir, is this room for?" I asked again.

"Right this way, sir," he said, pointing to another exit. I started to rephrase the question. He cut me off. "This way, sir," he said, pointing to the exit, his tone clipped and flinty.

Perhaps he was just doing his job. Without an answer, I filled in the gaps. I was convinced this museum had expansion plans, readying itself to house the memories and artifacts of the *next* genocide.

The exit led outside. Adjusting my eyes to the piercing sun, I noticed a lush garden and patio. That seemed to leave out the option that the empty space was a meditation room. As I walked, I came upon a grave holding a casket and a wooden cross whittled from two branches. A sign above it in capital letters read: "PLEASE, DO NOT STEP ON MASS GRAVES. NE MARCHEZ PAS SUR LES TOMBES, SVP. NTIMUKANDAGIRE KU MVA."

I repeated the words in English. "Please, do not step on mass graves. Please, do not step on mass graves. *Please*, do not step on mass graves."

Below, children were playing football in an area cleared between a clutch of homes, some assembled from scrap metal and wood, others from stucco. In the distance, homes and small farms dotted every hill. Just 3 kilometers from where I stood, I could see building cranes in downtown Kigali.

We left the parking lot and edged out to the street but had to wait. Joggers were streaming by.

Chapter 16

How Could This Happen Again?

Jane Goodall invited me as her guest at the United Nations International Day of Peace. She had been named a UN Messenger of Peace, along with Muhammad Ali, Michael Douglas and Elie Wiesel. It was UN Week again. Streets were blocked so that limousines and horses could travel unimpeded. Sharpshooters paced on roofs. Secret Service agents talked into their shoulders. A steady parade of ambulances whoop-whooped.

Jane introduced me to Kofi Annan, Secretary-General of the United Nations. Though shorter and sadder-looking than I had imagined, he radiated gentleness, humility and elegance. Annan announced to the assembled, "Please follow me," and ushered me ahead of him to a small garden outside the reception area. We stood in silence as he strode up to the Peace Bell, donated by the United Nations Association of Japan to the General Assembly in 1954. Housed in a structure modeled after a small temple symbolizing the Buddha's birthplace, the bell rests on a stone base donated by Israel. Cast from coins and medals collected by children from around the world, the Peace Bell is bonged with a wooden mallet at each vernal equinox and again on 21 September, the International Day of Peace.

The Secretary-General faced the assembled and spoke. "A month ago, almost to this very hour, an act of unspeakable brutality struck our friends and colleagues in Baghdad. Today we ring this bell for them, for their families and loved ones.

We ring it for the people of Iraq whom our colleagues were working to assist. We ring it for people of every nation who need our prayers and peace." He raised the mallet and struck the bell gently. Its resonance throbbed and floated above and inside us, invisible and hypnotic. No one moved.

The power of that day did not lie in quick encounters with global luminaries or in a solemn moment of international communion, but in a question asked following a panel discussion with the UN Ambassadors of Peace. Seated in the front row, Jacqueline Murekatete raised her hand. She looked directly at Elie Wiesel. In 1994, she was 9 years old, living in an orphanage in Rwanda. Her entire immediate family had just been butchered, as well as most of her extended family. Granted asylum to the United States in 1995, Jacqueline moved in with her uncle. As a sophomore at New York University, she attended a lecture by David Gewirtzman, a Holocaust survivor, who spoke in graphic terms about what he had witnessed and his journey as a survivor. Stirred by the lecture, Murekatete penned Gewirtzman a note. "At one time, I, like you, had a feeling of guilt for being alive," she wrote. "Now I'm thankful I was left."[41] Jacqueline and Gewirtzman traveled together, telling their stories.

The facilitator of the panel pointed to Jacqueline. She introduced herself and described how her six siblings and her grandmother were dragged to a river, hacked to death and dumped there, never to be recovered. She said she had read all of Elie Wiesel's books.

And then her question.

"How could this happen, again?" she asked. "What happened to *never* again'?"

Three hundred of us in the room held our collective breath. Photographers jostled for the best position to capture this, camera motor drives popping and whirring from Wiesel to

Jacqueline and back again. Wiesel straightened up and shielded his eyes, scanning the audience for the source of the young woman's voice. Seeing her, he sighed and thanked her for the question. He described how world leaders had been certain that, after the Holocaust, such horrors would be considered inconceivable, a relic of history. Never forget, never forgive, never again. And yet, he said, genocide continued. How the Americans knew what was going on in Rwanda but did nothing to stop it. How he had implored other major world leaders to intervene, but to no avail.

Wiesel mused about how he had longed to embrace the ebullience and optimism in anticipation of a new millennium. "Lots of fireworks and speeches about world peace," he said. He continued to describe how, at last, we would close the chapter on the bloodshed of the twentieth century and open a new era of peace, inclusion and opportunity.

And yet, soon after the Rwandan genocide, he said, there was Darfur, "like a chapter in a history book in which we tear the pages out one by one until we have nothing left." He spoke about how we were hearing testimony for the dead *and* the living.

He stopped and met Jacqueline's gaze again. He told her that he had sought his entire life to answer that exact question, that even though he did not know why or how it continues to happen, one's efforts to prevent genocide cannot flag. "I have dedicated my life to preventing it from happening again."

He paused, took a sip of water, and continued. "I know this: we cannot hate in return. There's even something worse than hate. The opposite of love is not hate, but indifference." He told her that he wished he could reach across generations, across time, across race, across religion, just to hold her. Members of the audience began to weep.

The panel facilitator had the good sense to end there. Elie Wiesel was the first to rise. He crossed the stage and walked down the stairs directly toward Jacqueline. He placed his arm on her back as they walked out.

Jacqueline went on to work with Miracle Corners of the World, a nonprofit devoted to empowering "youth to become positive agents of change in their communities." At a 2011 commencement speech at Washington University in St. Louis, Elie Wiesel peered out at the crowd and talked about his visits to Bosnia, sent by President Clinton as a Presidential Envoy, and spoke: "I would go literally from person to person, from family to family, from barrack to barrack, from tent to tent, asking them to tell me their stories. And they always began, but they stopped in the middle. Not one of the people I interviewed or interrogated ended the story."[42]

I promised to meet Jane in the morning. I needed air. It was a beautiful late September afternoon. Outside, a small group posed in front of "The Knotted Gun," a bronze statue of a large .357 Magnum revolver tied into a knot. A little boy ran around, thumb and forefinger extended, shrieking, "Bang! Bang!" His mother grabbed his arm as he tried to climb up and reach the trigger.

I crossed the street to walk through Ralph Bunche Park, named after the first African American winner of the Nobel Peace Prize for his key role in the armistice between Egypt and Israel. Prior to the Nobel, Bunche helped draft the UN charter. For years after the prize, he worked in the Sinai, the Congo, Yemen, Cyprus and Bahrain. He attended the 1963 March on Washington and the 1965 Selma to Montgomery March.

I stopped at a curved wall at the entrance to read the well-known inscription:

They shall beat their swords into plowshares. And their spears into pruning hooks. Nation shall not lift up sword against nation. Neither shall they learn war anymore.

I wondered why the documentation of voices of grief and pain does not stop humans from bringing upon themselves and the world such premeditated horror and the steady parade of swords and machetes. I wanted to block everything I had seen and heard over the past several years. Communities leveled by neglect. The abject deprivation of basic human rights. A teacher wishing that he, rather than his daughter, had perished in a school constructed by a greedy contractor who cut corners. The rage of a government official in the Niger Delta fouled by waste and purple with oil. Raphael's funereal description of what he had witnessed. I had just seen an Auschwitz survivor console a Rwandan survivor of genocide. I tried to shake it off, but Jabriil's voice seemed to have taken up a permanent residence in my head. "How about *now*?"

But then other voices drifted in. Jihad's confident "the village will take care of it." Deepmala's children urging us not to let the lights go out. The voice of the teacher who, despite the violence in Gujarat, wrote that "teachers do not kill each other." Sameena's lack of fear in the service of girls' education, human rights and livelihoods. That forklift driver stunned at the prospect he could apply his skills to make a difference. Solmaz's use of science to strengthen community safety. Sister Donata's soft and Salomon's exclamatory voices of resilience. And, of course, there was Jane's voice: a pant-hoot to pay attention, a warning about our stewardship of the earth, and this steady refrain: "Let's get to work."

Orange cones led to confusing detours. I got lost again. I didn't care.

Chapter 17

I Want to Meet the King of America

You probably have seen Steve McCurry's iconic 1985 *National Geographic* photograph and story, "The Afghan Girl."[43] Sharbat Gula's haunting sea-green eyes staring straight ahead at us, through us. That burnt-orange, well-worn headscarf. Her story of suffering and endurance walking across Pakistan and sleeping in caves for protection against Soviet attack.

In 2002, with help from the inventor of iris recognition, McCurry located and photographed her once again. Along with the new photograph, McCurry wrote: "So many here share her story." In her review of McCurry's photographs, Cathy Newman agrees: "Consider the numbers. Twenty-three years of war, 1.5 million killed, 3.5 million refugees: This is the story of contemporary Afghanistan."[44] Sharbat's green eyes had lost their light. Her face showed betrayal, more fear and bitterness. The world had all but forgotten her.

In 2016, Sharbat was arrested for alleged forgery of identity documents. A mother of four and sick with Hepatitis C, she faced prison time and an exorbitant fine. Amnesty International came to her defense. Pakistan deported her to Afghanistan. In December 2017, *National Geographic* reported:

Sharbat Gula was greeted by President Ashraf Ghani, who handed her a key to a new apartment and promised her children would have health care and schooling. "I welcome her back to the bosom of her motherland," Ghani said in a small ceremony.[45]

Had Afghanistan exploited her for the sake of its national image? Probably. Haven't we all?

Let's take a breath here, dear reader, because an elephant just tiptoed into the room. It's true. I looked it up. Elephants walk on their tippy toes.

First, the background of the photograph itself. Vlogger Tony Northrup has uncovered a disturbing back story. According to Northrup, Sharbat never received any money from the use of her image, let alone for prints sold at auction for over $175,000. Afghan girls could not show their faces, yet McCurry may have pressured her teacher. Photographs were forbidden and certainly were not to be publicized. Then, Northrup claims, McCurry set her up in another room with better lighting and a clean background for a perverse glam shot with enough space above her for the magazine title. Sharbat was not only scared but angry, and hightailed it out of the room.[46] McCurry has been accused of photoshopping the truth, both of her experience and of how he came to take the photograph. In short, the operational word here is *take*, as in ripped off, staged, boundaries crossed, a person turned into a poster child for poverty. Sharbat may have been at greater risk *because* of the photo.

Second, it's worth examining some of the headier implications once the magazine flew off the shelves. It riled up the fury of those convinced that her image reinforced the classic "orientalist trope of veiled Muslim women."[47] That it amplified the characteristic "one-dimensional" narcissism of Western rhetoric about "'saving' the exoticized, eroticized [critics point to our obsession with her green eyes as evidence] victims of Oriental oppression." Yet another high-stakes example of "white men saving the brown women from brown men."[48]

The objectification inherent in focusing on a single name and a tragic face must be taken seriously. Teachers Without Borders has consciously chosen to avoid the trap of pandering to the instinctual human wellspring of love and protection for children in need. We reach the people who reach those children.

But then again, enter Vasila Hosseini, yet another challenge to my rhetoric.

When I first heard about Vasila, she was 11 years old, living in tight quarters in the Kārte Se neighborhood of western Kabul. She was a standout in the Afghan Mobile Mini Circus for Children (MMCC), the brainchild of a Danish couple determined to help Afghan children experience joy in childhood. At the time, without the Taliban stranglehold on the Afghan people, they maintained, children should express themselves and make others laugh. The MMCC was a combination of circus camp and after-school program. The children picked up rudimentary English, sang, learned to juggle bowling pins on the street, and performed acrobatics and skits about proper hygiene, malaria and dysentery. Audiences of children squealed with delight every time.

Vasila was a firecracker, a leader and a crowd-pleaser. She would step out from the chorus, puff out her chest and sing the loudest of her peers, veins bulging on her neck. During breaks, she gave piggyback rides to bigger children just to show off her strength.

Filmmaker Stacia Teele first learned about Vasila while on a return trip to Afghanistan, where she and other Americans had once lived and attended high school during the 1970s. She and her crew were shooting a short feature, *Back to Afghanistan*, to capture the contrast between the Kabul of her youth and the present.

Stacia had stumbled upon the Mobile Mini Circus for Children and met the founders, who introduced her to Vasila and her father, Armand (an unemployed truck driver), and permitted Stacia to follow her daily life. Vasila was the beating heart of Afghanistan's children.

Stacia soon learned that Vasila's heart *was* the problem. She had been diagnosed with a congenital heart defect known as Patent Ductus Arteriosus (PDA). Symptoms include an enlarged heart, fatigue, difficulty breathing and cyanosis (blue coloring of the skin).

Before a baby enters the world, a blood vessel essential for fetal blood circulation connects the aorta and pulmonary arteries, bypassing the lungs because oxygen is provided through the mother's placenta. Once the baby is born and the lungs fill up with air, the blood vessel usually closes and it's all systems go. If it remains open, blood does not circulate normally between the lungs and the heart.

Doctors can easily identify the defect through a routine examination by stethoscope to listen for a raspy *phfft-tum-phfft-tum* sound of blood squirting through the opening, like water through a garden hose partially covered and uncovered by a finger. It can also be detected through more sophisticated diagnostic means like electrocardiograms, X-rays, echocardiograms and cardiac catheterization.

Prompt treatment is essential. Depending upon its severity, PDA can be treated with medication or a trans-catheter device. If that does not work, extensive surgery is the next option. Untreated, PDA can cause hypertension, an infection of the heart's inner lining, or heart failure. To take care of it, one needs resources, fast.

Dr. Vishant Tivari must have sighed, twisted his stethoscope back into his white lab-coat pocket and delivered the news that Vasila's life was at risk. Afghanistan did not have the proper facilities. India might work, he had thought, but he had been calling around for pro bono services, and there were no takers.

Only a global appeal could help fund an operation in the United States or Europe. The sooner, the better.

Meanwhile, Stacia had been documenting visits to Vasila's family, interviews with Dr. Tivari and footage of Kabul. Stacia described Vasila's family as:

> squatters who live with six families in a bombed-out house riddled with bullet holes. They have no electricity or plumbing. The eight members of her family live in one room that just has two pillows on the floor — all of them sleep lined up with their heads on the pillow and their legs on the floor. The twenty or so kids that live in the house have no toys. They only had one doll that they shared between them — a little plastic doll that had no arms and no legs.[49]

Stacia put her feature on hold and, with her colleague, Edward Robbins, wrote and produced a short documentary, *Vasila's Heart*.

Stacia asked Marnie Gustavson, her friend and classmate in Afghanistan, for help. She, too, had made several return trips to her neighborhood after the fall of the Taliban and has since dedicated her life to Afghan widows, public health, girls' education and human rights.

* * *

Marnie had already connected a classroom in South Colby, Washington, and one in Kabul through an exchange of postcards. Her film, *Pen Pals*, profiled each classroom and children's reactions to hearing their postcards about hobbies, play, food and dreams read aloud to their peers thousands of miles away. With surprising consistency, students defined themselves as if answering the question "Who am I?" and moved quickly to inquiring: "Who are you?" After several exchanges, Marnie and her team interviewed students in both settings. Afghanistan had a face and Afghan children had names. America had a face and American children had names. Curiosity led to friendship, to "Who are we?"

Attendance at parent events at one under-resourced school had traditionally been low. The night I attended, every parent or guardian came. Marnie had displayed the postcards, shown videos and discussed the program. Children made enthusiastic presentations. "We thought Afghanistan was in the Middle East and they spoke Arabic," one said. Another: "But it's in Central Asia and they speak Dari and Pashto." Another child chimed in: "They speak up to 40 languages and some of them learn it from TV!" Students described their new friends. One Afghan boy said that, at night, he looks up to the heavens, points out a star, and hopes that his new friends will do the same.

Making global connections through postcards and digital storytelling was no longer a luxury reserved for elite private schools or a temporary boost in motivation. As the program unfolded, teachers in both settings described how students were more attentive to their schoolwork. Longer paragraphs. Fewer absences. More questions and curiosity. Global education is not just a feel-good "nice to have" — it's an engine for academic achievement.[50]

* * *

A few weeks after the parent meeting, Marnie wanted to discuss something other than classroom exchanges. Marnie is not known for being vague. I could tell she had a plan that would involve a considerable amount of homework at my end.

"We have to help Vasila to get that operation in the United States." I fully expected her to channel Raphael and say that "time is not on our side."

Sharbat Gula's face came to mind. I launched my defense. "There are millions in need. Why just pick one?" Marnie was silent. "Marnie, even a cursory glance at Afghanistan's history can tell you that outsiders are perceived as pernicious invaders. This could cause more harm than good. I understand the urgency, but aren't we as exploitative as all those organizations who pull at heartstrings to get to the purse strings?" No reaction. "What about her life when she returns? Will authorities disown her family? Will they think she was infected by the US? What if she brings back a Barbie?"

More deafening silence.

I took a more pragmatic approach. "You know better than anyone that the Kabul NGO directory is the size of a municipal phonebook: filled with well-funded, do-nothing organizations. I've heard about all those perfectly manicured lawns and reinforced fences and spotless Range Rovers. Why not guilt them into doing something useful?"

"Do you *really* want an answer to that?"

I realized that this was her verbal rope-a-dope strategy. I would swing away, jabbing my excuses here and there, eventually tiring myself out. I was Frazier. She was Ali.

Marnie pulled a photo album from her purse. Vasila's laughing eyes. Vasila on her father's lap. Vasila in her purple dress and green chador, singing and playing with the tiny mirrors and beads on her sleeves. Playing hide and seek, hiding behind a blue tarp, ready to jump out to scare someone. Straining on a swing, hoping to complete a circle.

Marnie dug in her purse for a USB stick of *Vasila's Heart* to deliver her knockout punch.

My argument started to wobble. I tried to assert TWB's mission of supporting educational change. We could redouble our efforts and show the world that Afghan children's hearts beat like all other children's.

"First, that's off point," she said. "Second, Vasila needs an operation, not a teacher workshop."

Dear readers, put yourself in my shoes. It is difficult for any bleeding-heart liberal to say no to an actual bleeding heart.

Marnie knew she had won. "Project Kids Worldwide, founded by Stephen B. Colvin, MD, Chair of the Department of Cardiothoracic Surgery at NYU Medical Center, will help collect funds and NYU will do the surgery pro bono."

She wasn't finished. Stacia had already sent *Vasila's Heart* to Ted Koppel and *Nightline* at ABC. "We find out in two days if they will air it. If they give the green light, we'll have a week or two before it airs. That means you will need to publicize the show, then have an online donation site ready. You'll have to keep records, provide donors with receipts and thank-you letters for tax purposes, and get the funds to Stacia so she can plan for the family to come to New York, pay for post-op care, and help Armand, her father, buy a truck once he returns to Kabul after the operation. We'll need somewhere around $35,000."

The story unfolded as Marnie predicted. *Vasila's Heart* aired on *Nightline* and donations flooded in as the show made its way across the country. Together, Project Kids Worldwide and Teachers Without Borders exceeded the fundraising target.

The entire troupe of the Mobile Mini Circus for Children, a tearful family and a community of well-wishers saw Vasila off for the trip to the airport and a flight to the United States. Stacia had arranged for Vasila and her father to stay with a prominent Afghan family in Manhattan. The surgery was a success. Vasila recovered beautifully. A few days after her release, I flew to New York to meet her.

She was the Vasila I expected. Cheery, bold and comfortable in her own skin. She loved playgrounds and parks, squinted at skyscrapers and connected with other children. We watched like proud relatives.

Ted Koppel wanted to meet her in Washington, DC. When we walked into the *Nightline* offices, the staff jumped out from their workstations to meet her. An intern said, "Our favorite episode by far!" The staff lined up to shake her hand. Vasila plunked the keys on Koppel's typewriter, on display for visitors.

Koppel entered. "There she is!" he said, grinning. Vasila posed for snapshots. A staffer let her play in the control booth. Vasila climbed up on the swivel stool, whirled around, and slid knobs up and down. When other staffers crowded in, she shouted something in Dari. The interpreter blushed. "She said, 'I'm a movie star!'"

We spent the remainder of the day touring DC. She stopped at every public park, asking us to push her harder and harder on the swings. At 1600 Pennsylvania Avenue, she grasped the black uprights of the cast-iron fence in front of the White House. Her father gently asked, "What do you see, Vasila?"

"A white castle!"

Someone told her who lived in the white castle. "I want to meet the king of America!" she exclaimed. We all smiled. An ice-cream truck came to a stop nearby, featuring Donatello, the Teenage Mutant Ninja Turtle: muscular, green, purple eye mask with white eyes, baseball catcher's chest protector. To distract her, I asked, "How about one of those?"

She inhaled it, her tongue purple and blue. "*Tashakor!* Thank you!" Undeterred, however, she posed her question again.

That afternoon, Stacia found the White House public affairs office, prepared to tell Vasila that such arrangements are rare or that the president was busy or out of town. A few hours later, a White House staffer informed Stacia that President George W. Bush would, indeed, meet Vasila at the Diplomatic Reception Room the following day.[51]

After Stacia, Vasila, her father and the interpreter emerged from the White House, we took Vasila to another playground.

She turned to a child on the next swing over and said, in Dari, "I met the king of America!"

The child looked puzzled, then chased her onto the merry-go-round.

Postscript: 2021

President Ghani has fled. Kabul has fallen. As the evacuation continues, I cannot connect to my Afghan colleagues. My NATO colleagues tell me that they are working 48-hour shifts to locate families and map out alternative roads to the airport. I don't know where Vasila is. She's a young woman now. What must she be thinking? Is the Mobile Mini Circus for Children still in operation? What will become of the thousands of firecrackers like Vasila, who want only to play, learn, and feel safe and loved? Will the Taliban ban kites and music again, shut down the circus, and stone women? Will they hunt down journalists and kill the teachers?

Postscript: 2022, 2023

Foreign reserves amounting to over 50% of the Afghan government's budget have been frozen. Civilian casualties have dropped precipitously, but detentions, torture and extrajudicial killings by the Taliban are on the rise. The Ministry of Women's Affairs has been abolished. Women are forbidden access to public areas unless their faces are covered and they are accompanied by a male guardian. The Taliban has reversed its promise to educate girls past the sixth grade. Around 95% of households cannot meet basic needs. The country is plagued by malnutrition and drought. News reports have circulated about desperate Afghans selling their kidneys to feed their children. Children sold for survival. My God.

Chapter 18

Multiple Intelligences in Kabul

Marnie and Teachers Without Borders established a Community Teaching and Learning Center in Kabul. This one, Marnie said, would be housed at a high school run mostly by women. She wanted me to find computers, monitors and surge protectors, and ship them to a DHL office in Kabul. Local leaders would take it from there. Najia, a principal, wanted to introduce new teaching techniques.

I returned to my old sources for computers with an appeal to support women's empowerment in Afghanistan. DHL once again agreed to palletize and fly them to Kabul for free. Marnie had worked out the details with government offices to ensure there would be no value-added taxes or extortion.

* * *

Touching down at Kabul's international airport, I spied the rusted shells of Russian tanks. As we disembarked, soldiers funneled us to the terminal. Ahead, citizens waved and whistled to passengers from a viewing deck below an enormous "Welcome to Kabul" sign. Guards shouted *"Burro, burro"* (go, go), singling out nonresidents from the others. One guard shoved a Foreigner's Registration Form in my hand. When I had completed it, I slipped it into the passport. A few minutes later, a guard tugged at my passport. I held on.

One stern look from him was all that was necessary. My passport was his. I swallowed back a burning feeling in my throat and breathed through the adrenaline panic and the stages of grief: denial, anger, bargaining, depression, and landing on resignation. No passport, no life.

Up ahead, an official held a dozen passports in his left hand, licked the thumb of his right, fanned through each like a card pro and slipped it to the bottom of his deck. I watched for one with a US insignia and familiar security clearance stickers, but he drifted off. At 5 feet 5 inches, it is close to impossible to find people in a crowd. I lost him.

I felt a hand on my shoulder. I turned to face an official who shoved another empty Foreigner's Registration Form at me. I gave him a helpless look and mimed the story of giving up my passport and hall pass. He looked me up and down, pulled out a deck of passports to find mine, stared at the picture, back down at me, and shoved it into my pocket. The form was still there.

Passport stamped, I joined the anthill swarming over a mountain of luggage, found my bags and entered the reception hall to scan faces for any sign of Marnie. I spotted her immediately. The curse of being lost in a foreign land might have finally lifted.

Marnie nodded to a young boy to gather up my bags. I hurried behind, not letting my possessions out of my sight. We reached the driver, a one-legged man on crutches, leaning against the passenger-side door, smoking. Marnie signaled to him. He flicked his cigarette and popped the trunk. Once the young man slammed the trunk, I said *"Tashakor!"* to both. The driver folded himself into the car, popped the clutch, and we jerked our way forward. Marnie said, "Well now, Fred. *Tashakor*: very nice touch!"

Outside my window, I could see birds in cages, sparks flying from an electric lathe, meat vendors, turkeys, piles of striped melons, apples, rugs, meat, and an array of burlap sacks filled with pepper, cardamom, cumin, tamarind, turmeric, mint piled into perfect cones. Shops selling *bolani* (fried flatbread). Women in blue and green burqas. Boys with arms around each other. Older men in *pakol* (a wool brimless cap) or *koofi* (skullcap), and *khet partug* (a wide-sleeved tunic and string-tied loose pants) and argyle sweaters, walked along with their hands behind their backs. It seemed as if the entire city was dressed in layers for winter, though it was summer.

When we arrived at the guesthouse, Marnie announced: "Put your things down. Relax. I boiled some water for you." I sat on a couch way past its prime, shifting to avoid the springs. "Don't get too comfortable just yet," she announced, smiling. "We have about 20 minutes before the DHL office closes." She handed me a glass of tea.

At DHL, employees recognized Marnie, rolled up a garage door, and dollied computers to a truck. There were no hints at a bribe, no official "fees," no tangle of paperwork. An employee hopped in the back of the truck. I joined him. Marnie got in the cab to give directions. No one found that unusual.

The following day, we transformed a classroom into a computer lab and rearranged tables in another to create a seminar-style square instead of rows. Two days later, classes began.

* * *

Najia is well over 6 feet tall, confident and in charge. When we entered the classroom, I was struck by the immediate shift from noise to quiet. They did not seem intimidated by her. As is customary, I placed my hand over my heart and avoided direct eye contact. Many returned the greeting. Out of my element, I expected hostility. *Who is this guy and why is he here? What do you want us to do this time? Humor this dude? Feign appreciation for a lecture or "pearls of wisdom"? What's with the new shape of desks and chairs? If he's an American, why is he so short?*

I had my own questions. *Do they really want to hear my groovy American pedagogy? Will students respond only if called upon? Should I humor them? By arranging the room this way, was I implying that they have been doing it all wrong?*

I had discussed my reservations with Marnie, but she did not seem to care. "You teach honestly," she explained. "You offer ideas. What's wrong with that? Why are you so tentative about this?"

I said, "I am a man and they are women. I am an American and they are Afghans. I have power and privilege. They do not."

Marnie cut me off. "You're too sensitive to how you think they perceive the world and so afraid of offending them that you muzzle yourself. They know the difference between authenticity and some sanctimonious, pasty-faced schmuck mansplaining proper teaching. You have something valuable to share, so share it. Believe me, they won't take everything at face value."

I went ahead: "What are the pros and cons of teaching and learning by arranging the chairs and tables this way?" The teachers looked at each other. I flushed. Why had I posed this question as a quiz, expecting them to rattle off the answer?

I tried, "How might the shape of these tables and chairs work or not work in your classroom?" The shift worked. It was no longer a question directed to them, but for them.

They acknowledged that the new shape was cozier and more inclusive but asserted that most classrooms needed more room to pull this off. They began to talk with each other. The interpreter reminded them that I did not know Dari. Some liked the idea that a student couldn't hide. Others were concerned that some children would find it intimidating. One asked, "Do *all* students have to participate or can they just observe and learn that way?" Another asked what would happen if two tables faced each other for group work. "Would I lose control?" A teacher said she used groups often, but "there have to be rules." Still another: "People say lecture is bad. I tend to agree if the teacher uses lectures all the time. But does this shape mean the teacher can *never* lecture?" "When is this a bad idea?"

An older teacher cleared her throat. "There are places here where a circle or square of desks is against the law." The silence returned. Najia said something in Dari that the interpreter chose not to explain to me, then said it was time for a short break.

The throat clearer was the last to leave. We exchanged looks. Hers read: just so you entitled Americans get my point, not all teachers can do what they want here. Your fetishization of choice and carefree optimism are getting on my nerves. Mine read: I'm sorry.

The following day, I asked if students were familiar with Howard Gardner's "Multiple Intelligences" (MI). None were. Gardner challenged prevailing assumptions long held by psychometricians and behaviorists that intelligence was a quantity, measurable by IQ tests. He examined criteria, patterns and signs from observations and studies of exceptional individuals (those with brain damage, individuals with savant syndromes, and prodigies); development history; psychometrics; experimental psychological tasks; evolutionary history; and "end-state" performances. All factors had to be present to define the unique characteristics of each intelligence.

In his groundbreaking 1983 book, *Frames of Mind: The Theory of Multiple Intelligences*,[52] Gardner asserts that all humans exhibit eight intelligences applied to problem-solving within a cultural context. These intelligences were an exhibit of qualities, not a God-given gift or a life sentence. Gardner avoided recommendations about curriculum reform and distanced his work from learning styles. To date, Gardner has identified linguistic intelligence (word-smart), mathematical-logical intelligence (logic-smart), spatial intelligence (picture/place smart), bodily-kinesthetic intelligence (body-smart), musical intelligence (music-smart), interpersonal intelligence (people-smart), *intra*personal intelligence (self-smart) and naturalistic intelligence (nature-smart).

* * *

Dear reader, allow me to shoehorn a note here directed primarily to teachers familiar with Multiple Intelligences. Teachers grappling with MI tend to gravitate, naturally, to the application of theory to practice. Many conflate intelligences with learning styles. For some, the distinction is huge. Gardner grounds multiple intelligences theory in a theoretical framework and a cultural construct. MI is a representation of various intellectual abilities, not a recipe for how to teach. Learning styles are how one approaches various learning tasks. Gardner has never advocated for a particular teaching approach to meet particular intelligences.

That said, I admit to muddying the waters during my discussions with Afghan teachers. My fealty to Gardner's brilliant work notwithstanding, there was a higher goal here: introduce the ideas and let teachers grapple with them. All educational theories can be misinterpreted, abused, or packaged into dogma. Here, MI served as a worthy catalyst for reflection on the role of teachers as practitioners and researchers engaged in how children approach learning. It challenges one-size-fits-all pedagogies and connects teaching to observational research and common sense. MI also resonates with teachers around the world.[53]

Still, Multiple Intelligences (MI) has faced its fair share of skepticism. MI has been criticized for valuing individuals at the expense of the group, undermining the holy grail of assessment, shifting the locus of control from teachers to students, and de-emphasizing traditional subjects. It has been dismissed as an escape hatch for laziness and a facile way to describe talent.

Some have asserted that "multiple intelligences" blames teachers if students underperform, lowers standards in favor of self-esteem building, and can quickly disintegrate into categorization and marginalization of a particular ethnic group or class.

Substantial criticisms, indeed. I say, lighten up.

* * *

In class, I offered thumbnail sketches for each intelligence, and examples of how each may be recognized and integrated into teaching. For linguistic intelligence: poems, pamphlets, word games, debates, ancient tales, interviews and journals. For spatial intelligence: models, pop-up books, maps and jigsaw puzzles. For mathematical-logical intelligence: numbers, mysteries, investigative experiments. For bodily-kinesthetic intelligence: construction, movement, hands-on activities. I continued for each of the other intelligences.

The teachers mulled it over. One teacher took issue with the pendulum swing away from intelligence as a quantity or capacity issue. She argued that a certain amount of gray matter is necessary before one could talk about the nature of an individual's intelligence. Another asked whether someone might be smarter because s/he could demonstrate more than one form of intelligence: a *quantity* of qualities or *multiple* blends of intelligences.

I noticed a look of consternation on the older teacher's face and prepared myself for what might follow. As predicted, she reinforced her earlier point. "In some parts of the country, this would not be legal." I had never intended to use Howard Gardner's work in multiple intelligences to introduce "revolutionary" ideas. Najia and I had agreed on the topic because she found it interesting. She also told me to expect concern or resistance. "This is a safe space," she reassured me. "They are free to speak their minds here."

This teacher may have loved multiple intelligences and how these concepts could inform her classroom practice, but she was thinking ahead. She knew when to sow such seeds and how and where to water them. Even more, who might squash them.

If I gloss over her point, I thought, *I will reinforce every ugly perception of Westerners as heedless to danger, cavalier and ill-informed.* I did not dare to commiserate with her by discussing tragic parallels in the United States. Such unfair equivalencies would devalue her point.

I chose silence, tensing my butt like a third-grader who has just been told that his urgent request to go to the bathroom has been denied. Let her words take a stand on their own. Your job is to convene, not intervene. A glib answer would be hollow and destructive. This is *their* professional conversation, not yours. *Their* country. *Their* school.

What came out of my mouth would not exactly be an example of erudition. "I understand," I said.

Another question soon came. "How can we recognize a child's intelligence?" Better yet, this question was not directed to me. This teacher had embraced the notion that this discussion represented *their* challenge. "How about a checklist for teachers to observe how students approach classroom work?" Someone else blurted, "And how they play!" Still another, "And what they do to fix their mistakes!"

Another: "I think I can add a new way to teach Pashto language: with music." She began to hum, then sing the words to the Afghan National Anthem. While the interpreter was interpreting the words as fast as she could, someone called out, "The songs and the lyrics will probably change too!" Laughter.

The older teacher seemed to retreat, eyes narrow, lips tight.

For the next half-hour, one teacher after another identified her subject and how students might manifest intelligences.

They spoke over each other, but the room felt affectionate and alive. The interpreter began to wave her hands to slow the class down and give her a chance to keep me up to speed. Standing at the back of the class, Najia clapped her hands to get their attention. After a moment of silence, they were back at it, filling the room with innovative ideas.

The session had already run past its allotted time, but I felt compelled to ask, "What did you think of the class today?" I immediately wanted to take it back. If someone from another country gave a talk and asked how it went, basic hospitality and decorum would dictate that he or she was fishing for compliments.

The Pashto teacher exclaimed: "Maybe the seating arrangement worked too well!" The class tittered. Najia beamed.

I had been imagining Afghanistan as a time-lapse film in reverse: buildings once festooned with flowerpots cratering and pocked with bullets; majestic Buddhas carved into Bamiyan's cliffs in the sixth century exploding into a hollow, black outline. Hemlines becoming *chadri*. Cars reverting to oxcarts. Intact windows splintering, replaced with tarps. Intricate, rustic Baluchi prayer rugs of intersecting leaf and geometric patterns unraveling, then woven again into a cruder, blunt weave of AK-47s and helicopters.

And yet, in a country ravaged by war and treated like a doormat for empires seeking a foothold in Central Asia and beyond, women with eighth-grade educations and almost no professional training were exploring the essence of teaching and learning, challenging assumptions and asking hard questions.

I said, "*Tashakor!*" They giggled.

I wanted to apologize to the older teacher for my transgressions: condescension, pandering, ignorance, preferential treatment of others, and avoidance. As students filed out, I looked for her, but she seemed to have slipped away. I followed

Najia to her office, for tea. Students passed, half in headscarves and the other half in full burqas.

Outside the principal's office window, I could see them part ways at the end of a street. Those wearing burqas drifted off like a parade of blue and green ghosts.

Allow me to contradict myself. I believed in everything I had just taught about multiple intelligences as a set of qualities, not a quantity. But then again, as I have said before, brains are evenly distributed throughout the world. It was abundantly clear in Kabul.

The next day, teachers filed into the computer room. I kept my instructions to a minimum. Those with experience in internet cafés helped others. Some explained the purpose of a thumb drive. An official entered the room just when a monitor started to smoke and died. A teacher pointed out that she might be able to hook up her television.

* * *

Today, Marnie Gustavson is the Executive Director of PARSA, an organization devoted to "building healthy Afghan communities"[54] by focusing on youth leadership, economic empowerment, and social protection. PARSA began in 1996, when the Taliban first captured Kabul, and today works in 19 of Afghanistan's 34 provinces. PARSA aligns its efforts with the Red Crescent Society to "rehabilitate and modernize the Marastoons or 'places to find help,' an Afghan cultural tradition of social protection for vulnerable people." When there is a need, PARSA shows up.

Postscript: August 2021

I just heard the news that the war in Afghanistan is over and that the evacuation has begun. I am certain that the war against women will remain...and intensify. Women who have clawed their way to seats in Afghanistan's parliament face a government that, during their last rule, committed brutish abuses and will continue doing so. Girls who have flocked to school and embraced STEM are now afraid to leave their homes. Schools are closed. I'm horrified.

Postscript: 2022 and 2023

It is hard to believe it has been a year since the fall of Kabul. A year since desperate people found their way to the airport, flooded onto the tarmac and hung on to a C-17 on the runway. Local and international leaders have failed the Afghan people. Somehow, I am convinced those teachers will prevail.

Chapter 19

Noblesse Oblige, the Cologne of Colonists

Teachers Without Borders was selected as one of four grantees to execute a substantial foundation initiative in South Africa: a collaboration involving housing, internet access, community engagement and teacher professional development.

The first planning meeting in Silicon Valley was a nicely catered affair in an ultramodern conference room. High-level representatives of well-recognized organizations made characteristically lengthy introductions. Fiddling with the Aeron chair to appear taller, I pushed the side lever down, expecting it to crank me up like a car jack. Instead, I came close to banging my chin on the table. Everyone looked my way.

After several such meetings, the program officer suggested that we hold a few days of meetings in Johannesburg. Within weeks, we had assembled around another conference table of Zebrano wood inlaid with African mahogany, in a fine hotel. I picked up the scent of furniture polish, filtered air, high-end coffee, fresh flowers and expensive deodorant.

We went over our organizations' core expertise. Somehow, we would find common ground in a collaboration to meet selected communities' needs. I wondered, was this about developing cool solutions in search of problems? Too premature. I would not bite the hand that fed me. I chastised myself for coming to this conclusion; even worse, for using my privilege to cast aspersions about the intentions of the privileged. Dinners were cordial and the drinks stiff, but I could not loosen up.

Sunday was a free day. Someone suggested golf and asked for partners. Two others jumped at the chance. I returned to my room and noticed the blinking red light on the hotel phone. It was Yunus Peer.

Born in apartheid-era South Africa, Yunus and his Teachers Without Borders team had been facilitating science and community development education for South Africans since our early days. He wanted to show me the newest project—a learning center outfitted with computers and books in a prison— and show me what he had planned next.

Social justice runs in his family. He writes: "The apartheid government offered no math or science of any consequence in Black schools because they said clearly that Black people would never get the opportunity to use these skills since they were destined to be laborers anyway."[55] The government harassed his father for "his efforts to bring education to the Black, rural, poverty-stricken areas." Yunus's passport "was withdrawn for studying at Waterford School in Swaziland with the children of Bishop Tutu, Walter Sisulu and Nelson Mandela." For Yunus, an education denied is tantamount to stripping a human being of integrity, hope and a future. He has devoted much of his life to removing obstacles to education.

His message: "Be ready at 6:45 am tomorrow. Special day. Bring your passport." I set my alarm for 6:00 am. At 5:30 am, I awoke to a steady rapping of knuckles on the door. I fumbled for my watch. His eye met mine at the keyhole. "Traffic!"

My colleagues will be sleeping in, followed by golf and lunch. I will be going straight to the Odi Correctional Services Centre.

***

The guard tower was easily recognizable. The reinforced walls wore their typical hairdo of razor-wire. We entered two security checks before we were able to park. Yunus walked me to the entrance and chatted with a guard in bulletproof gear with extra leather pouches holding ominous objects. The guard motioned me forward. Yunus turned to me and said, "Back in an hour or so." The guard pointed to a sign: "Clearance at the next Gate. Show your ID."

I pictured my fellow grantees at a country club: exquisitely starched white linen, air-conditioning, a tuxedo-clad maître d' opening huge doors to a restaurant with oil paintings and chandeliers, attentive waiters holding button-studded leather chairs, bird-shaped napkins on gold-rimmed plates, and sommeliers with arm towels. My greeting at Odi: a sticky nametag, a pat-down, and my valuables scanned and whisked away. For my peers, rare African blackwood paneling. For me, cinderblock.

I walked past a small group of shirtless inmates and stifled the urge to ask them to explain the abstruse symbology of their tattoos—some crude, others intricate—ranging from dollar signs careening around a scar, cobwebs, barbed wire, roses and "Mom" to medieval warriors facing in opposite directions, GPS map coordinates, eyes, bar-codes, scorpions and women.

After staring me up and down, one asked, "Hey, little man, who are you? Why are you here?"

Two fair questions, I thought, both asked without malice. I wanted to answer with, "Funny you should ask. I was meaning to ask the same thing." I told him about the Teachers Without Borders project and Yunus. He seemed satisfied.

The Odi Correctional Centre had converted a storage room to a lab with eight computers, and bookshelves bowing from the weight of car-repair manuals, old textbooks and vocational training guides. Someone startled me with, "Hey, little man, c'mere." He wanted help making transitions in PowerPoint.

Men were sounding out words in a smaller room next door to the computer lab. "Hey, little guy! Little teacher guy! Teach us something! C'mere, little man! Can't you hear me? Check your batteries, little man!" I flushed.

I asked one of the unit staff for permission to play a quick game, whispered instructions to him, and got a nod. He left for paper and pencils, returning within seconds. I asked the inmates to count off in ones or twos. The guard distributed a piece of paper and golf pencils to both groups. Golf pencils, really? Funny, my colleagues on the links were using golf pencils too.

I asked each member of the group to write the letter of his first and last name in a separate column. Once completed, each team was to list as many words as possible beginning with that letter. A guard agreed to be the timekeeper. I turned to the men and instructed, "When he calls 'time,' stop writing and choose someone to read the words. The group with the most words is the winner." The game went well, though of marginal teaching value. No one got upset. I heaved a sigh of relief.

South African prisons are often described as overcrowded, unhygienic cages with a revolving door for the neglected, the poor, the angry and the marginalized. Most inmates I saw were Black. The Department of Correctional Services (DCS) requires the system to be "secure, safe and humane and that offenders are optimally rehabilitated to reduce their likelihood of reoffending."[56] Though recidivism is high, this felt redemptive.

After the exit pat-down, I scooped up my belongings and went outside, shielding my eyes against an unrelenting midday sun. I spied Yunus waving from the car. He didn't ask about my visit. He described the details of a potential benefactor's offer of prime real estate upon which we would build a school where teachers could spend a part of their sabbaticals as educators-in-residence. By day, they would instruct local children alongside their South African colleagues. By night, the facility would double as a health clinic. Yunus had been talking about this for at least a year. It was time to see the place and make some decisions.

I peppered him with questions. How many teachers have the opportunity or funding to take a sabbatical, no less an international one? The last time I checked, teachers in the United States were shelling out $1200 per year for school supplies. We were not Médecins Sans Frontières (Doctors Without Borders); doctors have the extra cash. How could a Sabbatical School make an impact beyond those lucky enough to make the trip? Who is the audience? Private school teachers? How would it be sustained?

Yunus listened attentively. Combining sanctimony and envy, he promised me that it "would be better than anything Oprah could pull off," a reference to her newly inaugurated school for girls emphasizing academics and leadership in a state-of-the-art facility.

My doubts aside, Yunus was a compelling spokesperson, someone who had always acted upon his ideas, a doer. He was successful before. He had transformed an ugly storage room at a correctional facility into a computer lab and reading center. This project would be unique and tangible. Teachers would interact online and face to face with colleagues they would never meet. We all have an inner empire-builder. Mine was starting to stir. But still, too good and too manic to be true.

Yunus pinballed around blind curves, cranking up Stevie Wonder's "Signed, Sealed, Delivered" (I kid you not). The membrane of his speakers thumped against my leg, like my heartbeat. Ahead, an 18-wheeler bore down on us. Was he in our lane? Would this song be the soundtrack of my imminent demise?

We arrived at what looked like a golf-course clubhouse and upscale housing development. My colleagues weren't here, were they? They were not. Soon after the pleasantries and customary card exchange, two spotless black Mercedes sedans appeared. We traversed through a hilly expanse of farmland, model homes and sugarcane.

Outside my window, I saw men and women, all Black, in rags. Men stooped over in the fields, wearing floppy felt hats, hoeing. Women bearing huge sugarcane stalks on their heads. I shot Yunus a look. He did not return my gaze.

I felt a lesson plan coming on. I set my camera to its sepia setting and pretended to snap landscape shots but aimed directly at a man resting on his hoe, staring at our car kicking up dust. I would display the photograph in class and ask students to guess when the picture was taken. I am assuming that we would place it in the 1930s or 1940s for its Dorothea Lange feel, like her masterpiece, "Sharecroppers. Eutaw, Alabama (1936)."[57] Just to be clear, there is no comparison here. Lange's photograph deserves its place in the Museum of Modern Art. Mine is a snapshot.

Still, it would drive the point home.

We entered a conference room. More exquisite polish. The landowner and chief architect had prepared preliminary sketches held down by crystal paperweights. The Sabbatical School would be built atop the division's 5000 acres overlooking the ocean. Charrette sessions would center on what buildings and grounds would work most productively for "our vision." I was assured that the land donation would serve as an easy catalyst for fundraising. I made a mental note. Fundraising is *never* easy.

I stuffed a brochure into my back pocket. We drove further up the hill, first on a smooth road, then crushed gravel that turned into a dirt road wedged through the sugarcane, like something out of *Field of Dreams*. An architect and passenger followed us.

We parked and walked through dried stalks to the highest point. The Indian Ocean, an expanse of turquoise and honeydew, met a milky-blue sky. *Field of Dreams* meets *The Sound of Music*.

They described the scope and sweep of the land. After a stroll around to think about it all, I returned to a group gathered around a smaller version of the plans. Someone asked the architect about the planned height of the Sabbatical School building. With a chilling nonchalance, the architect said, "See down there? The buildings must be tall enough and at an angle to hide the view of those slums down there. We need to keep these property values high."

There it was. Teachers Without Borders gets a piece of property to build our Sabbatical School. The developers get a tax write-off for their opulent real-estate venture and a visual barrier blocking out the nearby Black slums from the view of rich white homeowners. They sell homes and we sell our souls. They weren't interested in our vision, just sight lines—pure avarice masquerading as charity—the stench of *noblesse oblige*, cologne of colonists.

I pulled the brochure from my pocket and read: "Our heritage dates back over 150 years when our founder settled in KwaZulu-Natal." What heritage, I imagined, might that be? Which settlers? What did they settle? Plantations? What part of apartheid did I not yet understand?

We drove back to the conference room as we came: dirt path, crushed gravel and well-paved road. I was in no mood for idle chitchat. We assembled again. The developers discussed their plans for drawing up a contract. We posed for a group photo. Politely noncommittal, I thanked them and made tepid statements about more discussion with the TWB team. I promised to get back to them soon.

I remember the drive back to Johannesburg, well under the 120 km/h speed limit. Yunus and I needn't have discussed the project. Our decision was clear. He was raised in a family committed to justice, schools for rural children, and exposure to world-class teaching, particularly in science and math, all encoded as national priorities for South Africa but denied to those attending Black schools. His heart was pure...and broken.

That night, I informed the developers that we would not be moving to the next phase of the project. I felt relieved, if not downright giddy. The storage closets at Odi felt less claustrophobic than this hilltop view. There would be no land and no Sabbatical School. Most of all, no regrets.

The following day, meetings with partners continued. Our programs would not deviate from our core mission of connecting teacher leaders to information and each other. Local stakeholdership. Street cred. Programs would be led by those who conceived them. Our legitimacy would not depend upon a spectacular view of the Indian Ocean.

A small place like Odi would be just fine.

Chapter 20

El Mundo Es un Pañuelo:
The World Is a Handkerchief

Deyanira Castilleja (Deya) had been a TWB member for several years before she inquired about volunteering to translate our teaching materials into Spanish. Two years later, she was changing lives and leading our emerging Maestros Sin Fronteras network. She adapted our Certificate of Teaching Mastery to meet regional needs. She developed our Peace Education program in partnership with the Baja California Department of Education to create Zones of Peace for 12,000 teachers at 1500 K–8 schools. And she founded a nonprofit organization, Instituto Mejores Niños, in Saltillo, Mexico, to promote early childhood education for economically disadvantaged families. Let me emphasize, once again, that she did this *as a volunteer*.

I was sitting with Deya in a café. I had just seen her brilliant presentation about the power of Mexican teacher networks at a conference sponsored by one of Mexico's most prestigious universities, Tecnológico de Monterrey. Deya had described how Mexico's rapid rise in educational enrollment was encouraging, but its alarming dropout rate felt like an educational sieve. "Getting them into school is one thing. Keeping them in school and strengthening skills they need to pursue education for a lifetime is something else entirely. We've accelerated double shifts to accommodate more students, but we pay a steep price:

schools can no longer be local hubs for after-school activities. I don't want *that* picture outside my window."

She had challenged the assembled: "Where's our energy for change? Why do people always volunteer to travel to Mexico to help poor Mexicans? Our brains are here. I am not going to settle for the pity of others, handouts, stagnation or apathy."

Deya described the unacceptably low number of students aged 18 and older in Mexico who held a bachelor's degree and were considering a teaching career. She worried aloud, "Too many pre-service teachers fail their job-placement exam. Even more, a tiny percent of working teachers pass an exam that would give them a pay raise!"

Mismanagement or extortion of funds distributed to states was rampant, she explained, mincing no words. She bristled when she spoke about the teachers' union, Sindicato Nacional de Trabajadores de la Educación (SNTE). Mandatory membership required 1% of one's salary. Elba Esther Gordillo, the union president, was reputed to have been appointed for life and could make or break a presidency. Money laundering, embezzlement, wire fraud, Swiss bank accounts, plastic surgery, private planes, mansions, Hummers handed out like trick-or-treat candy in return for loyalty and favors, a seven-figure credit card bill at Neiman Marcus. No teacher believed Gordillo or the teachers' union had teachers' best interests at heart.

As far as Deya was concerned, *allá donde fueres, haz lo que vieres*. Wherever you go, do what you see. There was plenty of injustice in plain sight. Teachers and students did not feel safe on their way to, or at, school. Drug-related violence led to an unprecedented number of school closings. Mexico's homegrown version of implosive terrorism was rapidly reversing gains in every area of education. "Teachers say they're being extorted, kidnapped and intimidated by local gangs. They're refusing to return to their classrooms until the government does something to protect them."

Over our coffee, I asked Deya about Mexico's ambitious new national plan for education in areas in desperate need of attention: curriculum reform, greater autonomy for schools to focus on student learning, new governance structures that emphasize stakeholder participation and school-level planning, multiple pathways for teacher career development, and a greater focus on equity and inclusion. The plan ticked off all the checkboxes for promising educational research: twenty-first-century skills, critical thinking, digital competency, socio-emotional sensitivity, and the education of the whole child.

Lavar puercos con jabón es perder tiempo y jabón. Washing a pig with soap is to lose time and soap.

"Empty promises," she said. "It's trickle-down rhetoric. Education is political and Mexico's parties run the show, so it's ridiculous to hold our breath and expect change to come... They say we're decentralized, but the union controls 31 of the 32 states. I'm all for career pathway reforms. They're long overdue, but top positions are bought, sold, traded and handed down. They say they are reforming teacher preparation, but when? Where? Stakeholder governance? Great idea. They will never let that happen because officials would have to be held accountable, so they turn the tables and evaluate teachers on artificial appraisals. This is a special type of cruelty: don't prepare teachers, don't support them, don't encourage innovation, don't solve problems. And when it does not go well, you have a scapegoat: teachers."

Creerse la última Coca-Cola del desierto. To think of oneself as the last Coca-Cola in the desert.

"Deya," I said, "this sounds like an impossible mountain to climb."

She smiled. "Absolutely not," she said. "We must vent, even rage, against hypocrisy and inequality. Next, we climb that mountain together."

Teachers passing the café noticed her and waved. She waved them in. "Getting mad together, that's when the fun starts!" Teachers pulled chairs to our table. She continued, "There are some real efforts to support reform. More transparency. More equipment in schools. More resources for girls to study science. More parent education, early-childhood programs, literacy programs." I was confused. I thought she was about to continue her rant about more of Mexico's problems.

She shifted to, "But they're just pilots. They have no intention to scale them. The day after the cameras leave, in comes the steamroller of old habits, influence, fear, corruption and indifference. The emerging reform efforts are promising only if teachers are at the table." Teachers nodded. *¡Así es! ¡Exacto!* Yes, exactly!

"Deya," I said. "For someone so outspoken about the problems here, how come you come off as so optimistic?"

She beamed. *"Ella habla sin pelos en la lengua."* She speaks without hairs on the tongue (i.e. speaks candidly, frankly). "Just because I am angry, that doesn't mean I am unhappy. I am happy because we're making progress." A teacher gave her a high-five.

Teachers have embraced the Spanish version of the Certificate of Teaching Mastery because it is theirs. In turn, they have created self-paced and online learning opportunities fortified and reinforced by peer support and mentorships. Because of Deya, they search within their communities for cultural and contextual gems. If school leadership does not support them, their social networks serve as a platform for professional development.

* * *

Deya had prior plans to see her parents the following day, but had already arranged a visit to Plaza Hidalgo in downtown Mexico City. Sima Yazdani, a senior technology leader and Chief Data Scientist at Cisco Systems, joined me. Sima is an expert in collaborative knowledge building and discovery, and a pioneer in information modeling, machine learning and semantic ontologies.

So, what's a multiple patent holder and technology superstar like her doing in a place like this and with a ragtag organization like Teachers Without Borders? As part of Cisco's Corporate Social Responsibility initiatives, high-level employees had been placed in local and global community organizations to provide strategic guidance, promote best practices, and build capacities that help these organizations have a greater impact. Cisco had partially funded this project in Mexico and provided Flip Video cameras to teachers to record and share their lessons. It is one thing to offer a grant to a community or nonprofit organization. It is another to immerse oneself in an organization's daily life for a year.

Sima combines technical brilliance with a deep commitment to global inclusion and diversity, social justice, and global awareness about humanitarian crises affecting women and youth.

Ringed by shops and restaurants and anchored by an imposing municipal hall and a majestic church, the Plaza was alive with shoppers, lovers and families, people stooping down to hand their children ice-cream cones. Police paced about, their automatic rifles bouncing from their bulletproof vests. Pigeons typed on discarded cobs of grilled corn.

The public square was a soundtrack of public conversation, popular songs hand-cranked by organilleros (organ grinders), baritone sax riffs from a free jazz concert, and children chasing each other in their parents' T-shirts smeared with paint.

It was the week before Día de los Muertos (Day of the Dead). To celebrate the holiday, Mexicans mourn those who have passed by visiting cemeteries, where they sweep away debris from a special plot and leave marigolds. Families gather and eat sugarcoated, doughy *pan de muerto* (bread of the dead).

Neighbors visit each other, gossip, and honor La Calavera Catrina, "The Elegant Skull," by making clothes to fit tiny skeletons that often satirize contemporary political figures.

This year in Hidalgo Square, Día de los Muertos took on a different tone. As we rounded a corner, we heard strident pronouncements from a megaphone about gang deaths, unsafe communities and drug wars. We navigated around pop-up libraries, bins of free clothes, a circle of tents, and cardboard signs reading:

Si no nos dejan soñar, no les dejaremos dormir. If they don't let us dream, we won't let them sleep.

Me indigna la promesa y no sucede nunca. I'm outraged by the promise that never happens.

An assembly line of teenagers stapled and whitewashed crosses and tossed them onto a pile for others to space evenly on the sidewalk to represent a two-dimensional graveyard. Volunteers handed out water.

Sitting in an arc of benches, a group of people were embroidering messages on handkerchiefs for each person killed by gun violence. Many told an individual story, along with the birthday, date of death and the handkerchief maker's phone number. Some included flowers, lyrics or a favorite symbol. Upon completion, each handkerchief was passed along the line. People nodded, smiled, cried and clipped them to a clothesline crisscrossing a section of the square. There were dozens of them fluttering in a light afternoon breeze like a Mexican version of Tibetan flags:

[Nombre] que transitaba por las calles de la colonia Altavista y fue ultimado a bolazos por un grupo de sujetos armados. [Name] was

walking through the streets of the Altavista neighborhood and was shot to death by a group of armed individuals.

Some made statements:

No son cifras, tienen nombre: hijos, abuelos, hermanos, hermanas, amigos. They are not numbers, they have names: children, grandparents, brothers, sisters, friends.

One asked:

¿Dónde estás? Where are you?

A young woman noticed our curiosity and approached us. She explained that she was a member of the organizing group "Fuentes Rojas" (Red Sources), a group organized "to build a collective memorial made by citizens and a culture of peace."[58] She encouraged us to sit with the others and sew one of our own. Her voice was kind, solid and accessible.

She held up one of the linen handkerchiefs by its corners. A wooden hoop stretched the fabric in place, revealing a blood-red stitch halfway through a poem. She told us that her group would continue its project every day through the end of the year, then replicate it elsewhere. She offered me a starter handkerchief. Personally, I did not know of someone murdered senselessly in Mexico's drug wars. I asked for the name of the person I would honor. I struggled with the stitching. A grandmother came to my rescue. She whispered something to the others, who promptly held their hands over their mouths to keep themselves from breaking out into uproarious laughter at my incompetence. Sima, of course, took to it instantly.

Laughter, yet so much pain. It did not seem to matter. Over my shoulder, a sign read: *"Todos somos Juarez"* (We are all Juarez). Edward Steichen would have been pleased.

We called Deya. "Get her name and phone number," she said. "I'll talk to her. We'll put this activity in our curriculum and share their messages and pictures of the handkerchiefs."

I asked the organizer, "Are you a teacher?"

Over the years, I've often popped this question to strangers: truck drivers in Vietnam, Pakistani scientists, South African salesclerks and American servers at diners. Some respond with, "How did you know?" Others are surprised, say they have never considered the idea and ask why I raised it. She answered cordially, "I'm not a teacher in the *formal* sense. It was kind of you to ask." I explained that she had a plan she had executed beautifully.

Not a *formal* teacher, I thought, but someone with valuable information to share. A neighborhood group gathered to read these white flags of despair. And yet, there was a palpable sense of tragic, collective intimacy here, even hope. We *too* are a multitude. This is *our* world, *our* pain. We shall not be defeated. We shall wipe our tears and educate for safety and peace. *El mundo es un pañuelo*: The world is a handkerchief.

Deya found her in Hidalgo Square the next day.

* * *

Years after my conversation with Deya, Elisa Bonilla-Rius, an Antonio Madero Visiting Scholar with the David Rockefeller Center for Latin American Studies at Harvard, acknowledged the research-driven scholarship that has underpinned Mexico's educational reform initiatives and the challenges that remain.[59]

Progress, indeed, is underway, yet one must ask: how might measurable change take hold in a country of a quarter-million schools, where 62% of children reach secondary school, but 45% drop out? Where inclusion has been a protracted barrier for communities speaking 60-plus Indigenous languages? How might Mexico enlist the wisdom of the nonformal education sector? Address gender and poverty inequality, inertia, intransigence, corruption and entrenched power? Chart student achievement within the situated realities of their lives? How to engage the teachers' union to protect those who take risks?

Deya has been all over those questions but always returns to: "It has always been about the teachers. Find the great ones and the promising ones and remove obstacles so they can do their jobs." She has been doing just that, ever since, convinced that teachers can fling open their windows onto a world they have created. All they need is a leader from among their peers. Leaders like Deya.

In 2018, the winner of the Mexican presidential election campaigned on "canceling the education reform." In 2019, a rollback initiative was underway. In 2020, COVID-19 stopped everything in its tracks. Setbacks mean nothing to Deya. The years ahead are promising indeed.

La vida empieza al final de tu zona de confort: Life begins at the end of your comfort zone.

Chapter 21

Quick Quiz: What Is Suriname?

(a) *a native language in northern Alaska*

(b) *a Monsanto-owned grain from Canberra*

(c) *an island off the east coast of Africa*

(d) *a Caribbean country on the South American mainland*

(e) *the capital city of Uttar Pradesh in India*

(f) *none of the above*

No need to look at your phone. The answer is (d). If you didn't get it, join the club; I didn't either. Then again, I am an American. Geography is not our strong suit. When I got a call from Marie Levens, Suriname's former Minister of Foreign Affairs, I knew it was a country, but that would be it. I googled it while she was introducing herself.

Suriname is in the northern coastal region of South America on the Atlantic Ocean side, atop Brazil, sandwiched between Guyana, due west, and French Guiana, due east. It was formerly known as Dutch Guiana. That might ring a bell.

Indigenous settlements in Suriname were established as far back as 3000 BC. Historians point to the Arawak as its original Amerindian inhabitants, including the Lokono and the Taíno. Christopher Columbus is likely to have met the Taíno. In the 200 years from 1651 to 1850, the Dutch imported 300,000 West and

Central African slaves to Suriname.[60] The Netherlands abolished slavery in 1863, though it took ten years to release all the slaves. Mandatory work in plantations for minimal pay followed.

Descendants of West African slaves, the Maroon people of Suriname are known for having fiercely and successfully resisted colonial troops, resulting in a peace treaty with the Dutch in 1762 and the granting of their own land in the interior of the country, a full century before the abolishment of slavery. Gold mining brought drug smuggling, gambling and prostitution to the Suriname River. Maroons continued to fight for their rights and land ownership against encroachments from multinational timber and mining companies. In 2007, the Saramacca, one of six Maroon peoples, emerged victorious from a dispute for land rights, resulting in a compensation fund controlled by its Indigenous residents.

Today, Suriname is a mix of Amerindians, Creoles (descendants of Dutch Europeans and Africans), Maroons, Hindustani, Javanese, Chinese, Lebanese, Syrians, and a smattering of both Sephardic and Ashkenazi Jews. In the streets, the lingua franca is Sranan Tongo, a mix of Spanish, Dutch and West African languages developed by enslaved Africans in the seventeenth century, though not taught in schools or spoken by government officials. You can also hear Sarnami Hindustani, Surinamese Javanese, eight Amerindian languages, English and Dutch. Such linguistic diversity can also be traced back to a time when the Dutch could no longer rely on the loyalty of a slave workforce and so resorted to importing labor to produce coffee, cotton and cacao. Today, up to 40% of Surinamese are Hindustani descendants of Pakistanis, Indians and Sri Lankans, many of whom came to the country to work in the construction trades and on the land.

Paramaribo, Suriname's capital city, is known for its respect for all religions. The Ahmadiyya Anjuman Isha'at Islam Mosque is the largest mosque in the Caribbean, originally constructed by hand. Muhammad Ali was once a visitor. The mosque shares a parking lot with its next-door neighbor, the Neveh Shalom Synagogue, its floor covered with sand to symbolize the Israelites' 40-year exodus in the desert or, some claim, to muffle the sound of prayers from Marranos (Jews forced to convert to Christianity during the Spanish and Portuguese Inquisition, who fled to Holland and then set out for the Dutch colonies). Saint-Peter-and-Paul Basilica of Paramaribo, originally built on the site of a Jewish theater, is a ten-minute walk away. It is the largest wooden structure in the Western hemisphere. On a stroll in the area, I counted 11 Hindu temples, a Latter Day Saints church, a Baptist church, a First Presbyterian, and Assemblies of God and Foursquare Gospel churches.

Approximately 80–90% of the country is rainforest. Close to 50% of Suriname's 622,000 people live in Paramaribo or "Parbo," also the brand of its most popular beer. Tropical birds swoop from royal palms around a downtown that looks like a spaghetti western set with a Creole flair: buildings with brick foundations, white wooden frames, gabled roofs and shutters, some precarious, tilted, vulnerable, weatherbeaten, others restored. Inner Paramaribo is designated a United Nations World Heritage site.

Stores sport names like Secret, Cute as a Button, Black Tribal Tat'Shop, Jeruzalem Bazaar and Beni's Christmas Palace. Bars and restaurants are full and alive with laughter, someone always pulling up an extra chair for a friend walking by. After traveling for two days from Seattle to Suriname, I usually plunk down my bags at a hotel and walk to a nearby bar for either a Southwest Juicy (Texas-style) burger, a Quattro Formaggio pizza, or *nasi goreng*: Indian fried rice with garlic, egg, tamarind and chili. Tourist and open party buses outfitted with woofers the size of refrigerators blast Billboard hits, reggae, classical, hip-hop, Cajun-Zydeco, carnival party music, funk, Beyoncé, Adele and *kaseko* (a fusion of "big drums," big-band brass and calypso). I remember sitting at a table closest to the street during an 11:00 pm traffic jam. A party bus decorated with Simpsons characters played Lizzo's "Big Grrrl Small World," Nicki Minaj's "Anaconda," and a disco version of Beethoven's Fifth Symphony. Betting that the bus would be there a while, someone climbed down an attached ladder, handed me a Parbo beer, and ran off to jump back on just as traffic started to move.

You might ask, "Why the travelogue?" Believe me, dear reader, there is no attempt here to channel Anthony Bourdain or to present a picture of Suriname as a paragon of harmony. I cannot know the interior nature of this country any more than I can know the interior of any other human being.

My answer: in Suriname, homogeneity may not seem to cross the average person's mind. At the same time, Indigenous and tribal people in Suriname suffer from human rights violations, poor access to healthcare, exclusion from participatory government, and exclusionary land and resource laws. The religious, ethnic, geographic, culinary and cultural diversity a tourist sees belies a history of incalculable pain.

On New Year's Day, 1738, a West Indian Company slave ship carrying 700 abducted Africans from Ghana, bound for Suriname, could no longer steer through a strong tide and storm in the Maroni River and foundered in a sandbank, tilting and taking on water. Fearing an insurrection and a struggle for life rafts, the captain ordered crew members to nail tight the hatches and sit on them to ensure that none of the 644 people in the cargo hold could escape, all of whom suffocated or drowned. However, the ship's men did manage to retrieve a box of gold. The entire crew above deck survived. For the senseless murder of slaves, no punishment. Instead, dozens received a handsome reward.

For generations, colonizers reaped handsome rewards on the backs of the Surinamese people. Suriname's independence from foreign domination in 1975 led to its own forms of militaristic despotism, economic dependence, a weak rule of law, repression, marginalization and indiscriminate violence. In 1980, Dési Bouterse successfully launched a coup and established military rule from 1980 to 1991, assassinated 15 opposition leaders in 1982 and organized the massacre of Maroons in 1986. Bouterse was prosecuted for the 1982 murders, sentenced in 1999 for trafficking in cocaine, then elected to the presidency in 2010, given amnesty in 2012, elected again in 2015 and sentenced in 2019 (*in absentia*) to 20 years in prison. Chan Santokhi, a former chief of police, was elected on 13 July 2020, in an uncontested election.

In Suriname, the past and present collide. The Surinamese teachers I have met are aware that colonialism etches itself into the human psyche. They recognize that they are orphans living as an extended family. Everyone is an "other," each a descendant with a different narrative, yet similarly rooted in a legacy of misery and displacement as slaves or indentured laborers. In a world increasingly sensitive to the cruelty of cultural appropriation, the Surinamese never lose sight of who they are and are comfortable bringing the world in. Their identity of difference binds them to a singular destiny.

After hearing me whine about Donald Trump, a Surinamese doctor told me: "You Americans, did you really expect that, after you elected Obama, your original sin would simply evaporate? Did you not know that it just sinks for a spell, like a slave ship, only to be dredged up again? We Surinamese live our past. It allows us to move forward."

I have traveled to Suriname dozens of times. As an American, I have been conditioned to see the world through the lens of class, caste and color, or winners and losers. I have long ago dismissed the idea that true equality can happen in my lifetime. And yet, I invariably leave with a sense that familiarity can breed far more community than contempt.

* * *

Marie Levens had called from her office in Washington, DC, in her capacity as Director for the Department of Human Development, Education and Employment of the Organization of American States (OAS), a regional agency designed to defend solidarity in Latin America and the Caribbean, strengthen peace, promote cooperation, mediate conflicts, preserve diversity, support trade and ensure independence among its 35 member states.

For Levens, development, education and employment are inextricably connected to human rights. She experienced it firsthand, tragically, at home in Paramaribo. In the middle of the night on 7 December 1982, 13 students from the university were abducted from their homes for their criticism of the military dictatorship. Accused of orchestrating a countercoup that spring, they were transported to Fort Zeelandia, a fortress built by the French in 1640, and shot. Marie knew something tragic was about to happen to her friends. That night, she did not sleep at home. The December murders strengthened her resolve for education to stress critical thinking, human rights, cultural freedom and the joy of learning without fear.

As Suriname's Foreign Minister from 2000 to 2005, she led, or sent missions to, regional peace negotiations, fought for gender equity, and enhanced Suriname's standing as a legitimate trading partner. The people viewed her then and view her now as their advocate and a moral voice of reason.

As a director at the Organization of American States (OAS), Marie Levens created a Professional Development Scholarship Program for students to study in Latin America and the Caribbean or abroad and return home to build local capacity by sharing their wisdom. She established a Student Loan Program to keep higher education affordable, along with the Educational Portal of the Americas, a platform for online coursework in electoral cooperation and observation, education, sustainable tourism and economic development.

We chatted about TWB's work in Haiti, led by Fenel Pierre, a Fulbright Scholar who had solicited talented teachers, mentors, local institutions and NGOs to collaborate on innovative and practical professional development.

I could tell she was homesick. She was planning on retiring and returning to Paramaribo to develop a vision for building a culture of innovation in teaching and learning rooted in Surinamese diversity and supported by incorporating technology into daily teaching practice.

I agreed to meet her in Paramaribo. When I arrived, I met a group of Surinamese teachers, a professor from George Mason University and a group of professors from Vrije Universiteit Brussel (Free University of Brussels).

Over Coke Zeroes and kebabs, Marie described how Surinamese children who attend school often drop out at critical transition periods. "They become ghosts. Their families may walk among us, but we have lost them. That fact alone should haunt everyone."

Friends, well-wishers and fans feel free to interrupt Marie wherever she goes. A gaggle of teens or neighbors came by for a hug. She embraced them and got back to business. "The ones who cannot master Dutch and have nowhere to turn for consistent instruction become ghosts. The older ones who have attended school, but must repeat grades, feel humiliated for being the oldest or the largest of the class. They feel empty. Unnoticed, they fade to the margins. All ghosts."

She lamented that children with substantial gaps in basic knowledge lose self-respect, cannot envision a productive future, mistrust the powerful and get swallowed up in a vicious cycle of self-imposed discrimination.

She launched into a tirade about how school directors are afraid to take risks, how the lack of quality early-childhood programs in the country's interior guarantees marginalization, how no one has been listening to innovative teachers, how Suriname's curriculum ignores its diverse community, how high-stakes testing destroys morale, and how Eurocentric textbooks and colonial policies have caused stagnation and alienation.

Having assembled her team, Marie laid out her goals: develop a new undergraduate degree program for pre-service and in-service teachers that balances digital competencies with attention to culture. Build a cadre of such teachers to cascade their training throughout the country. If teachers could not get online, or if there was no electricity, teachers would still be able to enjoy and transfer the benefits of quality professional development to their classrooms. The program would enjoy the full endorsement of the government. "I know change must be gradual, but once stakeholders embrace what they help to create," she said, "it will take off." I was thinking this would take about a year. She looked at each of us. "Let's take three months for this." None of us got a chance to think it over.

For Marie, teaching must be practical, interesting, demanding and joyful. She wanted to see noisy, productive classrooms. She wants to surround herself with children pushing out their chests with pride to show adults that they know how to read, solve problems and climb the stairs of their accomplishments. To do this, she argued, Suriname must nurture and support its own talent rather than import solutions from the US or Europe. She second-guessed a question we had on our minds: "So, why are we here?"

Her answer was clear. "Suriname is a sovereign state," she explained, "but it suffers from deep-rooted scars of a country long dominated by foreign powers and self-inflicted wounds. We live a trans-generational life of impotence. Fear is an internalized ghost. It whispers, 'You're not up to the challenge. You're not worth it.' I heard those whispers as a child. No child, no teacher, no one should listen to that ghost." She continued, "A country burdened by the stranglehold and legacy of colonialism must rise on its own terms. Education is the path to achievement and dignity. The Surinamese are not at a loss for solutions. They will be the leaders. They need colleagues—people like you."

We got to work. We vowed to develop a teacher education program that would feel like a maker fair, a summer camp and a university all rolled up into one.

Students just out of high school and veteran teachers signed up at once. Some had computers; others borrowed money from family to buy one. They scrambled out of the classroom windows onto a third-floor ledge to hand off ethernet cables and extension cords to each other and rig up a Wi-Fi router.

One evening, my Surinamese teaching partner and I were exploring how wikis and Google Docs serve as examples of collaborative editing that could enable students to piece together their knowledge and construct learning. Just then, a storm knocked out the electricity to the campus and melted the electricity panel. When that happens, students instinctively pack up and head home. This time, they instinctively reached for their phones to turn on their flashlight app. One student suggested we use sticky notes instead of going online.

The rain was relentless. The roof started to leak. Two students excused themselves and returned shortly with two small metal trashcans. For the first ten minutes, a synchronized plunk punctuated our discussions with increasing frequency. Students collected more trashcans. The rain trilled across them, but no one seemed to care or packed up to go. For every plan A, they found a plan B.

Each year, the program added a new cohort of enthusiastic students, quickly becoming Suriname's largest degree-granting program at the Advanced Teachers' College. Politicians plastered slogans about technology to the sides of their campaign buses. In August 2017, the first cohort received their bachelor's degree in ICT in Education. They began to fan out across the country to introduce new teaching methods and coach other teachers for an emerging, modernized curriculum. Cohort after cohort followed. Today, a master's program is underway and on Suriname's own terms.

Once the program was solid, Marie assembled her team again. "I'm just getting warmed up." Suriname had taken on a loan from a regional development bank to build schools and reform its curriculum. In the first round, the country bought new textbooks from a publishing house in the Netherlands. "The students opened their textbooks and immediately asked their teachers to explain the illustrations of white children on snowboards or skis." She described how someone had decided to use colored pencils to color in faces to look more like Surinamese children. With a sad grin, she said: "It is not going to snow in Suriname anytime soon." Cultural obtuseness aside, the Ministry of Education had introduced new pedagogical techniques, but there was little attention to how they might fit into the unique contexts of Suriname's distinct districts.

Even worse, some districts had received a flood of new books with little or no accompanying support. Other regions received the books in a trickle. Still others received none at all. Teachers throughout Suriname had obvious and pressing questions. If we don't get new textbooks, are we supposed to teach the old ones in a new way? If we get new textbooks but no support, are we supposed to use the new teaching methods anyway? How do we teach effectively to students who speak different languages? How do we bridge the gaps? Marie lamented, "It's one thing to have a new crop of inspired teachers capable of transforming classrooms, but what will happen to them if we don't address teaching and learning itself? We have the talent, so let's use it!"

Marie took the lead for the second round of funding. Suriname must cease the textbook purchase program and commit to a reliance on indigenous intelligence to create and adopt educational resources for textbooks, support materials and teacher development one could identify as truly Surinamese.

After months of conversation, the Suriname-Belgium-American team began an ambitious national education reform project to investigate the gaps in grades K–6, rewrite textbooks for grades 7 and 8 to reflect the challenges, culture, diverse communities and curiosity of each of Suriname's ten districts, and build a culture that encouraged sharing content, resources and ideas.

Brains and courage are everywhere in Suriname, in downtown Paramaribo and in schools in the Amazon interior accessible only by river. The legacy of colonialism and historical disappointment may have weighed heavily on them, but they refuse to be haunted by ghosts. Marie Levens brought about transformational change in education and gender equity in the 1980s, fought for it in and out of office, and used her position at a hemispheric agency to set in motion tangible bottom-up initiatives. In Suriname, she has always been a national treasure.

Every time I see her, Marie says she is tired and wants to sit on her porch with her grandchildren. I could predict she would be too restless, too engaged, too in love with education not to have a hand in building the country she loves. Within months of her seventieth birthday, the national educational reform project was completed. During the COVID crisis, I couldn't travel to Suriname for several parties in her honor. Dozens of us sent in videos. We could not imagine she would be sitting still.

In July 2020, Marie Levens was appointed Minister of Education, Science & Culture. She had not wanted to be a minister, but the country sent her an unambiguous message:

she *had* to be. By mid-April 2021, her positions were clear. The issue of dropouts would be a priority. Suriname would no longer mandate a "sixth-grade test" that had unfairly determined or dampened students' futures. Large classes of over 40 students would be reduced to a maximum of 24. Today, teachers have a larger voice in curriculum development and teaching practice.

Suriname's national motto is: "If you put a stick in the ground, it will grow." The ground for fruits, vegetables and homegrown pedagogy is equally fertile. Its diversity has led to a cross-pollination of ideas. Ms. Levens has been planting seeds, and this nation is bearing fruit. The Surinamese will never forget their pain.

They are, however, exorcising their ghosts.

Chapter 22

"So I Will Walk Toward Them"

Two days after Russia invaded Ukraine on 24 February 2022, I knew that my graduate course on Global Education and Development at the Free University of Brussels (Vrije Universiteit Brussel) would never be the same.

I logged into Zoom early. The students were already there, consoling each other, horrified at what was unfolding. Anastasia, a Russian student, had been texting me about her concerns for the safety of her family, worried about her family and the arrests of protestors in downtown Moscow. In a course revolving around the critical role of teachers in emergency education, girls' education, peace and human rights, there would be few hypotheticals. Over the next two hours, we experienced a raw mix of despair, anger and a desire to do something to address the graphic brutality broadcast around the world. I asked, "Who is thinking about the schools on the border?" Hands shot up in dozens of Zoom squares.

A week later, I received a phone call from one of those students, Simbarashe Manyike ("Call me Simba"). He was timid at first, then blurted it out: "I want to walk to the Polish border from Brussels to raise awareness about the role of teachers in emergencies and raise money for Ukrainian refugees and the teachers who serve them. Prof., if you say no, I won't go, but I am a teacher. I am thinking about my students back home in

Zimbabwe. People are suffering. I can't concentrate unless I do something to take the first step."

* * *

I had not yet met Simba in person, only on Zoom and WhatsApp calls, but within the next several weeks I would come to know him well. I will never really know what inspires a humanitarian impulse in some and not others, but Simba's drive is pure. How could I say no to something like that?

Simba's parents divorced early, then both died. He was passed around, destined to work on a resettlement farm. His great-aunt took him in and encouraged him to get an education and ignore those who called him an SRB (Strong Rural Background), a backhanded way of saying that if you come from a rural area, you have nothing valuable to offer. In 2014, his community had enough solar power to enable him to read at night.

The Capernaum Trust's Higher-Life Foundation took an interest in him. Focused on support for orphaned and vulnerable children, Higher-Life promotes healthcare, crisis response, and a scholarship program that has enabled children to access mentorship, psychosocial support and pastoral care. They scout talented young people who show great leadership promise. Naturally, they found Simba.

His mentor required his mentees to pray for one hour a day, take breakfast, and spend several hours each day walking around. While walking, they were to keep in mind this question: "What did you notice?" Many of his colleagues pointed out what they observed in nature. Simba noticed people, what they were doing, their living conditions and what could improve their lives.

* * *

Within a month, students conceived and set in motion a "Walk the Peace Talk" project. The Russian student had initially told me that being involved would be too painful. Three days later, she called to say it would be too painful *not* to be involved and took a leadership role. Students formed committees to map Simba's path, find places for him to stay with families and students, and reach out to schools, universities, businesses, NGOs and government agencies. They contacted the press to interview him and wrote a steady drumbeat of stories on social media. Anyone could walk with him, document his journey, share his purpose and teach peace. The head of the university's internationalization initiatives alerted partner universities en route.

There is something deeply symbolic about Simba's journey. He is the first to say that he is walking as a proud African.

"Many people automatically associate Africa with war, famine, disease and refugees. But I know this: suffering is universal, and we Africans are generous people. As long as I walk this earth, I will do what I can to alleviate pain and promote education, anywhere. If teachers truly *are* change agents, then I must walk *my* peace talk." I wanted to call Raphael on the spot and tell him about a Sustainable Development Goal Ambassador in the making. Simba continued, "Ukrainian people are forced to walk away from a country they love, so I will walk *toward* them. Education cannot wait. If we don't act now, then when?"

Dear reader, let's take a breather from my stories *about* others. Let's hear Simba's *own* voice from his journal entries.[61]

25 April

The human toll of Russia's invasion of Ukraine is immeasurable. Up to 5 million people have fled Ukraine. Half of all children in Ukraine have been displaced. Cluster bombs have reduced inhabited towns to ruins, leaving trenches for mass burials in their wake.

Rape and torture of minors are war crimes. Every 90 seconds, a youngster from Ukraine becomes a refugee. I hear that teachers have been advised to avoid the subject because the youngsters have already been exposed to the media. A teacher in my class on Global Education and Development went ahead anyway. She invited me to her class and introduced the crisis in Ukraine and our project. The students wanted to know what I want to accomplish. I told the class that teachers are changemakers and peacemakers and that I was walking to raise awareness about education in emergencies. I told the class that hate is a cancer that has metastasized. I said that tyrants might blow up bridges, but education builds them back up again.

1–4 May

The journey begins. The organizing committee met me on campus early this morning. Two students decided to walk with me on the first leg of the journey: 31 kilometers. On day two, my internet connection was not working properly and so I was not sure I was walking on the right path. My team had a backup plan, though, so I kept the faith that things would get on track soon. What happened next was miraculous...a car pulled over and offered to take me to wherever I was headed. The driver mentioned something about having seen my bright yellow "Walk the Peace Talk" shirt the day before and, as luck would have it, was seeing me again. I was suspicious and declined the offer. The person insisted, so I explained what I was doing: walking to raise money for deserving organizations working with Ukrainian refugees and awareness about the role of teachers in emergencies. I told him about the symbolism of refugees forced to walk away from their homes and my effort to walk toward them.

He understood and gave me his address, just three kilometers from my destination. Near his house, he said, there is a lady who owns a home currently unoccupied, so she offered it to a Ukrainian family. I had to see this!

I walked to the house, met the family and filmed her talking about her journey, using Google Translate to get the gist of what she was saying. Her sadness was deep. The wife of the owner of a grocery had taken it upon herself to take care of this family. I remembered that, as I was leaving campus for the first leg of the journey, two of my classmates, Yan Liu and Ana Margarida Maia Magalhães Ferreira, handed me an envelope with €45 and a gift card. I had already spent €25 on food for my walking companions and myself. I offered the remaining €20 to the family, but they refused!

By this time, I was comfortable with the man who had spoken with me on the road. He and his wife handed *me* €20 and told me that if I ever found myself in need, the money would help. Imagine that!

What happened next moved me in a way I will never forget. He took me to his child's innovative school focusing on fostering each child's strengths. He turned to his son to explain what Walk the Peace Talk was all about. After listening intently, his son sweetly looked at me and, unsolicited, offered his football to take to the Ukrainian kids in Poland. I told him how much I appreciated his kindness but that it might be difficult for me to carry it since I was walking. He understood. Without hesitating, he handed me a cookie to eat along the way. It was the most delicious cookie I have ever tasted.

5–6 May

This invasion has sparked Europe's worst refugee crisis since World War II. The crisis here goes back further, too, to Stalin's aggression, particularly the 1932–33 famine, often called the Holodomor, a term derived from the Ukrainian words for hunger (*holod*) and extermination (*mor*).

As I crossed into the Netherlands and into Germany, I thought of the Ukrainian woman I interviewed back in Tienen. As I walk, I am not only thinking of Ukrainian refugees but child refugees in Eritrea, Ethiopia, the Central African Republic, Somalia, Sudan, the Democratic Republic of Congo, Myanmar, South Sudan, Afghanistan, Syria and Yemen. Refugees need our attention.

In spare moments, I have been reading about how Ukraine has captured much of the world's attention because those with means can relate and fear that it could happen to them, too. *Vox* reports that "race, culture and religion certainly play a role in the warm welcome fleeing Ukrainians have received."[62] I can see the point. I know that Poland had put up barriers to refugees from Afghanistan and Iraq who attempted to cross from Belarus to Europe.

But where does that leave us? We cannot turn away from this ugly reality. We are not neglecting the children and refugees from around the world when we walk this Ukrainian path to peace. We cannot be selective in whom we serve. Isn't that the very definition of discrimination against people: based on their country of origin?

7 May

I arrived in Cologne and made my way to the Catholic Cologne Cathedral (Kölner Dom), a breathtaking UNESCO World Heritage site and the tallest two-spired church in the world. On any other day, I would spend time inside the church, sitting in silence amongst the believers, craning my neck to see the intricate handiwork, or feeling the vibration of its enormous bells.

Today, though, I noticed a group of performing and visual artists who assemble every day on a promenade outside. I met Maryo Andrey, a Romanian artist, who was drawing flags on the ground. People threw money on the flag of their country. I told him that I was expecting to see a Zimbabwean flag. He flipped through a notebook to find it and quickly produced one.

I also saw a large heart in Ukraine's colors as an expression of solidarity. I noticed several coins tossed there as well. He assured me the money collected from tourists would go to Ukraine. I came to learn that he is an honest man. I saw messages of solidarity everywhere, convinced they were reaching the 20,000 visitors Kölner Dom welcomes every day. One message read, "We may have different languages and different color skin, but we all belong to one human race!"

8 May

It is Victory in Europe Day today. We honor those who perished for the sake of democracy over tyranny. If ever there was a lesson in learning from history, today is it.

The National Socialism Documentation Center of the City of Cologne is both a memorial and a learning and research center. This was the site of the Gestapo house where prisoners were held in the basement. The website describes inscriptions and drawings "written with pencil or chalk, sometimes with lipstick; or scratched on the cell walls with iron nails, screws, or even the prisoners' fingernails."[63]

10 May

Walk the Peace Talk is getting attention. The coordination team has been fielding inquiries. Everywhere I go, meetings with students have been set up. Some are walking with me!

Today is the anniversary of the book burning of 10 May 1933, where students from dozens of university towns across Germany lit over 25,000 books on fire. It is hard to believe that, given an opportunity to study, minds could be so easily swayed to buy into this. Joseph Goebbels declared that "the era of extreme Jewish intellectualism is now at an end."[64]

He went on to say that "It is to this end that we want to educate you…and thus you do well in this midnight hour to commit to the flames the evil spirit of the past." Education by itself is not the answer because it can be so ruthlessly corrupted. Education must be a moral endeavor.

In Bonn's market square, a memorial plaque opens to reveal a chest holding books. Each year, volunteers empty it and give the books away, filling them up again with more.

13 May

Today I met the Mayor of Marburg, Dr. Thomas Spies! Dr. Spies was joined by a student group at Marburg University devoted to peace. They call themselves: BRUK (for Belarusian, Russian, Ukrainian and Kazakh students).

Dr. Spies makes the connection between his field of medicine and politics. He talked about the social causes of illness. "Poverty is the number one cause of disease, and unemployment is the number two cause. Poor people live ten fewer years than rich people. That's unbearable." He believes that for every dollar one spends on war, one must pay the same amount to rebuild communities. He said that Marburg is a welcoming and inclusive city and made a commitment in front of reporters to investigate how the Marburg city budget could allocate funds to help Ukrainian refugees.

A Ukrainian woman pointed out that sometimes she is afraid to walk around because there are several Russians living in Marburg. Whenever she hears the language, she feels uncomfortable. Soon after she arrived, an early-morning trash truck on her street suddenly brought back the sound of Russian tanks. For two days, she could not leave her house. Russian and Ukrainian students talked about their Telegram groups mobilizing against the war.

14 May

Germans seem to have addressed the Holocaust directly and bluntly. The permanent exhibition at the Bonn Memorial and National Socialism Documentation Center depicts the exclusion and persecution of political opponents.

The Russian propaganda machine cloaks the invasion of Ukraine as a campaign of denazification. This is cruel nonsense. Their invasion has perpetuated Nazi-like atrocities. After World War II, the universal message was: "Never Forget." And yet, 77 years later, here we are. We can't forget. The museum has integrated the invasion of Ukraine into its exhibition about Nazism. If teachers avoid discussing this travesty, the forgetting will continue.

Elie Wiesel, Nobel Peace Prize winner and Holocaust survivor, once wrote: "Whoever listens to a witness becomes a witness." In his Nobel Prize acceptance speech, he said, "Silence encourages the tormentor, never the tormented. Sometimes we must interfere. When human lives are endangered, when human dignity is in jeopardy, national borders and sensitivities become irrelevant. Wherever men or women face persecution because of their race, religion or political views, that place must—at that moment—become the center of the universe."[65]

15–20 May

In Marburg, Bonn, Weimar, Erfurt and Jena, I met with youth organizations that provide migrants with opportunities through entrepreneurship apprenticeships, revitalize diverse cultural heritage through augmented reality, create forums for migrants to tell their stories, and use radio and board games to teach youth about civic and democratic education and peacebuilding. They took all that creativity and turned it into service.

I saw an exhibit about "Reichskristallnacht," also known as Night of the Broken Glass, 9 November 1938. All that Jews owned was destroyed. Hospitals, homes and schools: all gone. Across Germany and Austria, hundreds of synagogues were decimated and people beaten, burned and shot. Antisemitism and racism are on the rise. Sometimes I just don't understand the human condition. I am both exhilarated by the selflessness I have seen and distressed by the slow pace of change. Why does hate tear apart generation after generation?

21–23 May

1 in 3 children in developing countries is impacted by this war. Crop access has declined by over 25% and, with the blockade of the Black Sea, the World Food Program is predicting widespread famine. And yet, television crews follow me. I read posts on Twitter and Instagram. Radio interviews and newspaper articles give me an opportunity to spread the word about teachers as change agents and education for a sustainable future.

25 May

I met with African students who had fled Ukraine and enrolled in German universities. They appreciate this generosity but wonder when it will end. They spoke about a double standard toward third-country nationals. Others are getting residence and work permits, along with social welfare support, but they are not. One student said that all the efforts toward inclusion are real but so too is replacement theory. "It feels like 'Make Germany Great Again,'" one said. Holocaust deniers, Islamophobes and xenophobes subscribe to an identitarian ideology that promotes the protection of Western culture from any ethnocultural identity not their own. The Alternativ für Deutschland (Alternative for Germany or AfD) movement sends chills up my spine. Sure, the government is investigating them as an extremist group, but they have a substantial following.

Each night, I talk with Dr. Fred about the generous people I've met, how Germany has confronted its dark past and how they teach young people not to succumb to hate. I also told him that I am increasingly uncomfortable, but I can't quite name the reason. The more I travel east, the more I see empty buildings that could house refugees. I am staying with John, a TWB member in Dresden. He told me about Björn Höcke, the head of the AfD branch in the region, who spoke here to push for a "180-degree turn" in Germany's "politics of memory." John convinced me to take a train with him to Berlin so that the last leg of my journey in Germany would go smoothly. I am too exhausted to say no.

28 May

One of my classmates, Nicola Battistuta, met me in Berlin. What a welcome sight. Downtown, we joined a youth demonstration about the Sustainable Development Goals! The global pandemic has jeopardized hard-won gains in education. This war has turned back the clock on development.

30 May

Today I crossed the border from Germany to Poland. My team arranged for another train to take me to Warsaw. From here, Maria Jasiorowska, another dear classmate, made plans for me to talk about Walk the Peace Talk at a school on a registration day for the upcoming school year. A woman listened for a while and then broke down in tears. Registering her children for school was a clear sign that her family was not going home. Ukrainian and German teachers surrounded her with love.

I could tell that these youngsters were not ready to accept the fact that they had to flee their country. They asked questions I could not answer. Will this war drag on? Could it happen again? What could we do right now to prepare for it? Those two hours at the school today felt like a year. One Ukrainian student walked with me as I left the school. He stayed close. I felt as if my new companion was Ukraine's soul, urging me on.

31 May

As this walk ends, I will remember the Ukrainian people's pain. It was easy to read it on their faces: forced to leave home, to carry their belongings, their past, their grief, their uncertainty. Many have left a father, a brother or a nephew behind to fight. I have come to know more about the death camps 77 years ago than I ever learned in school. And yet, last month, another act of genocide in Bucha, Ukraine. *I* will never forgive, never forget.

I have seen their resilience, too, and the world rise to the challenge of supporting Ukraine. I do have faith in humanity's inherent kindness. I believe this most when I think about that little boy, unaware of the depth of this catastrophe, imbued with enough moral integrity to know what good looks like when he offered me a football and a cookie.

You are not fully human until you hear others. You can't hear others unless you can feel them. I haven't walked in *their* shoes, but I have shared their journey.

2 June

I have landed in Brussels. Walking through customs, I saw the smiling organizing committee waving. I rushed home to hug my wife and my son.

Postscript: February 2023

It has been a year since Simba set off from Brussels. He is about to launch an updated version of Walk the Peace Talk. It will include a course, a network, and a platform for anyone to walk *their* peace talk and share it with the world. One thing is certain: there are millions of Simbas out there who have shown up to do the right thing during these terribly wrong times.

Chapter 23

Progress Report:
The World's Fair or a Fair World?

My mother and father often told me that my great uncle, Tobias Miller, designed the folding chair. I didn't believe them, though I searched everywhere for evidence. Years after they had passed, I summoned the Google muse one day, keying in "Tobias Miller, folding chair." Up came a set of drawings entitled: "Auxiliary Seat. U.S. Patent 1302828. Tobias Miller. Publication date: 6 May 1919. Cleveland, Ohio."[66] My parents also claimed that he designed the Trylon and Perisphere: the iconic symbol of the 1939–40 New York World's Fair. Credit for the Trylon and Perisphere goes, without question, to Wallace Harrison and J. Andre Fouilhoux of the Harrison-Fouilhoux architectural firm. To date, the Google muse has come up empty. No matter. My internet perambulations have been worth it. I have learned a great deal about my family and, most of all, about progress, teaching and the power of human agency.

* * *

At a cost of $160 million, the 1939–40 World's Fair was a snow globe of modernity and marketing built on reclaimed swampland, the Corona Dumps, at Flushing Meadows in Queens. F. Scott Fitzgerald in *The Great Gatsby* modeled his Valley of the Ashes after the soot spewing from its coal-burning furnaces. The Trylon, a 610-foot spire, rose phoenix-like, phallic and triumphant from those ashes. Visible from the top of the Empire State Building, it was reachable via the world's largest escalator from the Perisphere, a moon-like orb constructed of steel and plasterboard housing its flagship exhibition: "Democracity," a scaled model depicting the metropolis of the future: "The World of Tomorrow."

The typical reverential homage to science and technology characteristic of most World Fairs was in full display, but this unabashedly went for the pocketbook. It was an art deco, futuristic, Coney-Island commercial funhouse of color photography, nylon, air-conditioning, the View-Master, Smell-O-Vision and the fluorescent lightbulb. An assembly line of workers packaging bacon for Swift Premium Meats. A "Mrs. Modern" versus "Mrs. Drudge" dish-washing contest. "Elektro, the Westinghouse Moto-Man," performing tricks, and by his side, his robot dog Sparko: barking, begging and wagging his tail. Carnival rides, too! At *this* World's Fair, corporations would outnumber countries. The National Cash Register corporation even built an enormous replica that displayed the daily attendance in 2½-foot numbers.

An average family could escape their daily crushing grind and take in the exotic wonders of 60 countries in a single day, step into the promise of a prosperous future, and snap up souvenirs and collectibles: bookends, clocks, aprons, salt and pepper shakers, earrings, cigarette lighters, paperweights, coins, kazoos, belt-buckles, toy airplanes and coasters.[67] The New York Yankees, New York Giants and Brooklyn Dodgers wore a Trylon and Perisphere patch on their sleeves. Wearing a brand *outside* one's clothes became fashionable.

In the World of Tomorrow, driverless cars end congestion, the air is fresh, parks are accessible and, in a nod to redlining, neighborhoods are separate, each tidy city block an entity unto itself. A historian at the Gotham Center for New York City

History writes: "There was no crime in the city of tomorrow, no slums and no poverty. The heroic efforts of planners and designers had eradicated human conflict and hardship. Progress was presented as inevitable and uniform."[68]

The future was within reach, freshly scrubbed, that is, except for its burlesque side. Men slipped away "to talk business with a friend," stamped out their cigarettes and entered Salvador Dali's *Dream of Venus* exhibit "through pillars shaped like a pair of women's legs."[69] One nude Venus lay in a bed of flowers on top of a taxi, another in a 36-foot bed shared with lobsters. Naked mermaids swam in two enormous pools. A couch was shaped like Greta Garbo's lips. Dali defended his erotic exhibit in a manifesto, *The Declaration of the Independence of the Imagination and the Rights of Man to His Own Madness,* in which he railed about "hideous mechanical civilization" and the "right to love women with the ecstatic heads of fish."[70] That is, if they didn't get caught. Close by, at the Cuban Village, the vice squad raided a "Miss Nude Show." Tomorrow included a wildly popular peepshow for just 25 cents.

World's Fair planners faced two challenges. The first was how to finesse their way around public suspicion that corporate greed had plunged the country into the Great Depression. The answer was simple: better marketing. The Fair "[married] the product with the consumer and the consumer with the notion of good. And underneath that came the whiff of patriotism— capitalism dressed up as being good for America."[71] It would be only natural, then, that the world would follow America's perspicacious lead. Unshackled from regulation, capitalism's invisible hand would work its magic to spin a utopian future in which there would be no winners and losers, only winners. Certainly, fairgoers would open their wallets for this!

Second, the Fair had to convince Americans that capitalism and progress would be the truest, fastest path to peace. Up in the clouds of the Trylon, a publicist writes: "spectators will find themselves cast in the role of the gods of old, from Olympian heights, to pierce the fogs of ignorance, habit and prejudice that envelop everyday thinking, able to gaze down on the ideal community."[72] The Fair would be a gathering place for world leaders to negotiate peace. Simply put, the carnival atmosphere would surely "charm dictators." Opening festivities included a "Pageant of Peace," an "Altar of Peace," and a "Court of Peace."

Something for everyone. The confident, baritone CBS radio commentator, H.V. Kaltenborn, rhapsodized about the secret sauce of science, technology and American-style democracy against an Ira Gershwin soundtrack, "Dawn of a New Day."

Dear reader, I ask for your indulgence and take my parents' word for it that Tobias was a player at the Harrison-Fouilhoux firm. Enter the theater, please, for a short daydream of his thoughts.

Stage directions: lights dim, then open on a recognizable big city thrumming with the city noise of commerce and construction, *circa* 1937. Upstage: brick tenements, fire escapes, laundry strung across buildings with faded advertising slogans, and traffic lights suspended from cables on either side of intersecting streets. Grills, headlights and the front part of the hoods of cars peek out from the wings, stage right and left. At a green light, people wearing hats cross the stage/street, while others wait at a red light, except for a gaggle of absent-minded shoppers who walk into traffic. Cue the honking horns, flashing headlights and drivers' angry admonitions. Traffic eases and the actors walk to the wings. The cars recede behind curtains. Traffic lights retract upward and out of view. The stage dims again. A scrim falls to obscure the city outside. In the dark, stagehands hurriedly set up the next scene, a top-floor workspace.

Footsteps. A spot illuminates a hinged trapdoor. Enter Tobias. He lifts the square door with his left hand, using his head to keep it open. He is work-weary yet resolute. He looks around. With each step up he takes, we see more: his worker's jacket with a bulging bottom-left pocket, a heavy tool bag on his left shoulder and the roll of plans pinched under his right arm. He heaves the plans upward and climbs onto the stage.

Once on his feet, Tobias switches on a light with his elbow, revealing an attic space transformed into a makeshift workshop. He spreads out his schematics and weighs down each corner with tools. Scattered about are a heap of tire rims, wire hangers, wood, rusted circulation vents and bicycle fenders. A school clock mounted on the wall reads 5:15 pm.

As Tobias steps away from his model of the Trylon and Perisphere to get a wider view, cue the voiceover in a less cinematic and more conversational tone: "Ladies and Gentlemen, meet Tobias Miller: inventor. He feels the world on his shoulders. He thinks: the world of tomorrow should be grand, yet not gaudy; extraterrestrial, yet grounded. Both structures should complement each other: one that jabs skyward like a spaceship ready to take off for a fresher, cleaner tomorrow. And beside it, a prototype city characterized by efficiency and cleanliness, round like a new planet ready to absorb a well-informed, larger population."

Tobias pulls out a flask from his jacket and takes a furtive sip, though he is alone, starts to put it back, takes another, then faces the audience: "A little fortification, folks!" He reaches in his other jacket pocket for a piece of whitefish wrapped in newsprint, pulls out a fork and stabs a bite.

Tobias returns to his schematics and pulls out a piece of charcoal to shade in one of his designs. He compares the drawings to the model and steps back for a bigger perspective.

Narrator: "He is onto something, wouldn't you agree?"

The clock's hands move to 6:30 pm. Tobias goes to the window, lifts it with two hands (cue the sounds of the city), props it up with a two-by-four, and sticks his head out to breathe it all in. Light from outside streams in to evoke those cinematic, crepuscular moments when the golden hour meets the blue hour. The narrator returns. "Our genius is satisfied, don't you think? No need to push his luck. That's enough for one day."

Tobias collects his tools, rolls up his plans, and starts to wrap up the greasy newspaper when he notices a headline with gloomy news from Europe. His face changes. Satisfaction gives way to doubt. He paces.

Narrator: "It's hard to design a future. The world does not travel at the same speed as our imagination."

I imagine myself in the audience, squirming and uncomfortable. What does all this mean? Tobias is not oblivious to the world around him. Was he distracted and haunted by Aldous Huxley's new, dystopian book, *Brave New World*? Was he worried that his designs would portend something bleak, sanitized and cold? Is the Trylon more a missile than a rocket ship? Is the Perisphere dome nothing more than a pathetic attempt to shelter and insulate a planet from forces trying to destroy it?

The narrator takes on a more ponderous, even portentous tone: "Tobias muses: what if the Trylon is nothing more than a gigantic pin and the Perisphere an enormous balloon? What if German designers laboring under huge, ominous klieg lights are putting the finishing touches on their *own* nefarious representation of tomorrow? What are *their* symbols?"

He picks up his toolbag, tucks his plans under his arm and turns toward the stairs. Narrator: "For now, folks, let's put all that apocalyptic thinking aside. Let us follow our dreams. Let's reach for the stars! Let's have fun! The future is bright!" Tobias lifts the trapdoor and twists his body to descend the stairs. Closing the door on top of him, the stage darkens and the house lights come on.

Narrator: "Tickets, please."

* * *

A General Motors promo film described the World's Fair as the

> true parliament of the world. Here the peoples of the world, like the Olympics, unite in amity and understanding, impelled by a friendly rivalry and working toward a common purpose: to set forth their achievements of today and their contributions to the "World of Tomorrow."[73]

In a breathless run-on sentence (abbreviated here), the voiceover drones on: "True, each of us may have different ideas about what that future will be," but science and communication will lead the way to "greater possibilities of the world of tomorrow as we move more and more rapidly forward, penetrating new horizons in the spirit of individual enterprise in the great American way!" Hopeful, but what does "penetrating new horizons" mean? Whose horizons?

Europe was, indeed, descending into hell, but on Sunday, 30 April 1939, 150 years to the day from George Washington's inauguration in Lower Manhattan, the clocks turned forward an hour for daylight saving time. RCA introduced television to the public. In NBC's first broadcast, President Roosevelt crackled to life.

Albert Einstein spoke:

> The World's Fair...is in a way a reflection of mankind. But it projects the world of men like a wishful dream. Only the creative forces are on show, none of the sinister and destructive ones which today more than ever jeopardize the happiness, the very existence of civilized harmony.[74]

On 15 March 1939, Hitler seized Czechoslovakia. World War II had begun. *The New York Times* reported that the "Czech Fair Center is Now an Orphan."[75] On 23 August, Germany and Russia signed the non-aggression pact. On 31 October, as the first season of the World's Fair ended, an editorial in *The New York Times* mused plaintively on the disconnect between aspiration and reality:

> In war and peace, prosperity and depression, scientific knowledge marches on...But it was clear, even at the Fair, that mankind has lagged in what have been called the social inventions. We have not yet invented a cure for war or a panacea for those destructive economic policies which preceded the present conflict...[76]

On 30 November 1939, the Soviet Union invaded Finland. The League of Nations expelled the Soviet Union and on 2 December Russia quit the Fair. Its four-million-dollar socialist-realist building, the tallest at the Fair (except for the Trylon), was to come down within 90 days.

The 100,000-square-foot lot was renamed the "American Common" and designated as "a performance venue given over to patriotic pageants and events celebrating democracy and American diversity." There, scholar and activist W.E.B. du Bois spoke during "Negro Week," 23–28 July 1940. W.C. Handy, the father of the blues, performed. "Negro Week" also featured the work of a fledgling drama troupe from Harlem, the Rose McClendon Players. Their dramatic adaptation of *The Life of Booker T. Washington*[77] starred Dooley Wilson, the actor who played the diminutive pianist Sam in *Casablanca*.

My father, another diminutive Sam in that same drama troupe, had initially constructed the lighting for their sets, but the Rose McClendon Players needed a white guy to play the part of President Theodore Roosevelt. He obliged.

I imagine my father coming to rehearsal each day that week, looking up with admiration and pride at the Trylon and Perisphere. Inside the performance space, actors are murmuring their vocal warmups: alliterations, tongue rolls and scales. Ossie Davis (who would later star in *Roots* and *Do the Right Thing*) would then call everyone to sit for a discussion. "When Booker T. Washington decided to cross the threshold of the White House and meet President Roosevelt, was this an audacious act of ethnic pride by a former slave or naïveté for believing he could earn the respect of whites?"

An actor might reflect, "What might happen to us if white communities see a depiction of Booker T. Washington and call us uppity?" Still another, "What will the Black community think if we portray Booker T. Washington as entirely passive and conciliatory?" My father is silent. He stares at his lines. He was just a neighbor, filling a role. A friend.

One of the actors might pull out a brochure for the World's Fair and read aloud: "The City of Tomorrow which lies below you is as harmonious as the stars in their course overhead — No anarchy — destroying the freedom of others — can exist here." Someone surely must have asked, "Do all these highways include us? Will these new machines free us, too?"

The organizing committee for "Negro Week" included Fiorello La Guardia, New York's 99th mayor; Hattie McDaniel, fresh from her performance of "Mammy" in *Gone with the Wind* (for which she was the first African American to win an Oscar); author Richard Wright; contralto Marian Anderson; and pastor Adam Clayton Powell Jr., born of a free woman at the end of the Civil War and the first African American from New York elected to the US House of Representatives. "Song of a City," by William Grant Still, considered "the Dean of Afro-American Composers," played on a continuous loop at "Democracity." Impressive indeed.

Someone interjects: "Is our country ready for full civil rights and political representation?" When the Fair opened, 500 African Americans picketed, protesting discriminatory hiring practices, for good reason. A memo circulated to hiring managers mentioned "no distinct foreign or racial types." Reverend Adam Clayton Powell met with the organizing committee to point out the hypocrisy of the Fair's theme: "You cannot have a World of Tomorrow from which you have excluded colored people."[78] Grover Whalen, president of the New York World's Fair Corporation, responded: "I do not see why the world of today or tomorrow of necessity has to have colored people playing an important role." Of the 391 Blacks employed (out of 4356), 191 were sanitary attendants. Most of the rest were maids, porters and entertainers.

This is progress?

Did the Rose McClendon Players frame a future of hope through education and self-reliance, or compromise and marginalization? Did they imagine that their children would go to schools led by creative teachers, or by an army of Elektros? In the future, would their children's teachers challenge, inspire and believe in them, or ignore them? Could they envision "the dwelling place the earth could be if men could only learn to work together"?

It had been just over 20 years since the 1918 influenza pandemic had killed with abandon but struck the poor and illiterate with a particular vengeance. Surely, we would make enough progress in science, literacy and equally distributed public health for that never to happen again—or, for that matter, another world war.

Originally launched with the slogan "Dawn of a New Day" and the promise of "The World of Tomorrow," the World's Fair was impacted by tensions mounting in Europe, compelling organizers in 1940 to change the slogan to "For Peace and Freedom." Close to bankruptcy, the Fair closed early. The World of Tomorrow met a wrecking ball. The Trylon and Perisphere were melted down and refashioned into armaments.

My father enlisted in the American army the day after Pearl Harbor, landed at Utah beach on D-Day, fought at the Battle of the Bulge, and, with the Ninth Infantry Division, liberated Nordhausen, a work-to-death concentration camp in Germany. He lost touch with his fellow thespians, but he held on to his hope, convinced life would get better, safer, more humane, equal and fair.

I wonder if the Rose McClendon Players shared my father's optimism. Ten years later, Langston Hughes was to publish his iconic poem, "Harlem." Would their dreams be deferred, still? Sugared or scabbed over? Too heavy a load to bear? Could they imagine that it took until 1954 for the Supreme Court to rule that segregation in schools was unconstitutional? Would the Players have felt comforted in this pace of progress?

The very next year, 14-year-old Emmett Till would be forced to carry a 75-pound cotton-gin fan on his back down an unpopulated road, be savagely beaten, disfigured and then thrown into the Tallahatchie River. Could the Montgomery Bus Boycott late that very same year be the beginning of the end for such racist depravity? At last, an era that valued justice and fostered human rights? Was progress just around the corner?

Were the Rose McClendon Players to dial up that time machine 20 years later, would they be impressed by the Civil Rights Act of 1960 and the assurance that voters would no longer be disenfranchised? That penalties would be exacted for obstructing voter registration? What might they have thought of Harper Lee's new book, *To Kill a Mockingbird*? Progressive? Paternalistic? Could they see themselves as one of the four students attending North Carolina Agricultural and Technical College who remained steadfast on those lunch-counter stools at a Woolworth's after having been refused service? Would they take heart the day six-year-old Ruby Bridges, escorted by four armed federal marshals, became the first Black girl to attend William Frantz Elementary School in New Orleans?

Was that what it would take?

On Mother's Day in 1961, a bus of Black and white Freedom Riders faced a white vigilante gang. A firebomb was lobbed through a smashed window. *The Smithsonian* reported that "arriving state troopers forced the rabble back and allowed the riders to escape the inferno. Even then, some were pummeled with baseball bats as they fled."[79]

Less than three years later, George Wallace would block Black students from registering at the University of Alabama.

Two months after that, a quarter of a million people marched on Washington. Dr. Martin Luther King, implored by gospel singer Mahalia Jackson, would describe his "promises of democracy." King would not mince his words. America's "bank of justice is bankrupt." The "unspeakable horrors of police brutality." The refusal to grant a weary traveler a motel room. "It would be fatal for the nation to overlook the urgency of the moment." America had "no time to engage in the tranquilizing drug of gradualism."[80]

Was the price for the world of tomorrow a world of sorrow? Less than a month after Reverend King's speech, four young girls would die in a bomb at the 16th Street Baptist Church in Birmingham, Alabama. And yet, Lyndon Johnson's signature on the Civil Rights Act of 1964 would prevent employment discrimination. In 1965, Malcolm X was assassinated and John Lewis and others beaten on the Edmund Pettus Bridge. In 1968, President Johnson would inch forward a bit more to sign the Fair Housing Act.

What would the Rose McClendon Players think, had they known all this? Was the whiplash of this shape and narrative of "progress" living up to the word's meaning in the original Latin:

"to step, walk, go"? Even with all that persistent, institutional discrimination in housing, voting and employment? Those police beatings?

Let's keep cranking the time machine forward, shall we? Sure, it was progress when Shirley Chisholm campaigned for the Democratic presidential election in 1972. Or when Barbara Jordan, Andrew Young and Thomas Bradley established their places in government, and Marian Wright Edelman founded the Children's Defense Fund. Would they, too, keep the faith, despite humiliations from self-help pundits attempting to blame Black communities for not lifting themselves up? Or when Black incarceration rates surged and Reagan's cuts to federal housing assistance and unequal revenue from property taxes left Black youth without a quality education?

Would progress have to wait until 1980, when Martin Luther King Jr.'s birthday would become a federal holiday? How about when *The Cosby Show* would try to normalize and socialize Black family life?

How about by 1990? More mayors, even in the south. More members of Congress. Would their hearts break again after the LA police beat Rodney King? How much patience and persistence might progress require? How wide and long must that arc bend before it reaches a vision that looks like justice or just snaps?

The year 2000? A new age, a new leaf, a fresh start? Surely when America elected a Black president less than a decade later. The day Barack Obama took the oath of office on his first day in the White House, I called my father.

"It's about time," he said wryly through tears of joy. "I'm too old to play the president, anyway."

Alas, I never got the chance to take my father to the Martin Luther King Jr. monument in 2011 at West Potomac Park, right next to the National Mall, but I do imagine he would have fingered those words from its inscription, etched in stone: "Out of the mountain of despair, a stone of hope."

Surely, Black lives would matter. Finally.

The morning after Donald Trump's election in 2016, I called my father from my university in Belgium. He was 101. Macular degeneration had clouded his vision. He had been sitting inches from a gigantic television, listening to an endless stream of pundits expressing shock and disbelief. I was in tears. He waded through my rants and sadness. He acknowledged the tragedy of the election and its blow to civility and progress, but then his tone changed. He had seen his share of poverty, war, disease and injustice, he said. "I fought the fascists. It's your turn. Freddy, remember what Joe Hill said?"

Near his end, Joe Hill, songwriter and labor activist, sent a telegram to Bill Hayward, the head of the Industrial Workers of the World (IWW): "Goodbye, Bill, I die like a true-blue rebel. Don't waste any time mourning. Organize!" Hill followed that telegram with another: "Could you arrange to have my body hauled to the state line to be buried? I don't want to be found dead in Utah."[81]

"But Daddy," I remember saying, "Donald Trump, President of the United States?" How could the pillars of a social contract based on fairness, decency, truth and progress dissolve so easily, like all those collapsed buildings I have seen in earthquake zones? Was democracy *that* flimsy? Were our social and educational fault lines *that* compromised? Disappointed at not hearing words of consolation, I answered his question, mumbling, "Daddy, Joe Hill said: 'Don't mourn. Organize.'"

During the Women's March in Washington the day after Trump's inauguration, I was by my father's side when the event was reported live on TV. I watched his bony elbows stiffen against the back of his favorite chair's armrests. Through the blur and blotches in front of him, a swirl of seaweed and darting schools of fish, he had pieced together that hundreds of thousands of protestors were both mourning and organizing. He began to stand. I moved toward him in case he faltered, but he shook me off and rose to express his support. He even began to march in place.

My father did not live to see the Unite the Right fascists in Charlottesville or witness news footage of George Floyd's murder. Sadly, neither could he celebrate the election of Kamala Harris, a Black South Asian woman, to the office of Vice President. Nor the election and re-election of Georgia's Reverend Raphael Warnock, a Black pastor holding the same pulpit at Ebenezer Baptist Church held by the Reverend Dr. Martin Luther King, to the United States Senate. He didn't see the insurrectionists swarming through the Capitol building, waving Confederate flags and wearing "Auschwitz Camp" T-shirts. If he had, he would still have told me to remember Joe Hill's words.

He would remind me that progress is fraught with failure, exasperating and painful. That it ebbs and flows in an uncertain continuum, but remains a trajectory, nonetheless. I am sure that I would promise him to remain patient and resolute. I would try, but when I see the growing number of attacks on the LGBTQI community, on the Jewish community, on Black and Brown people, and on Asian American and Pacific Islander communities, I wonder.

Cognitive scientist Steven Pinker's big-picture view of violence, *The Better Angels of Our Nature: Why Violence Has Declined*,[82] argues that life is, indeed, getting better. All that grisly carnage we scroll past—shootings in schools, faith communities, shopping malls, beauty salons, grocery stores, night clubs; sarin gas; car bombs; knees on necks; families torn apart by war or repression or climate change and forced to leave their homes—are, in the long view, exceptions to a trend-line of measurable, even considerable, progress. We are supposed to step away from the microscope and look through a telescope. Get the big picture.

According to Pinker, the chronic raiding of land has declined. Published before Russia's war on Ukraine, *Better Angels* points out that countries no longer attack each other with the same ferocity as the ancients, because the world is watching. Humanity's five demons—predatory violence, dominance, revenge, sadism and ideologically driven acts of violence—have given way to our four better angels: empathy, self-control, moral sensibility and reason.

This is where I struggle. There is no question that we have made progress in overall global development. But...but...in an era characterized by a precipitous swing to the far right, unregulated hate speech, Russian genocide against Ukrainians, the proliferation of gun violence, assaults on the truth, and an unprecedented rise in the number of families forced to uproot themselves and search for a better life, the world can look downright Pompeiian.

It's hard to have faith in our better angels when, at a moment's notice, the 8 billion people who inhabit this earth do not benefit equally from all those angels. How do we measure moral progress? It's difficult when the Sustainable Development Goals are receding. When a bright-eyed woman in Afghanistan one day is stoned to death the next because of a rumor of sexual impropriety or impertinence. When the residents of a city that once trusted its water supply now carry irreversible neurological trauma from lead poisoning in its pipes. When women's reproductive rights are reversed. Where are the empathic, moral, rational angels to stop the violence of climate change and ethnic cleansing?

I would lose the challenge to *Better Angels*, this painstakingly researched, exquisitely documented 800-page tome by a Harvard professor. I won't even try. I can only ask: who better to foster an equitable, safe, inclusive world of tomorrow than teachers?

Dear reader, you've met several: people with information to share, who show up, who mend and repair the world.

So many others have shown up and continue to show up. In Zambia, Mbao Mwiya-Ngula shows up to educate people about rising malaria infections, even after the wide distribution of medicated bed nets. Having observed that many nets were not used correctly, thus leaving children exposed, she designed a global competition for children to design the most effective use of a bed net. The winning entry was a game to construct a pup tent out of the net material, the children sleeping in a new home-inside-a-home. Malarial infections declined.

In Kenya, Joseph Muleka and Mathias Osimbo showed up to adapt our peace education program for a region torn asunder by post-election violence.

In Haiti, Fenel Pierre, a Fulbright Scholar, has shown up to build teacher capacity throughout the country, from teacher preparation to earthquake science and safety, following the devastating 2010 earthquake.

Teachers in Palestine, Israel, Morocco, Yemen and Turkey have shown up to create MYTecC (Mediterranean Youth Technology Club) so that youth may gain technology skills and connect to each other across borders.

In Sudan, Eiman Yousif has shown up to create an in-country and expat network of volunteer teachers to reach students using Telegram.

"Don't lose hope," I remind myself. When the going gets rough, the tough keep teaching. In every corner of the earth, and in all those intractable and desperate places written off as beyond hope or labeled as "failed states," teachers don't lose heart. They organize. They show up.

They teach science and safety so that families can feel comfortable sending their children to school. They construct child-friendly safe spaces to protect children from thugs in pickup trucks with black flags and masks, or white hoods and burning crosses. They educate girls, even when they or the girls themselves may be abducted, sexually terrorized or shot. They teach even when their schools have been occupied, bombed, burned, ransacked and turned into storehouses of munitions or fronts for fake polling places. When repressive regimes consider civic discourse or dissent an act of treason, teachers insist on being heard.

Teachers are the last ones to call themselves angels or heroes. They think heroics should be left for comic books. I agree. They have taught me that our fetish about heroes elevates a few and leaves the rest of us out. On the contrary, these teachers define themselves as catalysts and cattle prods.

When bullies and despots erect deep and artificial boundaries between nations and cultures, teachers emphasize comity and forge even deeper human connections. When the wall of bigotry inspires xenophobes blind with apocalyptic rage, teachers find a pathway for inclusion and safety. Teachers will not let their classrooms, their colleagues or their communities down. They can't; they never have and they never will. This is the ineffable, yet unmistakable, power of human agency and reciprocity built right into the profession.

In the world of fairness teachers build every day, children of families fleeing injustice or war are not someone else's problem. These teachers view their classrooms as a local patch of a global commons. In that fair world, they neither leave change to chance nor wait for Acts of Congress. They act from *conscience*. They don't depend on rich benefactors or celebrity endorsements. Instead, they fashion lessons from local materials and collective expertise.

These teachers care little about the tyranny of the urgent. They're more concerned about the urgency of tyranny.

I understand why my father insisted that I remember Joe Hill's "Don't mourn. Organize!" These teachers transformed their own mourning into mobilizations for social justice. I can hear him now: "Freddy, progress is not an escalator to the world of tomorrow, but it will go somewhere, I promise you." Maybe this is Pinker's point. Hard to tell.

Change might feel painfully slow, like watching a pearl descend in a curvy glass bottle of Prell. The odds that developing countries will emerge from a suffocating mountain of debt and the pernicious, generational impact of colonialism are not in our favor. The prospect that education can address the ravages of climate change, inequality and injustice, and reach those Sustainable Development Goals is, to put it charitably, Sisyphean. But then again, we have no other choice but to educate and act.

In a 2022 article for *The Nation*, Liat Olenick writes: "Healthy democracies don't hate their teachers."[83] Given a true voice, teachers can build the democracy and the world of tomorrow the world's children deserve.

Education isn't the answer to everything. The world needs roads, vaccinations, fresh water, sustainable livelihoods, equity, safety, the consistent application of the law, clean energy, climate change mitigation, protection against discrimination, and social justice. But without education and educators, the road falls into disrepair, the poor get poorer and sicker, good jobs drift even further out of reach, inequality widens, victimization deepens and racism festers. We lose hope.

Even hope, on its own, is not enough. Without a plan, a heavy dose of righteous indignation and a mobilization effort, hope alone is ephemeral, if not downright dangerous. Dr. Jane Goodall concludes her latest work, *The Book of Hope*, with this message: "Please rise to the challenge, inspire and help those around you, play your part."[84]

Greta Thunberg ruffles hope's feathers. She rages:

> I don't want you to be hopeful. I want you to panic. I want you to act as if our house is on fire ... All political and economic systems have failed, but humanity has not yet failed. Everywhere, lots of people show up, people of all ages. Things may look dark, but there is hope, and that hope comes from the people.[85]

The operational words here: show up.

You may not consider yourself a teacher, but if you have valuable information to share, you *are* a teacher. The world may be a cesspool, but if teachers like these can strap on their boots and show up to wade through the muck, so can you. Look outside your window. If the world you see doesn't look fair, then get out those timbales and cowbells and lesson plans, comrades, and make some noise. Don't give bigots and tyrants another vacation day. Flex your inner tattoo: *aquila non capit muscas* (the eagle does not catch flies).

And let these teachers remind us:

Sameena: "No fear!"
Raphael: "Time is not on our side!"
Deya: "*Habla sin pelos en la lengua.*" Speak without hairs on the tongue.
Simba: "If not now, when?"

Don't mourn. Organize, folks.

The clock's tickin'.

For More Information

Visit https://inthesmallplaces.net

Discussion topics are available for book clubs and high-school and college classrooms. You can also add your story or a story of a teacher changemaker. We will map stories and connect teachers.

Learn more about Teachers Without Borders (https://teacherswithoutborders.org), global development organizations we respect, and curated resources on education in emergencies, girls' education, and peace and human rights education.

* * *

For speaking engagements and general inquiries, please feel free to reach out to Fred Mednick: fred@twb.org and +1-206-356-4731.

About Teachers Without Borders

Teachers Without Borders (TWB) is an international teacher network and development organization launched in 2000, with a mission to connect teachers to information and each other in order to close the education divide. TWB views teachers as a sustainable army of community change agents and key catalysts of global development. Membership spans 177 countries. Teachers Without Borders is best known for its work in education in emergencies, girls' education, and peace and human rights education.

Jane Goodall is Teachers Without Borders' International Spokesperson.

Teachers Without Borders is made up 100% of volunteers. TWB offers free membership, free downloadable resources, free courses, internships, and graduate fellowships. All course content and workshop materials are governed by the least restrictive Creative Commons license to foster sharing across borders.

Raphael Ogar Oko, a Teachers Without Borders leader in Nigeria, was awarded the Champions of African Education Award for work to promote the Millennium Development Goals and the *Voice of Teachers* radio program. Teachers Without Borders is also the recipient of two peace prizes: the Luxembourg Peace Prize for Outstanding Peace Education Initiatives, and the Ahmadiyya Muslim Prize for the Advancement of Peace in recognition of TWB's "outstanding work in the promotion of peace through efforts to convene teachers from regions in conflict, provide unfettered access to courses and networks devoted to teacher professional development, and to ensure that Peace Education is integrated into all initiatives."

* * *

Please join Teachers Without Borders, subscribe to our newsletter, and get involved:

- https://teacherswithoutborders.org
- https://twitter.com/teachersnetwork
- https://facebook.com/teacherswithoutborders
- TWB *Burning Issues* Newsletter: http://bit.ly/TWB-subscribe

Endnotes

1   O'Connor F. *Everything that rises must converge.* New York: Farrar, Straus and Giroux; 1965.

2   Crossette B. Globalization tops 3-day UN agenda for world leaders. *The New York Times* [Internet]. 2000 Sep 3; Available from: https://www.nytimes.com/2000/09/03/world/globalization-tops-3-day-un-agenda-for-world-leaders.html?smid=em-share

3   Jane Goodall Institute. Home page [Internet]. Roots & Shoots. 2022. Available from: https://www.rootsandshoots.org/

4   Datta R. From development to empowerment: the self-employed women's association in India. *International Journal of Politics, Culture and Society.* 2003;16(3):351–68.

5   Enerson E. We want work: rural women in the Gujarat drought and earthquake [Internet]. Quick Response Research Report #135: Natural Hazards Research and Applications Information Center. Boulder, Colorado: University of Colorado; 2002 [cited 2002]. Available from: https://www.colorado.edu/hazards/qr/qr135/qr135.html

6   United Nations High Commissioner for Refugees. *Refworld* | General comment No. 8 (2006): The right of the child to protection from corporal punishment and other cruel or degrading forms of punishment [Internet]. United

Nations; 2006. Available from: https://www.refworld.org/docid/460bc7772.html

7   Morrow V. Beatings for asking for help: corporal punishment in India's schools [Internet]. *Guardian News*. Guardian; 2015. Available from: https://www.theguardian.com/global-development-professionals-network/2015/may/22/tough-boys-and-docile-girls-corporal-punishment-in-indias-schools

8   Timeline of the riots in Modi's Gujarat. *The New York Times* [Internet]. 2014 Apr 6; Available from: https://www.nytimes.com/interactive/2014/04/06/world/asia/modi-gujarat-riots-timeline.html

9   Chandhoke N. *Civil society in conflict cities: the case of Ahmedabad*. In University of Delhi: Crisis States Research Centre; 2009. Available from: https://www.lse.ac.uk/international-development/Assets/Documents/PDFs/csrc-working-papers-phase-two/wp64.2-civil-society-in-conflict-cities.pdf

10   Modi N. Speech at the Gujarat Gaurav Yatra public meeting. Public Meeting; 2002 Sep 9.

11   Roosevelt, E. Presentation of *In your hands:* a guide for community action for the tenth anniversary of the Universal Declaration of Human Rights. 27 March 1958. United Nations, New York.

12   Steichen E. *The family of man: the greatest photographic exhibition of all time*. New York: Museum of Modern Art; distributed by Simon & Schuster; 1955.

13   Shahn B. Letter to editor of New York Times [Internet]. Smithsonian Digital Volunteers. *New York Times*; 1955. Available from: https://transcription.si.edu/transcribe/44893/AAA-shahben00011-001031

14   Sandburg C. Prologue. In: *The family of man: the greatest photographic exhibit of all time*. New York: Simon & Shuster; 1955.

15   Towery T. *"The family of man"*: a reappraisal [Internet].
      towery.lehman.edu.   2015.   Available   from: http://
      towery.lehman.edu/photohistory/PhotoReadings/
      TheFamilyofMaAReappraisal.html

16   Tīfentāle A. *The family of man*: the photography exhibition
      that everybody loves to hate. *FK Magazine* [Internet]. 2018
      Jul 2. Available from: https://fkmagazine.lv/2018/07/02/
      the-family-of-man-the-photography-exhibition-that-
      everybody-loves-to-hate/#:~:text=The%20scholarly%20
      reception%20of%20The,historical%20specificity%20
      from%20this%20depiction

17   Easterly W. How the millennium development goals are
      unfair to Africa [Internet]. Washington, DC: The Brookings
      Institution; 2007 Nov. p. 4–19. Available from: https://
      www.brookings.edu/wp-content/uploads/2016/06/11_
      poverty_easterly.pdf

18   Payne E. Musharraf: Obama is arrogant [Internet]. *CNN
      Wire Staff*, editor. CNN. 2011. Available from: http://www.
      cnn.com/2011/WORLD/asiapcf/05/27/pakistan.musharraf.
      obama/index.html

19   Grimes W. Fathi Osman, scholar of Islam, dies at 82.
      The New York Times [Internet]. 2010 Sep 20. Available
      from: https://www.nytimes.com/2010/09/20/us/20osman.
      html?smid=url-share

20   Sexton A. Red Riding Hood. *The complete poems*. Boston:
      Houghton Mifflin; 1982.

21   Syed I. Shall I feed my daughter, or educate her? Barriers
      to girls' education in Pakistan [Internet]. Human Rights
      Watch.   2018.   Available   from: https://www.hrw.org/
      report/2018/11/12/shall-i-feed-my-daughter-or-educate-
      her/barriers-girls-education-pakistan#

22   Center for Global Development. Education and the
      developing world [Internet]. 2016. Available from:

https://www.cgdev.org/sites/default/files/2844_file_
EDUCATON1_0.pdf

23 Hassan N. Earthquake 2005: faulty towers—cursed by
nature, haunted by apathy [Internet]. *The Express Tribune*.
2011. Available from: https://tribune.com.pk/story/269546/
earthquake-2005-faulty-towers%E2%80%93-cursed-by-
nature-haunted-by-apathy

24 Alinsky SD. *Rules for radicals: a practical primer for realistic
radicals*. New York: Vintage Books; 1989.

25 Williams G. Earthquakes, consolation and the Senecan
sublime. Earthquakes. 2012 Apr 5;213–57.

26 Hsu A. Chengdu diary: caught in the earthquake. *National
Public Radio* [Internet]. 2008 May 12. Available from: https://
www.npr.org/sections/chengdu/2008/05/caught_in_the_
earthquake_1.html

27 Mohadjer S. How to Disarm Earthquakes. Solmaz Mohadjer
| TEDx Stuttgart [Internet]. TEDx Stuttgart. 2016. Available
from: https://www.youtube.com/watch?v=q1rFoN-DnS8

28 California Institute of Technology. 2004 Sumatra earthquake
[Internet]. California Institute of Technology. Cal Tech;
2019. Available from: http://www.tectonics.caltech.edu/
outreach/highlights/sumatra/what.html

29 United States Geological Survey. Earthquake Legends |
U.S. Geological Survey [Internet]. www.usgs.gov. United
States Department of Interior; 2004. Available from:
https://www.usgs.gov/programs/earthquake-hazards/
earthquake-legends?qt-science_center_objects=0#qt-
science_center_objects

30 United States Geological Survey. The MW 7.0 Haiti
earthquake of January 12, 2010. Series #: 2010-1048
[Internet]. USGS. USGS/EERI Advance Reconnaissance
Team Report; 2010 Feb. Available from: https://pubs.
er.usgs.gov/publication/ofr20101048

31 Shamasunder S. Sounds of Haiti. *Journal of General Internal Medicine* [Internet]. 2010 Nov 5 [cited 2022 May 2];26(3):349–50. Available from: https://doi.org/10.1007/s11606-010-1550-3

32 Benoit P. *The Haitian earthquake of 2010*. A True Book: Disasters Series. New York: Scholastic. Children's Press; 2012.

33 Mohadjer S. ParsQuake: earthquake education in the global Persian community [Internet]. parsquake.org. Available from: https://parsquake.org

34 Adichie CN. The danger of a single story [Internet]. TED Global Talks. TED; 2009. Available from: https://www.ted.com/talks/chimamanda_ngozi_adichie_the_danger_of_a_single_story?language=en

35 Gettleman J. First prize for a child in Somalia: an AK-47. *The New York Times* [Internet]. 2011 Sep 20. Available from: http://nyti.ms/LsdpgQ

36 The next frontier: human development and the anthropocene [Internet]. UNHDR. New York: United Nations Human Development Programme; 2020. Available from: https://hdr.undp.org/sites/default/files/Country-Profiles/BDI.pdf

37 UNICEF. Update on the context and situation of children. Country Report: Burundi [Internet]. UNICEF. 2021. Available from: https://www.unicef.org/media/115846/file/Burundi-2021-COAR.pdf

38 Reuters. Outgoing Burundi president Nkurunziza, famed for soccer and violence, dies. *Reuters News Agency* [Internet]. 2020 Jun 9. Available from: https://www.reuters.com/article/us-burundi-politics/outgoing-burundi-president-nkurunziza-famed-for-soccer-and-violence-dies-idUSKBN23G24H

39   Kigali Genocide Memorial: a place for remembrance and learning [Internet]. Kigali Genocide Memorial. Available from: https://kgm.rw/

40   Ubald Fr. Missionaries of Peace [Internet]. Father Ubald. 2012. Available from: https://frubald.com/about/missionaries-of-peace/

41   Birkner G. United by horror. *New York Jewish Week* [Internet]. 2005 Mar 4. Available from: https://www.jta.org/2005/03/04/ny/united-by-horror

42   Wiesel E. Commencement address [Internet]. Commencement Archive 2014–2019. Washington University, St. Louis; 2011. Available from: https://commencement-archive.wustl.edu/speakers-honorees/speakers/elie-wiesel-address-2011/

43   Artspace Editors. The story behind Steve McCurry's iconic "Afghan Girl" —and how he found her again 20 years later. *Artspace Phaeidon Folio* [Internet]. 2018 Aug 29. Available from: https://bit.ly/3qQMgus

44   Newman C. A life revealed: Seventeen years after she started out from the cover of National Geographic, a former Afghan refugee comes face-to-face with the world once more. *National Geographic*. 2002.

45   Strochlic N. Famed "Afghan girl" finally gets a home. *National Geographic* [Internet]. 2017 Dec 12. Available from: https://www.nationalgeographic.com/pages/article/afghan-girl-home-afghanistan

46   Karnad R. You'll never see the iconic photo of the "Afghan Girl" the same way again. *The Wire* [Internet]. 2019 Mar 19. Available from: https://thewire.in/media/afghan-girl-steve-mccurry-national-geographic

47   Johnson B. Symbolic oppressions: The rhetoric and the image of the veil in the West. [Internet]. *Prized Writing*. University of California, Davis; 2009. Available from:

https://prizedwriting.ucdavis.edu/symbolic-oppressions-rhetoric-and-image-veil-west

48 Spivak G. Can the subaltern speak? In: Nelson C, Grossberg L, editors. *Marxism and the interpretation of culture*. Urbana-Champaign, Illinois: University of Illinois Press; 1988. p. 271–313.

49 Koppel T, ABC Evening News: *Nightline*. Vasila's Heart. Vanderbilt Television News Archive; 2005.

50 Yuksel P, Robin B, McNeil S. Educational uses of digital storytelling all around the world. In: Proceedings: *Society for Information Technology & Teacher Education International Conference* [Internet]. Houston, Texas: University of Houston; 2011. p. 2–8. Available from: http://digitalstorytelling.coe. uh.edu/survey/SITE_DigitalStorytelling.pdf

51 Morse P. George W. Bush greets 11-year-old Vasila Hossaini in the Diplomatic Reception Room of the White House [Internet]. The White House. 2005. Available from: https://georgewbush-whitehouse.archives.gov/news/ releases/2005/06/images/20050602-13_w9w3799jas-515h. html

52 Gardner H. *Frames of mind: the theory of multiple intelligences*. New York: Basic Books; 1983.

53 Gardner H, Chen J-Q, Moran S. *Multiple intelligences around the world*. San Francisco: Jossey-Bass; 2009.

54 PARSA [Internet]. PARSA Afghanistan. 2022. Available from: https://www.afghanistan-parsa.org

55 Peer Y. Yunus Peer is closing the global education divide [Internet]. Punahou School. Punahou PFA—Teachers Across Borders/Teachers Without Borders; 2005. Available from: https://tab-sa.org/yunus-peer-closing-the-global-education-divide-punahou-pfa/

56 Correctional Services [Internet]. www.gov.za. South African Government; 2000. Available from: https://www. gov.za/about-government/correctional-services

57   Lange D. Sharecroppers: Eutaw, Alabama [Internet]. Museum of Modern Art, New York. 1936. Available from: https://www.moma.org/collection/works/52292

58   Visible Project: "Fuentes Rojas." Embroidering for peace and memory [Internet]. Visible Project. Fundazione Pistoletto Cittadellarte Biella and Fundazione Zegna; 2017. Available from: https://www.visibleproject.org/blog/project/embroidering-for-peace-and-memory-one-victim-one-cdmx-mxico/

59   Bonilla-Rius E. Education truly matters: key lessons from Mexico's educational reform for educating the whole child. In: Reimers FM, editor. *Audacious education purposes* [Internet]. Copenhagen University Hospital, Denmark: Springer Cham; 2020. p. 105–51. Available from: https://doi.org/10.1007/978-3-030-41882-3_5.

60   van Andel T. The reinvention of household medicine by enslaved Africans in Suriname. Social history of medicine [Internet]. 2015 Mar 12;29(4):676–94. Available from: https://www.researchgate.net/publication/273452790_The_Reinvention_of_Household_Medicine_by_Enslaved_Africans_in_Suriname

61   Manyike S, Mednick F. Daily Blog [Internet]. Walk the Peace Talk. Teachers Without Borders; 2022. Available from: https://walkthepeacetalk.net/journal

62   Zhou Y, Narea N, Animashaun C. Europe's embrace of Ukrainian refugees, explained in charts and a map [Internet]. *Vox*. Vox Media, Ltd.; 2022. Available from: https://www.vox.com/22983230/europe-ukraine-refugees-charts-map

63   Gestapo prison memorial [Internet]. NS-Dokumentationszentrum Köln. Museen der Stadt Köln; 2022. Available from: https://museenkoeln.de/ns-dokumentationszentrum/default.aspx?s=716

64   Schwartz D. The books have been burning: a timeline of 2200 years of book burnings, from ancient China to The

Book of Negroes [Internet]. *Liberal Studies Guides.* Ottawa, Canada: CBC News, Institute for Liberal Studies; 2011 Jun. p. 1–7. Available from: https://liberalstudiesguides.ca/wp-content/uploads/sites/2/2015/07/CBC-Timeline-Book-Burnings-since-WWII.pdf

65   Wiesel E. Hope, despair and memory [Internet]. Nobel Prize Lecture. Nobel Foundation; 1986. Available from: https://www.nobelprize.org/prizes/peace/1986/wiesel/acceptance-speech/

66   Miller T. Auxiliary seat: Patent [Internet]. 1919. Available from: https://patents.google.com/patent/US1302828A/en

67   Shepherd D. The 1939–1940 New York World's Fair: typical American families build tomorrow. *Student Research Submissions,* University of Mary Washington [Internet]. 2011 Dec 12;23:1–54. Available from: https://scholar.umw.edu/cgi/viewcontent.cgi?article=1011&context=student_research

68   Uvia K. Gasopolis: from the 1939 to the 1964 World's Fair [Internet]. The Gotham Center for New York City History. Gotham Center; 2010. Available from: https://www.gothamcenter.org/blog/gasopolis-from-the-1939-to-the-1964-worlds-fair

69   When Salvador Dalí Created a Surrealist Funhouse at New York World's Fair (1939) | Open Culture [Internet]. Open Culture. Open Culture LLC; 2021. Available from: https://www.openculture.com/2021/06/when-salvador-dali-created-a-surrealist-funhouse-at-new-york-worlds-fair-1939.html

70   Dali S. Declaration of the Independence of the Imagination and the Rights of Man to His Own Madness [Internet]. 1939. Available from: http://digitalarchives.queenslibrary.org/search/browse/*?fq[0]=sm_relation%3ACollection+on+the+1939-1940+New+York+World%27s+Fair

71 Mauro J. *Twilight at the world of tomorrow: genius, madness, murder, and the 1939 World's Fair on the brink of war*. New York: Ballantine Books; 2010. p. 105.

72 Ibid. p. 154.

73 General Motors. To new horizons [Internet]. Internet Archive. Handy (Jam) Organization (Public Domain); 1940. Available from: https://archive.org/details/ToNewHor1940

74 Einstein A. Address at Dedication of Palestine Pavilion at N.Y. World's Fair. 1939–1940 World's Fair; 1939 May 28.

75 Czech fair is now an orphan [Internet]. Times Machine. Times Wide World. *The New York Times*; 1939. Available from: https://timesmachine.nytimes.com/timesmachine/1939/03/17/94691504.html?pageNumber=9

76 Farewell—and hail! [Internet]. Times Machine. Times Wide World. *The New York Times*; 1939. Available from: https://timesmachine.nytimes.com/timesmachine/1939/10/31/94731745.html?pageNumber=20

77 New York World's Fair. "Negro week" records. New York: Schomburg Center for Research in Black Culture; 1940 Oct. p. 2–5.

78 Cope D. Racism: hope for a better "World of Tomorrow" [Internet]. Paul M. Van Dort. Sparks, Nevada; 1996. Available from: https://www.1939nyworldsfair.com/Ponderings/racism.htm

79 Holmes M. The Freedom Riders, then and now. *Smithsonian Magazine* [Internet]. 2009 Feb; Available from: https://www.smithsonianmag.com/history/the-freedom-riders-then-and-now-45351758/

80 Luther King M. I have a dream [Internet]. March on Washington; [cited 1963 Aug 28]. Available from: https://www.npr.org/2010/01/18/122701268/i-have-a-dream-speech-in-its-entirety

81 Whitfield SJ. *Roughneck: the life and times of Big Bill Haywood*. Business History Review. 1984;58(4):613–15.

82 Pinker S. *The better angels of our nature: a history of violence and humanity*. London: Penguin; 2012.

83 Olenick L. There is something very wrong with a society that scapegoats its teachers [Internet]. *The Nation*; 2022. Available from: https://www.thenation.com/article/society/covid-school-teachers/tnamp/

84 Goodall J. *Book of hope: a survival guide for trying times*. First Edition. New York: Celadon Books, division of Macmillan; 2021.

85 Toraya NV, Scott JP. *Greta Thunberg has given up on politicians*. Film Club: *The New York Times* [Internet]. 2021 Nov 4. Available from: https://www.nytimes.com/2021/11/04/learning/film-club-greta-thunberg-has-given-up-on-politicians.html

**CHANGEMAKERS
BOOKS**

Transform your life, transform *our* world. Changemakers
Books publishes books for people who seek to become positive,
powerful agents of change. These books inform, inspire, and
provide practical wisdom and skills to empower us to write
the next chapter of humanity's future.
www.changemakers-books.com

The Resilience Series

The Resilience Series is a collaborative effort by the authors
of Changemakers Books in response to the 2020 coronavirus
pandemic. Each concise volume offers expert advice and
practical exercises for mastering specific skills and abilities.
Our intention is that by strengthening your resilience, you can
better survive and even thrive in a time of crisis.
www.resiliencebooks.com

Adapt and Plan for the New Abnormal – in the COVID-19
Coronavirus Pandemic
Gleb Tsipursky

Aging with Vision, Hope and Courage in a Time of Crisis
John C. Robinson

Connecting with Nature in a Time of Crisis
Melanie Choukas-Bradley

Going Within in a Time of Crisis
P. T. Mistlberger

Grow Stronger in a Time of Crisis
Linda Ferguson

Handling Anxiety in a Time of Crisis
George Hoffman

Navigating Loss in a Time of Crisis
Jules De Vitto

The Life-Saving Skill of Story
Michelle Auerbach

Virtual Teams – Holding the Center When You Can't Meet
Face-to-Face
Carlos Valdes-Dapena

Virtually Speaking – Communicating at a Distance
Tim Ward and Teresa Erickson

Current Bestsellers from Changemakers Books

Pro Truth
A Practical Plan for Putting Truth Back into Politics
Gleb Tsipursky and Tim Ward
How can we turn back the tide of post-truth politics,
fake news, and misinformation that is damaging
our democracy? In the lead-up to the 2020 US Presidential
Election, *Pro Truth* provides the answers.

An Antidote to Violence
Evaluating the Evidence
Barry Spivack and Patricia Anne Saunders
It's widely accepted that Transcendental Meditation can create
peace for the individual, but can it create peace in society as a
whole? And if it can, what could possibly be the mechanism?

Finding Solace at Theodore Roosevelt Island
Melanie Choukas-Bradley
A woman seeks solace on an urban island paradise in
Washington D.C. through 2016–17, and the shock
of the Trump election.

the bottom
a theopoetic of the streets
Charles Lattimore Howard
An exploration of homelessness fusing theology,
jazz-verse and intimate storytelling into a
challenging, raw and beautiful tale.

The Soul of Activism
A Spirituality for Social Change
Shmuly Yanklowitz
A unique examination of the power of interfaith
spirituality to fuel the fires of progressive activism.

Future Consciousness
The Path to Purposeful Evolution
Thomas Lombardo
An empowering evolutionary vision of wisdom and the
human mind to guide us in creating a positive future.

Preparing for a World that Doesn't Exist – Yet
Rick Smyre and Neil Richardson
This book is about an emerging Second Enlightenment
and the capacities you will need to achieve success in
this new, fastevolving world.